ROY CAMPBELL

GARLAND REFERENCE LIBRARY
OF THE HUMANITIES
(VOL. 197)

Portrait of Roy Campbell by John P. Flanagan, 1924

ROY CAMPBELL

*A Descriptive and Annotated Bibliography
with notes on unpublished sources*

D.S.J. Parsons

GARLAND PUBLISHING, INC. • NEW YORK & LONDON
1981

Library of Congress Cataloging in Publication Data

Parsons, David Stewart Japp, 1925–
  Roy Campbell, a descriptive and annotated
bibliography, with notes on unpublished sources.

  (Garland reference library of the humanities ;
v. 197)
  Includes index.
  1. Campbell, Roy, 1901–1957—Bibliography.
I. Title.
Z8142.85.P37 [PR9369.3.C35]   016.821   79-7930
ISBN 0-8240-9526-X

Printed on acid-free, 250-year-life paper
Manufactured in the United States of America

*This book is dedicated
to
Mary and Teresa
Campbell*

CONTENTS

ILLUSTRATIONS

INTRODUCTION

From knowing Roy Campbell's elder brother, Archie, in Canada, my father became interested in his poetry and first made me aware of it, even though as an entomologist he was much more excited by Archie's world-famous butterfly collection. However, I date my serious involvement with Campbell's work from the time I heard him recite (a dim word, but shall we say as the minstrel might have "recited" Homer) some of his poems in Toronto in 1953. Subsequently, I met his widow and daughter Teresa in Portugal and his brother George and his wife in Durban. Such reference may seem extraneous, but to understand something of Campbell's writings, one soon realizes, one has to an unusual degree to approach his works with some knowledge of the man's life, with its exoticism and violent variety, and an appreciation of the personality informing it, one—particularly in his earlier years—of deceptive externals. Campbell's intensity, as much as his old-fashioned Romantic posturing, has encouraged many critics and commentators to seek the man in the poetry and the poetry in the man. At the same time, though, comment on Campbell's work with few exceptions displays a degree of inability to perceive this poet in all his parts. His variety and unevenness, amounting almost to a bewildering heterogeneity, whether as lyrical poet, satirist, polemicist, mystic, autobiographer, journalist, social and natural historian, translator or critic, make difficult a comprehensive view, in which perceptions of different sides of the man are made to inform one another. Contributing, no doubt, to the difficulty is the considerable bulk of his published work. Seldom does one feel when reading his critics that they are familiar with more than a part of it; yet even with the part they know they have seemed very often to have failed to achieve a balanced perspective—not, of course, that Campbell encouraged this.

My reason, then, for undertaking to publish a bibliography has been to provide evidence of Campbell's scope and diversity, and also to indicate the very wide range of critical response. As a first step in drawing attention to the relationship between his kaleidoscopic career, his ebullient yet complicated and troubled personality, and his output, I have provided—despite the lack of originality in doing so—a biographical chronology. Among other things it shows Campbell to have been very much a man of places and different cultural affiliations.

There is the need, too, to bring the record up to date at a time when, following a period of grave decline in his reputation, signs of a continuing interest in Campbell are manifest. Bibliographies attached to studies have been necessarily partial, and those provided by Valerie Davis and Fey Miller, in themselves not extensive, are now out of date, and I have long since perceived the inadequacies of my checklist published in 1976. My attempt has now been to make a full record up to the end of 1978.

The recent monographs by Rowland Smith and John Povey, and the forthcoming study by Peter Alexander, due to be published by Oxford University Press in the summer of 1982, attest to the need for a recognition, however belated, of the importance and range of Campbell. In spite of the vicissitudes of his reputation, and the critical hostility and sometimes harmful advocacy with which his work has met, especially at the end of his life, reassessment has been occurring and it has become apparent that he has gone on enjoying a following outside as well as within South Africa, where, until recently, the younger generation of poets and critics have been reacting against his earlier enshrinement. The bibliography undertakes to document not only the seldom realized bulk of Campbell's published work, but the extent of its posthumous publication, and to reflect the diversity and persistent vitality of critical interest in North America, Britain, South Africa and Europe—particularly Iberia.

So far no one study has been able to do justice to all sides of Campbell and none has shown clear evidence of having been based on all the major research sources available, no doubt because of their wide dispersal. An attempt at a full-scale biography has yet to be made; several were initiated and announced, notably by W.H. Gardner and Alan Paton, but for one reason or another fell by the wayside. Some academic attention has been given to Campbell as a satirist, but there is room for further treatment here. As yet very few theses or dissertations on him are on record. Academically he has been extensively studied only with respect to the literature of the Spanish Civil War; it is only now being acknowledged that, though seemingly fulfilling the role of outsider, Campbell was very symptomatic of the thirties and forties and should be fitted much more into their literary-cultural milieux.

In general, in the bibliography I have followed standard practice in the form and ordering of entries, and have tried to be consistently clear in meeting the objectives of identification and simple but sufficient description. Unless it is stated that an item has not been seen, its description or annotation results from perusal of the item itself or facsimile thereof. In the sections devoted to descriptions, title pages and statements of limitation have been transcribed exactly, but no attempt has been made to distinguish among type faces and sizes. Imprints and colophons have been copied without retaining capitalization or regard for lineation or relative spacing.

In my choice of methods of bibliographical description I have been influenced by several bibliographies published by Garland Publishing, notably by David K. Kermani's *John Ashbery: A Comprehensive Bibliography*, and in my annotating by the example in particular of Samuel Rees's *David Jones: An Annotated Bibliography and Guide to Research*. The format of the descriptions of the primary works follows a pattern. First, the particular edition or reprint to be described is identified. Such identifications provide the publishing history of the title to the extent that all first editions and all reprints are set down. Successive printings or impressions of first editions are merely noted within an entry, as are subsequent editions. Following the transcription of the title page, the collation and physical characteristics of the book are given.

In providing the collation the number of preliminary leaves is specified whenever the page numbering or page count does not total with the page count of the text. Likewise, any unnumbered leaves following the end of the text are enumerated; any blank leaves are also noted. On the other hand, when the text ends on an unnumbered page, the fact is signified by adding a 1 in brackets to the total page count, as in this example: 216, [1] pp. The same procedure is adopted to indicate that on an un-numbered page following the end of the text, a colophon or other printed matter occurs. In the description, reference to any unnumbered page is made by giving it a number in brackets according to count. Beyond this, there is no need to detail methods of specifying collation since they are mostly straight-forward. Outside dimensions are given to the nearest $\frac{1}{16}$ of an inch. Illustrations and their disposition are briefly indicated along with description of format, or, if numerous or of special interest, are described and located as part of the description of contents.

Simple descriptions of kinds of bindings, paper covers, or dust jackets, types of paper and colors printed have been em-ployed. Covers of books by Campbell tended rather monotonously to be gilt stamped or gilt lettered on fronts and spines; for some variety, and to avoid the ambiguity in "gilt," I have often stated "stamped"—or "printed"—"in gold," by which of course I merely designate a color. Distinction has been made between books sewn and books stitched, the latter description being reserved for those with widely spaced vertical stitches visible. All staining or trimming of edges of pages is noted; in those few instances where special paper has been used, an at-tempt has been made to provide proper identification. Flyleaves are not mentioned unless somewhat unexpected in the particu-lar format or of a color different from that of the book's pages.

In Sections A, B and C only a comparatively few exact dates of publication and statements of numbers printed have been given. For the most part the publishers of books by Campbell still in existence either no longer possess records, or have be-haved as though they do not. As my notes to various entries indicate, either because of wartime conditions or as a result of clearances undertaken to avoid being inundated by paper, some of the publishers no longer possess the relevant files. Many of the publishers written to, and more than I had expected, have declined to respond to inquiries, even when repeated. My at-tempts to make up for this lack of firsthand information by turning to booksellers' trade publications for data have been handicapped by not being at the right time in the right place where complete enough runs of these were held. To retrieve such data at this fairly late date for much of Campbell's work is not easy and would be in any event, perhaps, a labor disproportionate to the worth of the outcome in that the chronology of his publications is for the most part easily established. In those few instances of multiple publication within the same year, relative chronology can be fixed by resort to publishers' announcements of prior publications, references in letters, dates of appearances of reviews and the like.

Treatment of the contents of collections of poems, whether of originals or translations, has been affected by the great number of these and also by the fact that there is much repetition owing to considerable re-collection. For the larger collections containing many poems the solution adopted has been to list the divisional headings, with pagination for each, under which individual poems are grouped so as to indicate the scope of the collection. For the *Poems of Baudelaire* this same method of enumeration has been used for consistency, though an indication that the poems were arranged in the order followed by Yves Le Dantec in the "Pléiade edition" would be sufficient. Similarly, only generalized descriptions have been given of the translations appearing in *Lorca* and *Portugal*, along with the listings of chapter or part headings. Many of these poems were published individually in journals, and are indexed accordingly, or were subsequently collected in *Collected Poems*, Volume 3, 1960. Also, because the three volumes of Campbell's collected poems are readily available, their contents have not been itemized poem by poem. I have thought it more important to make clear that, with some exceptions, all of Campbell's earlier collections of poetry and published single poems are collected in either *Collected Poems*, 1949, or *Collected Poems*, Volume 2, 1957, as are the majority of his translations in Volume 3. In any case, listing and then indexing all the poems would be to duplicate the work already done by Fey Miller in her *First Line and Title Index to the Poetry of Roy Campbell* ([Johannesburg], 1961). It might be noted here that for greater clarity and convenience all references in the text to the major poetry collections are to CP49, CP57 and CP60 respectively.

Individual poems are listed as part of the descriptions of

contents when the total number does not exceed twenty-five. Observing this proviso has made it possible to list individually all poems appearing in the smaller, less well-known collections, and also in selected editions. Also given in appended notes are the lists of the poems in *Mithraic Emblems* not collected in CP49 and of those from *Talking Bronco* not collected in CP57. Whether poems are individually listed or not, in all instances an effort has been made to point out any significant differences between the final collected version and earlier ones.

It will be seen that the three volumes of collected poems are not placed together ahead of or among the other entries, as has occurred in other bibliographies, but singly within the chronological sequence; furthermore, CP60 is entered among the translations in Section C whereas the other two volumes are found in Section A. It was only retroactively, of course, that CP49 came to be considered as "Volume 1." This collection at the time brought together all of Campbell's earlier and, it is generally acknowledged, best poetry. The poems of CP57 mark a largely different phase of Campbell's poetry, one with only a faint and indirect relationship to what had preceded. Campbell's activity as translator also represents the writing of a new and again very different kind of poetry, and if one wishes to emphasize this, as I believe one should, then clearly the listing of CP60 with the other translations as a unit becomes logical and desirable. Similar arguments attach to the inclusion of the prose translations in the C section. Having the books of prose together with the books of poems makes more evident the extent of the publication of works in translation by Campbell and the degree of his immersion during the last part of his career in the Catholic and the Iberian world. The translations of the classic Spanish plays have necessarily had to be placed in Section D, along with the separate publication of the translation of Lorca's *Llanto Por Ignacio Sánchez Mejías*, but their listing is close enough for them to be easily associated with the other translations.

In his letters and to one degree or another in a number of bibliographies—notably that attached to *Hommage à Roy Campbell* (Montpellier, 1958)—various additional, mostly prose works by Campbell are referred to: an essay on Burns, a study of Wyndham Lewis, what was possibly a collection of translations of

Lorca, a book entitled *Marine Provence*, a "Bull book," and a history of the Spanish Civil War. None of these was published. Of them, only the first two need be considered, since they have actually been listed in bibliographies as published. About the former the Archivist at Faber and Faber Limited states, ". . . *Burns* was announced in our Poets on Poets series but in fact never came. I am afraid this does happen sometimes with series that are said to be 'in active preparation'. . . ." Concerning the latter, Mr. John Charlton of Chatto and Windus Ltd. replied, "I can confirm that we did not publish Roy Campbell's book on Wyndham Lewis. . . . It was accepted for publication in our Dolphin Books series, and indeed it reached proof stage. But in September 1932 it was agreed that the publishing rights should be transferred to Messrs. Boriswood Ltd. . . . I cannot tell what happened thereafter, but I do know that the type was distributed that same month." The only announcement of the book, in the *Cumulative Book Index* for 1932, was of it as a "Dolphin Book" and it did not subsequently appear, nor was it ever listed among Boriswood's titles.

In Section E, first appearances of individual poems in journals, annuals or works in series, poems with the same or similar titles are in several cases cited more than once because sufficiently significant variants in the versions would seem to warrant notice of more than just the first appearance. Some entries, on the other hand, besides giving the first appearance of a poem, note the second when the first was in an obscure journal or a newspaper and the second in a well-known journal. In addition, for several poems, differences in title between their first appearance and when they were collected are noted.

A few first appearances of poems in South African and, possibly, Rhodesian newspapers have probably been missed. It has been impossible in general to attempt systematically to hunt down Campbell's contributions to newspapers, or to retrieve press comment about him, especially from either South African or European sources. Undoubtedly, the section on his published letters could be augmented by newspaper submissions. References by Campbell himself and others suggest that a body of such correspondence and newspaper comment exists.

Aside from this limitation, though, I have endeavored to

account for Campbell's prefaces and other contributions to books by others, his broadcasts and incidental prose writing. Much of the latter is journalistic and ephemeral, some of it perhaps to be passed over with averted eyes because of the prejudice and intemperance at times expressed, but the necessary labor of recording it for bibliographical purposes is not altogether unrewarding. One does come across some good reviews, some vigorous and revealing pieces that can assist assessment, for instance, of Campbell's critical standards, reading interests, and prose style.

The listing in Sections, H, I and J of what can be found in standard works of reference, such as the *Annual Bibliography of English Language and Literature* and *Granger's Index to Poetry*, has not been eschewed. Together with what is more *recherché* and fugitive, such entries make for true comprehensiveness and a satisfying picture of the corpus of Campbelliana. One exclusion, however, that of entries in encyclopedias and like reference handbooks, has been largely abided by.

Section J, dealing with works about Roy Campbell, has been divided into three sets of entries: for extensive studies, brief discussions and selected reviews. The criteria applied in determining the extensive are, obviously, comparative length and scope; but their selection has also depended on what is judged to be their relative critical importance, an importance estimated partly from their apparent effect on the reception of Campbell's work. In this selection an element of subjectivity is inevitable. So be it; there has to be a limit to objectivity in such matters. In the annotations themselves pains have been taken to convey essences dispassionately and accurately; but here, too, some subjectivity has arisen in that occasionally impressionistic comment has been included when the epitome itself could not suggest particular qualities of an account, on the assumption that potential readers of or about Campbell wishing to add to their knowledge and insight might appreciate some initial guidance on priorities.

One of the reasons that the briefer discussions are so numerous is that they tend to divide among critical comment, remarks upon Campbell's life and personality, and reactions to his political ideas and actions. Particularly when treating these brief discussions, I have thought it useful in the case of comment rather obscurely imbedded or dispersed in a book to indicate in parentheses following the entry the pages on which the material occurs. When an entire book is annotated, on the other hand, the number of pages is given in brackets after the entry.

The selection of reviews has been mainly governed by the fact that they abound for some of the works, in particular *The Flaming Terrapin, Adamastor, Collected Poems*, 1949, and *Light on a Dark Horse*, and are almost nonexistent for some of the smaller or less well-favored works. As with choices of appearances in anthologies, however, other considerations have also affected the selection of particular reviews, when otherwise one could have had merely a repetitious accumulation. Beyond trying to reflect Campbell's literary reputation at all periods and the relative importance accorded individual works and collections at different times, there has been the attempt to represent often sharply contrasting viewpoints. In several instances reviews of or comments upon studies about Campbell have been included when these in themselves provide a direct evaluation of Campbell.

The format of the entries for the research collections in Section K has naturally been influenced by the nature of the materials in each case, as well as by the manner of their presentation *in situ*. At one time or another I was fortunate enough to have catalogues or lists made available to me, apart from what was to be deduced from file catalogue entries, by the Berg Collection of the New York Public Library, the Poetry Collection of the Lockwood Memorial Library at the State University of New York at Buffalo, the Department of Rare Books and Manuscripts of the University of Saskatchewan Library, and most recently by the Killie Campbell Africana Library, University of Natal, Durban, and the National English Documentation Centre, Rhodes University, Grahamstown, South Africa. This last is the only collection I have not seen. Cornell University obligingly once sent me photocopies of their collection of letters, notes and cards from Campbell to Wyndham Lewis, and I have benefited greatly from having been able to study materials on microfilm lent me by the Humanities Research Center of the University of Texas at Austin. But whether aided or not by a catalogue or copies, the compression and presentation of the various research materials is of course my responsibility and any inaccuracies or omissions are solely my fault. The latter part of this comment, of course, applies also to the bibliography as a whole.

The division of the longest section, J, into parts has resulted in some unavoidable clutter in the Index. I can only hope that its usefulness will outweigh the inconvenience. In order to avoid confusion surpassing any possible benefit, the Index does not include the contents of Section K, Research Collections. It did not seem advisable to attempt to mingle the published with the unpublished; the Index should relate solely to the bibliography proper. Furthermore, in many instances items in the research collections cannot be sufficiently particularized and separately identified for indexing with acceptable thoroughness. For these reasons, therefore, I trust the omission will meet with understanding and hope that the arrangement of Section K will make any need for indexing comparatively slight.

ACKNOWLEDGMENTS

Without the help of a number of people and institutions, the compilation of the bibliography would not have been possible. To both I am deeply grateful in almost equal measure. Such an ambiguity may seem surprising and rather artificial, for in dealing with the institutions one is surely engaging with those who represent them. But I feel I have been very fortunate in so often working in or gaining assistance from libraries or publishing firms with obviously good traditions of excellence and service. To name individuals alone out of gratitude, then, is not enough. Instead, it seems best first to list those institutions, represented by the many I cannot identify and the few I can, to which my thanks are due.

Those libraries in South Africa I gladly mention are the Killie Campbell Africana Library, University of Natal, Durban; the Johannesburg Public Library; the South African Library, Cape Town; the State Library, Pretoria; the libraries of the University of Natal, Pietermaritzburg, and the University of the Witwatersrand, Johannesburg. Of course, like so many, I have been a grateful user of those great international depositories, the British Library and the Library of Congress. I recall with particular pleasure working in the London Library.

Good memories attach as well to the visits made to libraries in North America, among them the Berg Collection of The New York Public Library; Cornell University Library, Department of Rare Books; the William R. Perkins Library, Rare Book Room, Duke University; the MacLennan Library, McGill University; the Poetry Collection, State University of New York at Buffalo; and the Academic Center Library of the University of Texas at Austin. It was through the courtesy of the Humanities Research Center of the latter that I was able to make copies of or notes on the extensive Campbell collection held there. I owe a real debt, too, to the National English Documentation Centre, Rhodes University, at Grahamstown, South Africa, for so very generously providing me with a detailed catalogue of their recently acquired collection. I am no less indebted to the Killie Campbell Africana Library for sending me a current list of their Roy Campbell holdings. In addition, I express my thanks without reserve for many acts of kind service received at the University of Saskatchewan Library.

Publishing firms whose cooperation I should like to acknowledge are Ernest Benn Limited; The Bodley Head Limited; Chatto and Windus Limited; Faber and Faber Limited; Greenwood Press, Inc.; Haskell House Publishers, Inc.; Jonathan Cape Limited; the Longman Group; Ohio University Press; Pantheon Books, Inc.; Scholarly Press, Inc.; and Yale University Press.

For providing me with much needed information I am especially obligated to Dr. Herbert Berry of the Departments of English and Drama, University of Saskatchewan; Dr. George Campbell; Mary Campbell; Teresa Campbell; Robert J. Bertholf and Eric J. Carpenter, University Libraries, State University of New York at Buffalo; T.E. Cochran, University of Natal, Durban; Leonard W. Conolly, Department of English, University of Alberta; Mrs. Constance B. Cruikshank, Archivist, Faber and Faber Limited; Ms. J.F. Duggan, Killie Campbell Africana Library, University of Natal; Dr. J.A. Edwards, Archivist, The Library, University of Reading; Miss L. Kennedy, City Librarian, The City of Johannesburg Public Library; Francis O. Mattson, First Assistant, Rare Book Division, New York Public Library; Mrs. F.D. Parnell, National English Documentation Centre, Rhodes University; Joseph T. Rankin, Curator, Spencer Collection, New York Public Library; Dr. Reinhard S. Speck, School of Medicine, University of California, San Francisco; Miss E.M. van der Linde, University of Natal Library, Durban; Miss Valeria L. White, Yale University Press; Mrs. Joan H. Winterkorn, Bernard Quaritch Limited (formerly of Cornell University Library).

For responding to my inquiries or otherwise being of material assistance, I am grateful to Dr. Peter Alexander (Department of English, University of New South Wales); Henry Bailey-King, Esq. (Ernest Benn Limited); Dr. Susan Gingell-Beckman (Department of English, University of Saskatchewan); Dr. William F. Blissett (Department of English, University College, University of Toronto); Dr. R.L. Calder (Department of English, University of Saskatchewan); Agnes Campbell; Viscondeza Anna de Carondelet; John Charlton, Esq. (Chatto and Windus Limited); Dr. Geoffrey Durrant (Department of English, University of British Columbia); Mrs. A. Falk (The Bodley Head Limited); David Farmer (formerly, Humanities Research Center, University of Texas at Austin); Margaret Farnell (Head, Reference Department, Rutherford Library North, University of Alberta); K.C. Gay (formerly, Curator, Poetry Collection, State University of New York at Buffalo); Stanley D. Hanson (Archivist, University of Saskatchewan Library); Mrs. Mary M. Hirth (formerly, Librarian, Academic Center Library, University of Texas at Austin); William R. Johnson, Library Assistant, Department of Rare Books, Cornell University Library; D.S. Lea, Esq. (Longman Group Limited); Miss Arlean McPherson, Head, and Glen Makahonuk (Special Collections, University of Saskatchewan Library); Ms. Holly Panich (Ohio University Press); Neil Richards (Reference Department, University of Saskatchewan Library); Ms. Brenda Rueger (Rare Books Librarian, Stanford University Libraries); Dr. John L. Sharpe III, Curator, and Mrs. Janet L. Thomason (Rare Book Room, William R. Perkins Library, Duke University); W.H.P.A. Tyrrell-Glyn, Esq. (Librarian, The South African Library, Cape Town); Dr. Elizabeth M. Vida (Department of English, University of Saskatchewan); Vivian Webb, Esq. (Jonathan Cape Limited); Victor G. Wiebe, Head, and staff (Reference Department, University of Saskatchewan Library); Dr. Kurt Wittlin (Department of French and Spanish, University of Saskatchewan).

To anyone I should have mentioned by name but have overlooked, my apologies; to the many besides those named whose helpfulness and courtesy have aided in the preparation of this book, my sincere thanks.

University of Saskatchewan   D.S.J. Parsons

CHRONOLOGY

1901   October 2, born Royston Dunnachie Campbell in Durban, Natal, South Africa.

1910–17   Attends Durban High School; holidays in Rhodesia.

1918   Enters Natal University College; leaves for England and Scotland.

1919   Stays briefly at Oxford University; joins Aldous Huxley and Russell Green in London.

1920   Goes to Paris with T.W. Earp; visits Provence; meets Wyndham Lewis and other notables; works as a seaman.

1922   Marries Mary Garman; lives in Wales.

1924   *The Flaming Terrapin* published. Returns to South Africa.

1925   Wife and daughter join him in Natal; period of teaching, writing, ill-health.

1926   With William Plomer and Laurens van der Post founds and edits the literary magazine *Voorslag*; after two issues resigns following violent opposition and withdrawal by the magazine's backers. Returns to England, having written *The Wayzgoose*.

1927   Lives with the Nicholsons in Kent.

1928   *The Wayzgoose* published. Leaves England for Provence; at Martigues begins a varied career as cowboy, fisherman, bullfighter, water-jouster.

1930–33   Returns to writing and publishing: *Adamastor, The Georgiad, Taurine Provence, Flowering Reeds*.

1933–34   Moves to Barcelona and writes *Broken Record*.

1934–35   Farms for a while at Altea, Alicante, before going to Toledo to take up the horse and mule trade. Becomes a Roman Catholic. At confirmation takes additional Christian name—Ignatius.

1935–36 Active in bullring; briefly imprisoned for alleged debt; lives of family threatened by anti-clerical elements.

1936 During the troubles preceding the Spanish Civil War the Campbells harbor Carmelite Fathers and hide the Carmelite archives from the mob; they are evacuated to England; *Mithraic Emblems* published.

1937 Briefly back in Spain as war correspondent; joins family in the Algarve, Portugal. Writes *Flowering Rifle*.

1938–40 Visits Rome. *Flowering Rifle* published. Returns to Toledo after the Civil War and is active in social work. Undergoes spinal operation.

1940–41 According to reports, does some undercover work for British Intelligence.

1941 Returns to London; acts as air-raid warden. *Sons of the Mistral* published.

1942 Joins up in the South Wales Borderers; trains at Brecon, Wales; is transferred to Intelligence and posted to the King's African Rifles, East Africa.

1943–44 Made a sergeant, trains recruits and undertakes coast-watching duties; following injury in a training exercise and recurrence of a hip ailment, is hospitalized in Nairobi.

1944 Invalided out of the army; is in a Durban hospital briefly before being returned to England.

1945 Clerk with the War Damage Commission; receives disability pension.

1946–49 *Talking Bronco* published. Becomes a B.B.C. talks producer. Lectures in Spain.

1949 *Collected Poems, 1949* published. Edits *The Catacomb* with Rob Lyle.

1951 *Poems of St. John of the Cross* published. Works intensely on translating Baudelaire. Revisits Spain.

1952 Awarded the William Foyle Poetry Prize. *Poems of Baudelaire* and *Lorca* published. Leaves London to settle near Sintra, Portugal.

1953 Goes on a lecture tour of Canada and the U.S.A. *The Mamba's Precipice* published. Begins translating Portuguese works.

1954   Visits Durban via Rome to receive an Honorary D. Litt. from the University of Natal.

1955   Second North American tour. *Selected Poems* published.

1957   April 23, on returning from the celebration of Easter in Seville is killed in a car crash near Setúbal, Portugal. *Collected Poems*, Volume 2, published posthumously.

1960   *Collected Poems*, Volume 3 [Translations], published.

Section A

Books of Poetry
by Roy Campbell

Dust jacket front and spine of *The Flaming Terrapin* (A1a)
(Courtesy of Poetry/Rare Book Collection,
State University of New York at Buffalo)

a. First English edition:

The | FLAMING TERRAPIN | by | ROY CAMPBELL | [publisher's
device] | Jonathan Cape Ltd | ELEVEN GOWER STREET LONDON

1 blank leaf, 94 pp., 1 blank leaf.   7-11/16 x 5-1/4 in.
illus.: frontispiece, signed by John Austen. In the first
state the cover was of beige quality paper printed in green
and dark brown repeat pattern over boards; green cloth backstrip; ochre label, 1-1/2 x 1/2 in., at top of spine printed
across between decorative borders. The later state, identical
otherwise, was covered in orange paper over boards with tan backstrip; sewn; fore edges of text pages only rough trimmed;
lettered [A] to F. Printed on laid paper; unwatermarked.
Pale ochre dust jacket printed on front in light orange, with
illus. centered.

Published early 1924 at 4s. 6d. *On verso of title-leaf*:
'First published in mcmxxiv Made & printed in Great Britain
By Butler & Tanner Ltd. Frome and London [publisher's device]'

Dedication on page [7] to Mary and Natalie Campbell.

Contents: Text divided as follows: Part I, pp. 11-20; Part II,
pp. 23-38; Part III, pp. 41-52; Part IV, pp. 55-72; Part V,
pp. 75-80; Part VI, pp. 83-94. Intervening pagination
accounted for by separate part title leaves.

Note: Vivian Webb of Jonathan Cape writes concerning their
publication of *The Flaming Terrapin* and *The Wayzgoose*: "At
Jonathan Cape, as with most other publishers it was not thought
that publication book files were of the highest importance,
that is until quite recently. As the books were published so
long ago there is no one in the building who could have memory
of their publication details and alas there is not even a file
copy of the book with which I can check even some of the sim-
pler questions such as jacket design." The edition went
through five impressions between 1924 and 1935.

b. *First American edition:*

The | Flaming | TERRAPIN | By Roy Campbell | [publisher's device] | Lincoln MacVeagh | THE DIAL PRESS | MCMXXIV | New York

3 leaves, 83 pp., 1 blank leaf. 8-5/16 x 5-11/16 in. Watered orange paper with charcoal motif over boards; spine in black cloth, stamped across in gold; pages stained salmon pink at top edges.

Copies sold for $2.00. *On verso of title-leaf:* 'Copyright 1924 by Dial Press, Incorporated The Plimpton Press Norwood [bullet] Mass [bullet] U.S.A.'

Dedication on page [5] to Mary and Natalie Campbell.

Contents: Text divided as follows: Part I, pp. 3-11; Part II, pp. 15-29; Part III, pp. 33-44; Part IV, pp. 47-62; Part V, pp. 65-69; Part VI, pp. 73-83. Intervening pagination accounted for by separate part title leaves.

Note: Recorded on microforms for on-demand reprinting by University Microfilms International (not seen).

c. *Reprint (1970):*

Collation and title page as in the first English edition, except that at the foot of the title page is added: 'Republished 1970 | Scholarly Press, Inc., 22929 Industrial Drive East | St. Clair Shores, Michigan 48080'

8-5/16 x 5-1/8 in. Probably bound in light blue cloth over boards, as are the other reprints of Campbell titles by Scholarly Press. The only copy obtainable for examination was bound by the Library of Congress in dark red-brown cloth over boards, printed in white down spine; sewn.

Copies sold for $7.50. *On verso of title-leaf* (following the imprint given in the Jonathan Cape edition): '... This edition is printed on a high-quality, acid-free paper that meets specification requirements for the fine book paper referred to as "330-year" paper'

Note: Several requests for information on the dates of publication and numbers printed of their various Campbell

reprints, as well as on the binding for *The Flaming Terrapin*,
finally elicited this anonymous statement typed at the foot
of the last letter sent to Scholarly Press: "The above information is not available. Original covers of books are
destroyed."

A2   THE WAYZGOOSE   1928

a. First edition:

THE WAYZGOOSE | A South African Satire | by | ROY CAMPBELL |
Author of 'The Flaming Terrapin' | [publisher's device] |
London | JONATHAN CAPE [bullet] BEDFORD SQUARE | 1928

61 pp., 1 blank leaf. 8-3/16 x 6 in. Tan textured cloth
over boards; stamped in bright blue down spine; gatherings
lettered [A] to D. Printed on laid paper, unwatermarked.
Beige heavy paper dust jacket printed in black on front flap,
on front and back and down spine.

Published early 1928 at 5s. *On verso of title-leaf:* 'First
published in 1928 Made & printed in Great Britain By Butler &
Tanner Ltd Frome and London'

Dedication on page [1] to Mary Campbell.

Contents: Text of the first part of the poem, pp. 7-31, begins
beneath decorative border and half title above 'I'; the divisional title 'PART II' occurs on page [33], verso blank;
balance of text, pp. 35-61.

Note: See comment from Jonathan Cape quoted in the note under
A1a.

b. Reprint (1971):

Collation and title page as in the first edition, except that
the blank leaf is at the front and that at the foot of the
title page is added: 'Republished 1971 | Scholarly Press,
22929 Industrial Drive East | St. Clair Shores, Michigan 48080'

8-1/2 x 5-7/16 in. Light blue cloth over boards; printed in
gold down spine; sewn.

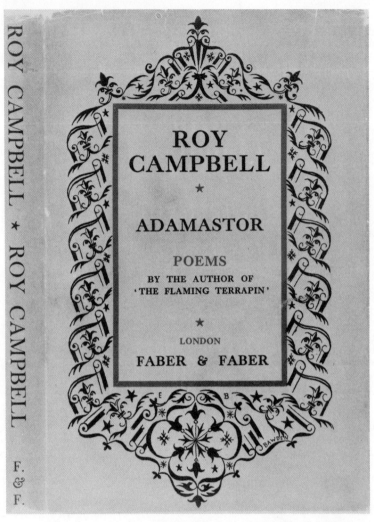

ROY CAMPBELL ★ ROY CAMPBELL F. & F.

ROY
CAMPBELL

★

ADAMASTOR

POEMS

BY THE AUTHOR OF
'THE FLAMING TERRAPIN'

★

LONDON
FABER & FABER

Dust jacket front and spine, first state, of *Adamastor* (A3a)
(Courtesy of Rare Book Room, Cornell University Libraries)

A3   ADAMASTOR   1930

a. First English edition, ordinary copies:

ADAMASTOR | POEMS | By | ROY CAMPBELL | LONDON | FABER &
FABER LTD. | 24 RUSSELL SQUARE

108 pp., 2 leaves. 8-1/16 x 5-9/16 in. Light red-brown cloth
over boards; stamped in gold down spine; stitched; pages stained
green at top edges; trimmed at fore and bottom edges; lettered
A to G. The dust jacket in the first state was of low-gloss
paper printed on front in black and red on a light green
ground, the design signed by E.B. Bawden, and the back and
flaps printed on green; on the spine was printed: 'ROY CAMPBELL
[star] ROY CAMPBELL F. & F.' Subsequently the printing on
the spine was altered to: 'ADAMASTOR [star] ROY CAMPBELL
F. & F.'

Published April 8, 1930; copies sold for 5s. *On verso of
title-leaf:* 'First published in mcmxxx By Faber and Faber
Limited 24 Russell Square London W.C.1 Printed in Great
Britain At the Westminster Press ...'; *on verso of last leaf:*
'[printer's device] The Westminster Press 411a Harrow Road
London W.9'

'DEDICATION | (TO MARY CAMPBELL) [poem, dated at end 'January
1929']', pp. 7-9.

Contents: Early Poems (Dedicated to C.J. Sibbett), pp. 15-38;
Adamastor, pp. 41-100; Satirical Fragments, pp. 103-06; Notes,
pp. 107-08. In each instance, except for "Notes," divisional
titles are found on the recto of an unnumbered leaf preceding
the text of the division.

Note: This edition was much in demand and went through three
impressions within two months of publication. In 1932 it was
reissued by Faber in a smaller format: 7 x 4-7/8 in.; green
cloth over boards; printed in gold across spine. Title-leaf
and collation as in the first edition, except that on page [1]
was printed: 'The Faber Library - No. 10 | [tapered rule] |
ADAMASTOR'; priced at 3s. 6d.; *on verso of title-leaf:* '...
second impression April mcmxxx third impression May mcmxxx
Reprinted in this new edition mcmxxxii ...' On page 10 under
'NOTE [Acknowledgments]' the following was retained: 'For
South African readers a supplement to *Adamastor* will be
published later.' Dust jacket: spine, front and back covers
printed on deep pink paper with blue-green decorative borders.

b. First edition, signed copies:

Title page and collation as in first edition, ordinary copies,
except that on the recto of the initial blank leaf occurs the
statement of limitation: 'This signed edition, printed on
English hand-made paper, is limited to ninety numbered copies.
Seventy-five copies only are for sale. This copy is number
[number written in] [author's signature beneath]'; also, the
last page [108] of "Notes" is not numbered and the printer's
colophon occurs on the verso of the first, not the second, of
the last two leaves, the final one being left blank.

8-1/16 x 5-9/16 in. Red cloth over boards; stamped in gold
down spine; stitched; top edges gilt; fore and bottom edges
rough trimmed. Acetate dust jacket; slipcase.

Note: The archivist at Faber and Faber, Mrs. C.B. Cruikshank,
states that this "small limited signed edition ... sold out
at once and curiously I find no trace of this in our bound
catalogues. From our cards I think it was priced at 25/--
which would be about right." It should be noted, though,
that ninety "Out of Series" copies were also printed. The
one such copy learned about by the compiler has a glassine
dust jacket and came in a slipcase covered in blue paper.

c. First American edition (1931):

[Enclosed within ornamental rectangular broken border simula-
ting logs laid end to end, with retangular rule inside:]
ADAMASTOR | POEMS | By | ROY CAMPBELL | Author of "The Flaming
Terrapin" | [publisher's device] | Lincoln MacVeagh | THE DIAL
PRESS | New York [bullet] MCMXXXI

1 blank leaf, 6 leaves, 103 pp., 1 blank leaf. 8-1/4 x 5-11/16
in. Paper with decorative motif in gold and navy blue over
boards; black backstrip; spine stamped across in gold; sewn;
top edges lightly gilt; fore edges trimmed.

Published February 1931; copies sold for $2.50. *On verso of
title-leaf:* '... Manufactured ... By the Vail-Ballou Press,
Inc., Binghamton, N.Y.'

Dedicatory poem to Mary Campbell on pages vii-ix, dated
'January 1929' at end.

Contents: Early Poems, pp. 3-28; Adamastor, pp. 31-94; Satirical Fragments, pp. 97-101; unnumbered leaves with divisional titles on rectos, including 'Early Poems | Dedicated to C.J. Sibbett', interspersed.

d. Selected edition in French (includes some poems from Flowering Reeds) (1936):

"LES CAHIERS DE BARBARIE" | PUBLIÉS PAR LES SOINS D'ARMAND GUIBERT | 12 | ROY CAMPBELL | ADAMASTOR | PRÉFACE ET TRADUCTION D'ARMAND GUIBERT | ÉDITIONS DE MIRAGES | 46, RUE DE NAPLES - TUNIS | Dépôt à Paris : Librairie R. Van den Berg | 120, Boulevard du Montparnasse

1 blank leaf, 88, [1] pp., 2 blank leaves. 7-15/16 x 5-3/4 in. Red-brown cloth over boards (apparently library bound, not original binding, in only copy seen: likely paper cover originally); stamped in gold up spine. Sewn; pages trimmed.

Printer's colophon, p. [89]: 'Achevé d'imprimer sur les presses de J. Aloccio, a Tunis, le 18 Février 1936.' *On verso of title-leaf:* 'Il a été tiré d'<<Adamastor>> douzième <<Cahier de Barbarie>> et quatrième de la deuxième série. Douze exemplaires sur Hollande van Gelder Zonen marqués de I a XII, et 300 exemplaires sur Alfa numerotés de 1 a 300. [Below:] Exemplaire [no. stamped in]'

Dedication, p. 8: 'A la chère mémoire de PIERRE RAFFRAY qui, fils d'une île australe, fut durant sa courte vie amoureux de deux langues et écartelé entre deux patries, -- les chants de ce poëte [sic] que nous n'avons pu aimer ensemble. A.G.'

Contents: Préface [close: 'Armand Guibert'], pp. 9-23; text, pp. 27-88; Dédicace (à Mary Campbell) -- En doublant le Cap -- Pour faire un poëte [sic] [prose trans.] -- Chant pour le peuple [prose trans.] -- Le Serf -- La fille Zoulou -- A un cobra favori -- Clair de lune africain -- Poëtes [sic] d'Afrique [prose trans.] -- Les zebres -- Buffel's Kop -- Tristan da Cunha [prose trans.] -- Les soeurs [prose trans.] -- Chevaux en Camargue -- Saint Pierre des Trois Canaux -- Messe à l'aube -- Estocade -- Automne -- Le Jardin -- La Flamme -- La Route d'Arles -- La Muse secrète -- Le roseau fleuri / A Charles Maurras -- <<La Clemence>> -- La Fleur -- Le choix d'un mât.

"LES CAHIERS DE BARBARIE"

PUBLIÉS PAR LES SOINS D'ARMAND GUIBERT

12

ROY CAMPBELL

ADAMASTOR

PRÉFACE ET TRADUCTION D'ARMAND GUIBERT

ÉDITIONS DE MIRAGES

46, RUE DE NAPLES - TUNIS

Dépôt à Paris : Librairie R. Van den Berg
120, Boulevard du Montparnasse

Title-page of *Adamastor* (selected edition in French) (A3d)

Notes: On p. 4, facing title page, eight titles in the "Première Série" of "Les Cahiers de Barbarie" are listed, and in the "Deuxième Série," four titles are given: '9. Paul Souffron ..... L'Eau Lustrale -- 10. F. Garcia Lorca ..... Chansons Gitanes (traduites de l'espagnol par Mathilde Pomès, Jules Supervielle, Jean Prévost et Armand Guibert.) -- 11. Anna Denis-Dagieu ..... Montherlant et le Merveilleux -- 12. Roy Campbell ..... Adamastor (traduit de l'anglais par Armand Guibert.)' Under "A Paraitre" three titles are listed.

Acknowledgments (under heading, "Avertissement") are of interest, as they differ somewhat from those in the English edition of *Adamastor*: 'L'éditeur présente ses remercîments [sic] les plus vifs à l'auteur, qui a bien voulu approuver cette traduction; et, à travers lui, aux journaux et revues suivants: *The New Statesman, The Cape Times, Voorslag, Die Burger, Ons Vaderland, The Zululand Times, The Bulawayo Chronicle, The South African Nation, The Nation, The Outspan, Die Huisgenoot,* ainsi qu'à M. C.S. [sic] Sibbett de Hout's Bay, Western Province, Cap de Bonne Espérance. Les 19 premières pièces du présent recueil sont tirés de *Adamastor* ... le reste, de *Flowering Reeds* ...'

e. Reprint (1950):

ADAMASTOR | By | ROY CAMPBELL | WITH A PREFACE AND | SEVEN DRAWINGS | CAPE TOWN | PAUL KOSTON | [publisher's device]

1 blank leaf, 101 pp. illus. by author. 10-1/2 x 8-5/8 in. Light blue cloth over boards; black leather backstrip and corners; stamped in gold on front and down spine; sewn.

Copies sold for 42s. *On verso of title-leaf:* 'First Edition Published in 1930 by Faber and Faber Limited, London This Edition Published SEPTEMBER 1950 Printed in South Africa by The Peninsula Press Limited Paarden Eiland'

Contents: Preface [close: 'Roy Campbell' and dated 'London | June 24, 1950'], pp. [5-7]; Dedication (to Mary Campbell), pp. 11-12 [at end dated 'January 1929']; text, pp. 15-101. Black and white illus. on pages counted but not numbered: pages [10], [30], [36], [44], [66], [78], [84]; also, each group of poems is preceded by a divisional title on the recto of a separate leaf counted but not numbered: Early Poems, p. [13]; Adamastor, p. [35]; Satirical Fragments, p. [95]. One change in order from that of the first edition occurred:

"Solo and Chorus from 'The Conquistador'" was moved down to
follow "The Making of a Poet" and to precede "A Song for the
People." That is, it was transferred from the "Early Poems"
section to the "Adamastor" section.

Note: In 1954 this reprint was distributed for Paul Koston by
Faber and Faber at 21s. a copy.

f. Reprint (1971):

ADAMASTOR | By | ROY CAMPBELL | WITH A PREFACE AND | SEVEN
DRAWINGS | [publisher's device] | GREENWOOD PRESS, PUBLISHERS |
WESTPORT, CONNECTICUT

349 copies published at $8.00 each.   9-1/4 x 6-1/8 in.   illus.
Collation identical to that given above, except that the preliminary blank leaf is lacking.   Black textured cloth over
boards; lettered in gilt down spine, author's name at top
enclosed in border doubled at ends; sewn.

A4   POEMS   1930

First edition, signed copies:

POEMS | ROY | CAMPBELL | HOURS PRESS | 15, Rue Guénégaud --
PARIS 6^e | 1930

2 leaves, 18 pp., 1 leaf.   11-9/16 x 7-15/16 in.   cover illus.
Vermilion paper over boards; on front, line drawing by author
of picador and bull, and on back line drawing by author of
olive tree, both drawings centered (p. [1] has: 'POEMS | by |
Roy Campbell | Covers by Roy Campbell'); brown leather back-
strip; lettered in gilt up spine; stitched; first eight leaves
rough trimmed on fore edges; all twelve leaves and flyleaves
rough trimmed at bottom; Canson-Montgolfier paper; unwatermarked.

Colophon, p. [19]: '200 copies of this book set by hand and
privately printed on hand-press each copy has been signed by
the author This is No [number written in], [author's signature beneath]'

POEMS

*ROY
CAMPBELL*

HOURS   PRESS
15, *Rue Guénégaud* - *PARIS* 6ᵉ
1930

Title-page of *Poems*, 1930 (A4)
(Courtesy of William R. Perkins Library, Duke University)

Published July 1930 at 40s.

Contents: The Louse Catchers (After Rimbaud) -- Reflections --
La Clemence -- The Secret Muse -- The Resonnador [sic], ["While
in your lightly-veering course ..."] -- The Olive Tree -- The
Olive Tree (2) -- The Albatross (After Baudelaire) -- A Sleep-
ing Woman -- From 'The Georgiad' (1) ["Next him Jack Squire
through his own teardrops ... Will lift his leg for Lawrence
on his bier"] -- An Anatomy of the Veld: From an Epistle to
William Plomer ["Have you not heard the call of Open Spaces?
... There's nothing underneath to fall into ..."] -- From 'The
Georgiad' (2) ["The hoary sage for dinner having dressed, ...
'Archmistress of the slowly crawling theme ...'"]

Note: One of the copies examined by the compiler was numbered
"230." Evidence suggests there was a considerable overrun.
Nancy Cunard in *Those Were the Hours: Memories of My Hours
Press, Reanville and Paris 1928-1931,* edited with a foreword
by Hugh Ford (Carbondale: Southern Illinois University Press,
1969), p. 139, states: "Campbell's name was such that his
Poems ... was oversubscribed far before publication and ...
my delight was great at being able to send him royalties of
£80 or so."

A5   THE GUM TREES   1930

a. First edition, ordinary copies:

[On front (in lieu of title page):] THE GUM TREES by ROY
CAMPBELL | [line drawing of trees] | DRAWINGS BY DAVID JONES

[4] pp. 4-13/16 x 7-3/8 in. col. illus. Limp bright green
paper covers flapped in over stiff flyleaves; watercolor reproduction of rows of trees in light brown, light olive green and
white over pen and ink outline, p. [1]; laid paper; stitched and
tied with ivory-colored string. Copies with salmon pink
covers also seen.

Copies sold for 1s. On back: 'This is No. 30 of THE ARIEL
POEMS Published by Faber & Faber Limited at 24 Russell Square,
London, W.C.1 Printed at the Curwen Press, Plaistow'

Contents: The text, pp. [2-4], under 'THE GUM TREES | (To
M.W.C.)', begins, "Half hid by leaves, in lofty shoots, ..."
and ends, "Their old antagonists arise." 17 quatrains.

Note: Concerning the Faber Ariel Series, Mrs. Cruikshank, the archivist, comments: "These were small booklets, each containing one unpublished poem by a leading poet and one or two illustrations by carefully matched artists. They ... are now very much Collectors' items. Coming as they did in the very early days, they did much to establish the prestige of this firm."

b. First edition, signed copies:

THE GUM TREES | BY | ROY CAMPBELL | Drawings by David Jones | London | Faber & Faber Ltd | 1930

8 leaves, text printed on rectos only. 8-3/4 x 5-11/16 in. col. illus. (line drawing, p. [3]; illus. in light brown and black, p. [8]). Red-brown paper over boards; printed in gold on front; pages rough trimmed on fore and bottom edges; stitched and tied with ivory-colored thread; English hand-made paper, including flyleaves.

Copies sold for 7s. 6d. Statement of limitation, page [1]: 'This large-paper edition, printed on English hand-made paper, is limited to four hundred copies This is Number [number written in], [author's signature beneath]'; *on verso of title-leaf:* 'Printed in England at The Curwen Press'; the rest of the printed matter on the back wrapper for the ordinary copies is found on page [15].

Note: Some of the enlarged, limited signed editions in the Ariel Series subsequently had special envelopes for Christmas use. That of *The Gum Trees* and of *Choosing a Mast* (see below) may have done so.

A6   THE GEORGIAD   1931

a. First edition, ordinary copies:

THE GEORGIAD | A satirical fantasy in verse | by | ROY CAMPBELL | [publisher's device] | LONDON | BORISWOOD LIMITED

64 pp. 8-7/8 x 5-7/8 in. Light blue cloth over boards; front cover has author's signature gilt-stamped at lower right;

stamped down spine in gold. Lettered [a] to d. Sewn. Dust
jacket of beige laid paper printed on front, back, flaps and
up spine. Reproduction on front center of line drawing (identified on front flap as by C) of charging bull with four banderillas in at base of neck; subtitle given -- A Charlotade --
differs from that on title page.

Copies sold for 5s. On verso of title leaf: 'Printed at The
Alcuin Press Chipping Camden Gloucestershire First published
in 1931 by Boriswood Limited 15a Harrington Road London S.W.7'

Contents: Text, in three parts and with occasional footnotes,
pp. 9-64: Part I, pp. 9-25; Part II, pp. 29-48; Part III,
pp. 51-64.

b. First edition, signed copies:

Title page and collation the same as for the first edition,
ordinary copies, except that on page [3] in place of a list
of other works the colophon is given: 'This special edition
of THE GEORGIAD, printed at The Alcuin Press, Chipping Camden
Gloucestershire, is limited to 170 copies signed by the
author, of which those numbered 1 to 20 are printed on Goat-
skin Parchment paper, and those numbered 21 to 170 on English
hand-made paper. There have also been printed fifteen copies
for presentation. [Below: number written; author's signature]'

Bound in silk over boards; silk has floral motif in silver,
blue, gold and charcoal. Tan leather backstrip, stamped up
spine in gold. Pages gilt at top, trimmed at front and bottom.
Clear acetate dust jacket.

Note: There may also have been a limited number of signed
copies bound in vellum. Not seen.

A7   CHOOSING A MAST   1931

a. First edition, ordinary copies:

[On front (in lieu of title page):] CHOOSING | A MAST | BY |
ROY CAMPBELL | DRAWINGS BY BARNETT FREEDMAN [title and author's
name superimposed on line-drawn version of col. illus. on

page [1]; inset at center of this illus. is line drawing of
sailboat, not in col. illus.]

2 leaves. 4-13/16 x 7-3/8 in. col. illus. Limp buff paper
covers flapped in over stiff flyleaves; p. [1]: watercolor
reproduction of trees in green, blue and brown over pen and
ink outline on recto of start of text; laid paper; stitched
and tied with ivory-colored string.

Copies sold for 1s. On back cover: 'This is No. 38 of THE
ARIEL POEMS Published by Faber & Faber Limited at 24 Russell
Square, London, W.C.1 Printed at the Curwen Press, Plaistow'

Contents: The text, pp. [2-4], under 'CHOOSING A MAST', begins:
"This mast, new-shaved, through whom I rive the ropes, ..."
and ends, "Shall fly, the feathered arrow of the foam."
Author's name printed at end. Eight 8-line stanzas.

b. First edition, signed copies:

CHOOSING A MAST | BY | ROY CAMPBELL | [rule] | Drawings by |
BARNETT FREEDMAN | [rule] | LONDON | FABER & FABER LTD | 1931
[page [3] reproduces what had been printed on the front wrapper
of the ordinary copies]

6 leaves. 8-11/16 x 5-9/16 in. col. illus., p. [7]. Tan
paper over boards, stamped in gold on front; English hand-made
paper, including flyleaves; pages trimmed at fore and bottom
edges; stitched and tied with light ivory-colored string.

Copies sold for 7s. 6d. Statement of limitation, page [1]:
'This large-paper edition, printed on English hand-made paper,
is limited to three hundred copies. This is Number [number
written in], [signature beneath]'; *on verso of title-leaf:*
'Printed in England at The Curwen Press'; the rest of the
printed matter on the back wrapper for the ordinary copies is
found on page [12].

See note to A5b.

A8   [POEMS]   1931

First edition:

[Outside front cover constitutes title page, counted as page
[1]; within double rule border is ornamental border enclosing
a single rule rectangle containing.] THE AUGUSTAN BOOKS OF |
POETRY | [rule] | ROY | CAMPBELL | [rule] | LONDON: ERNEST
BENN LTD. | BOUVERIE HOUSE, FLEET STREET

Verso of front cover lists new titles for series for 1931;
last title given under Bibliography, page [31], is "*The
Georgiad* (a satire), Boriswood. 1931."

30, [1] pp. 8-11/16 x 5-7/16 in. Paper covers, printed on
front and back; stitched and tied with light ivory-colored
string. On page [31]: 'Printed in Great Britain by Billing
and Sons Ltd., Guildford and Esher'

Contents: Biographical-critical note, followed by Acknowledg-
ments, p. [3]; table of contents, p. [4]; text, pp. 5-29:
Dedication ["When in dead lands ... The calm blue mirror of
the stars and moon"] -- The Making of a Poet -- The Zebras --
The Festivals of Flight -- African Moonrise -- The Sisters --
A Veld Eclogue: The Pioneers -- Tristan da Cunha -- The
Sleeper -- Horses on the Camargue -- Mass at Dawn -- Autumn --
An Open Window -- Sonnet ["The teeth of pleasure ... Before
a bull with lowered head."] -- From "The Swords" ["The third
is like a rainbow spun -- ... And heroes fought upon the
strand."] -- The Olive Tree [1] -- The Secret Muse -- The
Garden -- The Palm; Notes, p. 30 [those found in *Adamastor*
applying to "Adamastor," "A Veld Eclogue," "The Festivals of
Flight," "Horses on the Camargue"]; Bibliography, p. [31].

Notes: In answer to inquiries, Henry Bailey-King of Ernest Benn
replied: "We have to say that we are unable to give you any
information. Most of the books of Augustan poetry were very
slim, and in many cases there was no contract. In any case
most of our records of this era are very incomplete owing to
wartime upheavals."
        CBI 1928-32 gives price as 6d.

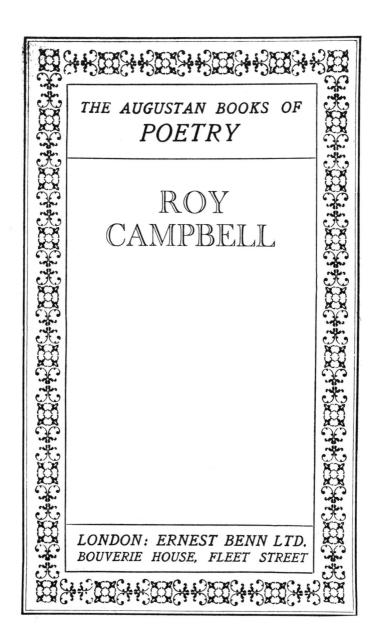

THE AUGUSTAN BOOKS OF
POETRY

ROY
CAMPBELL

LONDON: ERNEST BENN LTD.
BOUVERIE HOUSE, FLEET STREET

Title cover of [*Poems*], [1931] (A8)

A9   POMEGRANATES   1932

a. First edition, ordinary copies:

POMEGRANATES | A poem by | ROY CAMPBELL | with drawings by |
JAMES BOSWELL | LONDON | BORISWOOD LIMITED | 1932

6 leaves, 1 blank leaf. 7-5/16 x 5-3/8 in. col. illus.
Stiff light pink paper covers; front printed in dark blue.
Illus. in color signed by James Boswell, p. [3]; sewn; fly-
leaves.

Copies sold for 1s. 6d. *On verso of title-leaf:* 'Printed at
the Alcuin Press Campden Gloucestershire First published in
1932 by Boriswood Limited ...'

Dedication, p. [7]: 'To Mary Campbell'

Contents: Text, pp. [9-12]: poem of 14 quatrains: "Sung by
the nightingale to birth ... Whose changing reveries they seem."

Note: Some differences in punctuation, mainly between the
second and third stanzas, from the collected version. Also,
the latter was dedicated to Thomas Earp.

b. First edition, signed copies:

Title page and collation the same as for the first edition,
ordinary copies, except that there is an additional leaf and
that on page [1] there is a black and white illustration; on
page [3] of additional leaf the statement of limitation
occurs: 'Ninety-nine numbered copies of this edition have
been printed on English hand-made paper and signed by the
author. Ten presentation copies have also been printed.
[number written in], [author's signature]'

7 leaves, 1 blank leaf. 7-11/16 x 5-3/4 in. Beige textured
cloth over boards, printed in red on front and down spine.

Copies sold for 12s. 6d.

a. First edition, ordinary copies:

ROY CAMPBELL | FLOWERING REEDS | poems | 1933 | BORISWOOD
LIMITED

47 pp. 7-9/16 x 5-11/16 in. Textured green cloth over
boards; stamped in silver down spine; on front cover author's
signature stamped in silver at lower right. Light cream flyleaves. Dust jacket of stiff textured linen paper printed on
front in apple green and black, also down spine and on back
and front flap.

Published July 1933 at 5s. *On verso of title-leaf:* 'Printed
at the Alcuin Press Campden Gloucestershire First published
in 1933 by Boriswood Limited ... Copyright'

Dedication, p. [7]: 'Dedicated to My Mother'

Contents: Text, pp. 13-47: The Flowering Reed -- Canaan --
Song -- The Shell -- Autumn Plane -- The Flame -- The Road to
Arles -- The Flower -- The Blue Wave -- Wings -- Swans --
Vespers on the Nile -- On the Top of the Caderau -- Choosing
a Mast -- The Secret Muse -- The Rejoneador -- La Clemence --
Reflection -- The Louse Catchers (after Rimbaud) -- The Olive
Tree (1) -- The Olive Tree (2) -- A Sleeping Woman -- The
Albatross (after Baudelaire) -- The Gum Trees -- Overtime

Note: The ordering of some of the poems is slightly different
from that of CP49. In "Autumn Plane," "Vespers on the Nile,"
"The Secret Muse" and "Overtime," punctuation differs here
and there from that in the collected edition. Occasional word
changes or line drops occur in the collected versions of "On
the Top of the Caderau," "Vespers on the Nile," "Choosing a
Mast" and "Reflection."

b. First edition, signed copies:

Identical to the first edition, ordinary copies, in collation
and as to title page. On page [3], the statement of limitation
reads: 'Sixty-nine numbered copies of this edition have been
printed on English hand-made paper and signed by the author.
Eight presentation copies have also been printed. [Number
given], [author's signature]'

Beige cloth over boards; backstrip of brown cloth. Facsimile
of author's signature stamped in gold on front; stamped in
gold down spine. Pages gilt on top, trimmed at front and
bottom; sewn; lettered [a] to c. Copies sold for 21s.

c. Reprint (1971):

Title page same as for the first edition, except that at foot
is added: 'Republished 1971 | Scholarly Press, Inc., 22929
Industrial Drive East | St. Clair Shores, Michigan 48080'

Collation differs from that of first edition, ordinary copies,
only in that an initial and a final blank leaf are added, and
the half title leaf, pp. [11-12] in the first edition, is
moved back to become pp. [5-6]. 8-9/16 x 5-7/16 in.

Bound in medium blue cloth over boards; stamped on front in
silver: 'FLOWERING REEDS | [diamond] | Campbell | Scholarly
Press'; glued. Stiff beige flyleaves. Published at $8.50 a
copy.

A11   MITHRAIC EMBLEMS   1936

a. First edition, ordinary copies:

ROY CAMPBELL | MITHRAIC | EMBLEMS | poems | "... sin otra luz
y guía | sino la que en el corazon ardía." | SAN JUAN DE LA
CRUZ | BORISWOOD : LONDON

175 pp. 8-5/16 x 5-13/16 in. Bright blue cloth over boards;
publisher's emblem blind stamped on back cover at lower left.
In the first state, lettered down spine in gold and tops of
pages gilt; thereafter, printed down spine in black. Pages
trimmed at fore and bottom edges; sewn; lettered [A] to L.
Glossy paper dust jacket printed on back and front flap in
light blue and black on white; upper two-thirds of front and
spine printed in white on black and lower third of front
printed in blue on black. Cameo illus. in black and white of
Mithras and the Bull on front.

Copies sold for 7s. 6d. *On verso of title-leaf:* 'Made and
printed in Great Britain by Stephen Austin and Sons Limited,

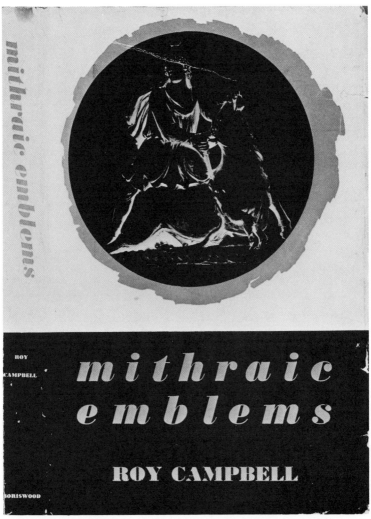

Dust jacket front and spine of *Mithraic Emblems* (A11a)
(Courtesy of Rare Book Room, Cornell University Libraries)

Hertford for Boriswood Limited ... First Published October
1936 Copyright'

Dedication, p. [7]: 'To Mary Campbell'

Contents: Text under three main divisional headings: 'I /
Mithraic Emblems', pp. 17-85, including 'Author's Note' on
p. 39, verso [40] blank; 'II / Toledo, 1936', pp. 89-101;
'III / Horizon', pp. 105-72. Gaps in paging accounted for
by separate divisional title leaves; also, preceding the text
of "Mithraic Emblems" is an additional subtitle leaf with
heading 'Mithraic Emblems -- a symbolic poem' followed by an
epigraph in the form of a quotation from Mistral; an extra
leaf preceding the text of the third division carries an
'Author's Note'. Notes occupy pp. 174-75.

b. First edition, signed copies:

ROY CAMPBELL | MITHRAIC | EMBLEMS | poems | "... sin otra luz
y guía | sino la que en el corazon ardía." | "... Aunque es
de noche." | SAN JUAN DE LA CRUZ | BORISWOOD : LONDON

175 pp.   8-3/4 x 5-5/8 in.   Bound in tangerine-orange textured
linen over boards; on front in gilt stamp: 'Roy Campbell';
publisher's device blind stamped on back cover at lower left;
gilt lettering down spine. Top edges trimmed and gilt, side
and bottom edges untrimmed; sewn; lettered [A] to L; endpapers,
one free and one paste-down. Laid paper; watermark: 'E.P.
Mathers | [device]'.

Statement of limitation on recto of tipped in leaf preceding
title page: 'Thirty numbered copies of this special edition
have been printed on hand-made paper and signed by the author.
Eight presentation copies have also been printed [author's
signature] [inscribed number]'

Publisher's imprint, dedication and contents as in ordinary
copies. Copies sold for 42s. net.

First edition:

FLOWERING RIFLE | A Poem from the Battlefield of Spain | By |
ROY CAMPBELL | Longmans, Green and Co. | LONDON [centered
diamond] NEW YORK [centered diamond] TORONTO

157 pp., 1 blank leaf. 8-3/4 x 5-3/4 in. Light red textured
cloth over boards; printed across and up spine in mustard
yellow; sewn; gatherings lettered A to K. Dust jacket printed
on front and up spine in black on orange and lemon; flaps
orange and lemon edged, otherwise printed on white.

2000 copies published February 6, 1939, at 6s. *On verso of
title-leaf:* '... First published 1939 Printed ... By Western
Printing Services Ltd., Bristol'

Dedication, p. [5]: 'To Mary Campbell'

Contents: Author's Note, closing 'VIVA FRANCO! ARRIBA ESPANA! |
ROY CAMPBELL. | Airosas Toledo. III° Año Triunfal', pp. 7-9;
text, pp. 13-157: Part I [begins under half title], pp. 13-28
-- Part II, pp. 31-67 -- Part III, pp. 71-102 -- Part IV, pp.
105-19 -- Part V, pp. 123-31 -- Part VI, pp. 135-57.

Notes: A "Cheap Edition" was published, according to *Notes on
Books,* v. 14, p. 101, on July 21, 1941, at 3s. 6d. Dr. J.A.
Edwards, Archivist, The Library, University of Reading, reports
that in the Longman archives the Impression books for this
title "do not contain a separate entry for the cheap edition.
Since the 'Code number'--18509--for the cheap edition and for
the first edition are identical, it may be that the cheap edition simply represents a reduction in price. The format and
make-up was, so far as I can see, precisely the same in both
editions."
   In CP57 *Flowering Rifle* consists of five parts, beginning
with the original Part II as Part I, the following parts re-
numbered accordingly; the old Part I was turned by C into a
separate poem and collected as "A Letter from the San Mateo
Front." The collected *Flowering Rifle* has more footnotes,
Part III opens with a new line added, and the couplet, "The
dirtiest of the elements in chief, / That loves the chill,
webbed hand-clasp of the thief" is a change from "The least
fastidious element we know, / That loves the chill, webbed
hand-clasp of the Jew." A new finale of 125 lines was added
to Part V.

A13   SONS OF THE MISTRAL   1941

First edition, selected poems:

SONS OF THE | MISTRAL | by | ROY CAMPBELL | Faber and Faber |
24 Russell Square | London

79, [1] pp. 7-1/2 x 5 in. Light blue paper over boards, printed
in red on front and down spine; stitched; lettered [A] to E.
Pale blue dust jacket printed in red.

Published January 23, 1941; copies sold for 2s. 6d. This
edition of selections was very popular despite wartime conditions: there was a second impression that August; third,
April 1943; fourth, July 1945; and further ones in 1948, 1955,
1958--seven in all. *On verso of title-leaf of first impres-*
sion (there were later changes of printer): 'First published
in mcmxli by Faber and Faber Limited ... Printed ... by Western
Printing Services Ltd., Bristol ...'

Contents: Select Bibliography, p. 5, contains error "Flowering
Record" for "Flowering Rifle," not changed in subsequent printings; text, pp. 9-78 [each poem under superscribed number in
heavy type]: Hialmar -- Mazeppa -- A Veld Eclogue: The Pio-
neers -- Georgian Spring -- Rounding the Cape -- The Making
of a Poet -- A Song for the People -- The Serf -- The Zulu
Girl -- To a Pet Cobra -- The Albatross -- In the Town Square
-- To a Young Man with Pink Eyes -- African Moonrise -- Poets
in Africa -- The Zebras -- Tristan da Cunha -- The Sisters --
Resurrection -- The Sleeper -- Horses on the Camargue -- The
Palm -- Estocade -- Autumn -- Sonnet -- The Garden -- The
Snake -- On Professor Drennan's Verse; Notes, pp. 79-80.

Note: Among photocopies of bindings seen is one measuring
approximately 9 x 5-1/2 in., but further information on a large-
paper edition has not been forthcoming.

A14   TALKING BRONCO   1946

a. First English edition:

[Hollow caps:] TALKING BRONCO | [rule] | by | ROY CAMPBELL |
FABER AND FABER LIMITED | 24 Russell Square | London

91 pp., 1 blank leaf. 8-13/16 x 5-9/16 in. Orange-red cloth
over boards; stamped down spine in gold. Lettered [A] to F.
Dust jacket printed on front and down spine in cream white on
red; printed on back and flaps in red on white.

Copies sold for 7s. 6d. Second impression, August 1946. *On
verso of title-leaf:* 'First published in mcmxlvi by Faber and
Faber ... Printed by ... R. MacLehose and Company Limited The
University Press Glasgow ...'

Dedication on p. [5] to Mary Campbell.

Contents: One Transport Lost -- Luis De Camoes -- Snapshot of
Nairobi -- The Beveridge Plan -- The Hoopoe -- Dreaming
Spires -- The Skull in the Desert -- The Volunteer's Reply to
the Poet -- San Juan de la Cruz -- Heartbreak Camp -- Washing
Day -- The Clock in Spain -- After Ruben -- Colloquy of the
Sphinx -- Moon of Short Rations -- Nyanza Moonrise -- Reflec-
tions -- Imitation (and Endorsement) of the Famous Sonnet of
Bocage -- Wars Bring Good Times for Poets -- Jungle Eclogue --
The Carmelites of Toledo -- On the Martyrdom of Garcia Lorca
-- How It Works -- En Una Noche Oscura -- Monologue -- Talking
Bronco -- Poems for Spain -- Auguries; Glossary for Civilians
[divisional title in text reads: 'Glossary of words from Ara-
bic, Swahili, Army-English and Elsewhere']

b. First American edition (1956):

Roy Campbell | [rule] | TALKING BRONCO | [publisher's device] |
Henry Regnery Company | Chicago, 1956

91 pp., 2 blank leaves. 9-1/4 x 6-1/4 in. Dark green mesh pattern printed on light olive green paper over boards. Light olive
green label, 4-3/16 x 3-1/4 in., printed in green within green
decorative rectangle pasted on front at upper right. Collation the same as in the English edition; stitched.

Priced at $2.50. *On verso of title-leaf:* 'This edition © 1956
by Henry Regnery Company ...'

Dedication: 'This Edition is Dedicated to Henry, Eleanor,
Susan, Alfred, Henry (Junior), and Margaret Regnery.'

Note: Many of the poems in this edition are dated at the end.
And many are rededicated also. The last part of the text is
headed simply "Glossary."

Dust jacket front and spine of *Collected Poems* (A15a)
(Courtesy of Rare Book Room, Cornell University Libraries)

Repeated requests to the publisher's successor for details concerning this and the other titles published by Regnery have had no result.

A15   COLLECTED POEMS   1949

a. First English edition, ordinary copies:

The Collected Poems of | ROY CAMPBELL | [publisher's device] |
THE BODLEY HEAD LONDON

297 pp., 1 blank leaf. 8-3/4 x 5-3/4 in. Bound in green cloth over boards; on front cover: red-brown panel enclosed by double rule in gold and stamped in gold inside, this repeated at top of spine, with stamping across; sewn; gatherings numbered [1] to 19; tops of pages stained light purple. Front and spine of dust jacket printed in light blue, brown and black on beige; back printed on light blue and beige, flaps on beige; stiff paper.

Copies sold for 15s. *On verso of title-leaf:* 'First published 1949 Made and printed in Great Britain by William Clowes and Sons, Limited, London and Beccles for John Lane The Bodley Head Ltd. 8, Bury Place, London, W.C.1'

Dedication, p. [5]: 'To Mary'

Contents: The titles collected are distributed under parts headed 'Lyrical', pp. 15-171, and 'Satirical', pp. 175-289, and, unless first published as single poems, are grouped under the name of the original collection to which they belong. All the single poems, including *Flowering Rifle*, previously published separately and all the poems of earlier collections are included, with the exception of a considerable number of those in *Mithraic Emblems* (see below) and *Talking Bronco*; however, the balance of the latter's poems were subsequently collected in CP57. "Kwa-Heri!" appears in CP49 with the *Talking Bronco* poems listed under "Satirical," even though it was not originally in that collection. The rest of the text consists of Notes, pp. 291-94; Index of Titles, pp. 295-97.

Notes: The poems in *Mithraic Emblems* not collected are "The 'Aficionado,'" "After the Riots," "The Argonauts," "The Bonxie," "Born too Late," "A Bouquet for my Wife," "The

The
Collected Poems of
ROY CAMPBELL

THEODORE BRUN LIMITED, LONDON

24 MUSEUM STREET, W.C.1.

Title-page of *Collected Poems* (A15b)
(Courtesy of William R. Perkins Library, Duke University)

Circle," "The Cowboy's Knife," "Dedication of a Tree," "A
Fable for my Children," "The Family Vault," "The Guid Auld
Mon," "Herdsman's Song," "Klipspringer," "Law," "Passing an
Examination," "Prologue," "Procession to the Sun," "San
Anton's Day," "A Schoolmaster," "To all Fascists and Commu-
nists," "To my Daughters in the Bullring," "To my Horses,"
"To the Red Indian, Michawago," "To the Springboks in
England," "Vaquero's Hearth."
    Recorded on microforms for on-demand reprinting by Uni-
versity Microfilms International (not seen).

b. First edition, deluxe copies, signed copies:

The │ Collected Poems of │ ROY CAMPBELL │ [publisher's device] │
THEODORE BRUN LIMITED, LONDON │ 24 MUSEUM STREET, W.C.1.

Collation as for the first edition, ordinary copies, except
for two added leaves and, tipped in, a black and white reproduction of the portrait of the author by Augustus John. The
first additional leaf has half title on recto, verso blank;
the second, the statement of limitation on recto, and on verso,
the colophon: '[publisher's device] Editions De Luxe Limited
The Collector's Book Club 24 Museum Street, W.C.1 London Catalogue No. 25 Produced for The Collector's Book Club by Theodore
Brun Limited, London De luxe binding by G.A. Cramp & Sons Ltd.,
Mitcham, Surrey'; this second leaf precedes the half title
leaf as in the first edition, ordinary copies, between which
and the title-leaf the portrait is tipped in.

8-5/8 x 5-3/4 in. Bound in red pebbled leather; publisher's
device stamped in gilt on front; stamped across spine in gold,
including floral designs. Top edges of pages gilt; white-gold
ribbon marker; endpapers and versos of flyleaves marbled.

Statement of limitation: 'This Limited de Luxe Edition is
published by special arrangement with Messrs. John Lane The
Bodley Head Ltd., London, and appears simultaneously with their
first edition. One hundred and seventy five copies have been
printed for sale, of which copies No. 1 to No. 75 have been
autographed and are available to members of The Collector's
Book Club only. In addition, twelve copies, numbered I to
XII, have been struck off as presentation copies.'

c. First American edition (1955):

SELECTED POEMS | [ornament: silhouette of charging bull from
drawing done by author] | ROY CAMPBELL | Chicago HENRY REGNERY
COMPANY 1955

Collation and binding same as for CP49.

Copies sold for $6.50. *On verso of title-leaf:* 'Henry Regnery
Company, Chicago, Illinois 1955 All rights reserved Printed
in Great Britain'; from front flap of dust jacket: '[Campbell]
... fell in with the gilded literary bohemians of the twenties,
and married one of them at the age of nineteen.... He has received an honorary D.Litt. at Natal University and was made a
Soci of Provençal Poeti at Avignon. In addition, he is well
known for his numerous translations into English of the literature of Norway, France, Spain, Provence, Catalonia and various
sections of South Africa.' Jacket printed in dark olive green
on light olive green.

Contents: Same as CP49.

A16   NATIVITY   1954

First edition:

Nativity | by | Roy Campbell | illustrated by | JAMES SELLARS |
[line drawing in block broken at sides] | FABER AND FABER |
24 Russell Square London WC 1

2 leaves. 8-1/2 x 5-1/2 in. col. illus. Pale salmon paper
covers, printed on front and back; stitched and tied with light
ivory-colored string. Illus. of nativity scene on verso of
title-leaf, facing beginning of text.

Copies sold for 2s. Colophon at foot of inside front cover:
'First published in mcmliv by Faber and Faber ... Printed ...
by Jesse Broad & Co. Ltd., Manchester....' On back: 'Ariel
Poems (new series) ...'

Contents: Beginning under title, 5 stanzas rhyming abcabc;
opens, "All creatures then rejoiced, save that the Seven ..."
and closes, "The tears of Man should shine in God alone."
Beneath close of text is a larger version of the black and
white illus. appearing with the title.

A17   COLLECTED POEMS, VOLUME 2   1957

a. First English edition:

The Collected Poems of | ROY CAMPBELL | VOLUME 2 | The Bodley
Head [bullet] London

256 pp. 8-11/16 x 5-5/8 in. Gold brown cloth over boards;
stamped in gold across spine, author's name and title near
top in brown panel, 1-9/16 x 1 in., enclosed in double gold
rule. Magenta stain on tops of pages; sewn; lettered [A] to
Q. Straw-colored dust jacket printed in dark brown. Portrait
of author reproduced on back flap.

Copies sold for 21s.; distributed in Canada by British Book
Service at $4.25 Can. a copy. *On verso of title-leaf:* 'First
Published 1957 This book is copyright under the Berne Conven-
tion.... Set in Centaur and printed in Great Britain by The
Camelot Press Ltd., London and Southampton for The Bodley
Head Ltd., 10, Earlham Street, London, W.C.2.'

Dedication on page [v] to Rob Lyle.

Contents: Preface by the author, p. xi; Early Poems (1926-
1939), pp. 13-58; Later Poems (1939-1956), pp. 58-256. The
text of the last poem, "Flowering Rifle (Revised Version),"
begins on p. 139, being preceded by the divisional title and
an epigraph consisting of two quotations from Bernard Shaw
on p. 135 and by "Author's Note Added to Proofs in September
1938," pp. 137-38. The revised version of "Flowering Rifle"
is divided as follows: Book I, pp. 139-77; Book II, pp. 178-
208; Book III, pp. 209-23; Book IV, pp. 224-31; Book V,
pp. 232-56. These divisions represent Books II to VI of the
1939 version; in the revision Book I became a separate poem,
"A Letter from the San Mateo Front," included under "Early
Poems (1926-1939)."

Note: The poems collected from *Mithraic Emblems* are "To my
Jockey" (re-titled "In Memoriam of 'Mosquito'"), "Thank you
very much" (re-titled "Driving Cattle to Casas Buenas") and
"Pillion to Talavera."

b. First American edition:

The | Collected Poems of | ROY CAMPBELL | CHICAGO | HENRY
REGNERY COMPANY 1957

On verso of title-leaf: 'First Published in the United States
1957 All Rights Reserved Henry Regnery Company 64E Jackson
Blv'd Chicago 4. Illinois Printed in Great Britain'; copies
sold for $6.50.

Identical in all other respects to the first English edition.

A18   POEMAS   1958

Selected first edition, in Spanish, incl. numbered copies:

ROY CAMPBELL | POEMAS | Selección, versión y prólogo | de |
AQUILINO DUQUE | [publisher's device] | ADONAIS | CLVII |
EDICIONES RIALP, S.A. | Madrid, 1958

67 pp., 8 leaves. 5-3/4 x 4-1/4 in. Dark red textured cloth
over boards; printed down spine in gold; gatherings numbered
[1] to 5; sewn; stiff flyleaves.

Colophon, recto of last leaf: 'Esta primera edición de
《Poemas》, de Roy Campbell, Vol. CLVII de la colección Adonais, se acabó de imprimir el día 20 de Sept. de 1958, en los
talleres artes gráficas 《Arges》 en Madrid': *on verso of title-
leaf:* '... De esta primera edición de Poemas ... se han hecho
seiscentos ejemp. en papel de edición y ciento viente en papel
especial, de los cuales, setenta (numerados del 1 al 70) para
los suscriptores de lujo de ADONAIS, y cincuenta (numerados
del I al L) para los suscriptores de honor.... Ediciones
Rialp, S.A. - Preciados, 35. Madrid'

Contents: Prólogo, pp. 9-12 [closes: 'Sevilla, junio de 1958.
Aquilino Duque']; poems, pp. 13-67: Buffel's Kop (En La Tumba
de Olive Schreiner) -- La Muchacha Zulu / A.F.C Slater --
Doblando el Cabo -- El Poeta [The Making of a Poet] -- El
Siervo -- En la Plaza del Pueblo -- Silencio -- Las Cebras --
Las Hermanas -- Tristan da Cunha -- Caballos en la Camargue --
Misa de Alba -- Otoño -- La Serpiente / A Liam O'Flaherty --
Eligiendo un Mastil -- Luis de Camoes -- San Juan de la Cruz /
Para Eve Kirk -- Dia de Lavado -- Sale La Luna en Nyanza --
La Muerte del Toro -- Al Sol -- Toledo, Julio 1936 -- Condu-
ciendo Ganado a Casas Buenas -- La Mancha en Tiempo de Guerra /
A C.J. Sibbett -- Sobre los Planos del Arquitecto para el
Escorial -- Rastreando un Angel / Para la Dama Comendadora
Edith Sitwell; Textos Utilizados, p. 67; Indice, pp. 71-72;

Suscriptores de Honor de ADONAIS, pp. 73-74; ADONAIS colección de Poesía ... Volumenes Publicados (1943-1958), pp. 75-81.

Note: The compiler has not seen any of the numbered copies.

A19   POEMS OF ROY CAMPBELL   1960

First edition:

POEMS OF | ROY CAMPBELL | chosen and introduced by | UYS KRIGE | MASKEW MILLER LTD. | 7-11 BURG STREET | CAPE TOWN

3 leaves, 142 pp. 7-1/2 x 5 in. Red cloth over boards; stamped in gold up spine; sewn; lettered [A] to I.

Copies sold for 10s. 6d. *On verso of title-leaf:* 'First published 1960 ... Printed in 11 on 12 point Bembo by The Standard Press Limited, 34 Glynn St., Cape Town ...'

Reprinted in 1973.

Contents: "The Poetry of Roy Campbell: A few aspects" [introductory essay in 4 parts by Uys Krige], pp. 1-32; text, pp. 35-142: selections from *The Flaming Terrapin*, *The Wayzgoose*, *Adamastor*, *The Georgiad*, *Flowering Reeds*, *Mithraic Emblems*, *Talking Bronco*, "Translations," "Later Poems (1946-57)."

A20   SELECTED POETRY   1968

a. First English edition:

Roy Campbell | [rule] | [hollow caps:] SELECTED POETRY | EDITED BY J.M. LALLEY | [publisher's device] | THE BODLEY HEAD | LONDON SYDNEY | TORONTO

221 pp., 1 blank leaf. 8-13/16 x 5-13/16 in. Navy blue cloth over boards; spine printed down and across in gold; sewn; lettered [A] to O. Salmon-colored dust jacket of laid paper printed in blue and red on front and on back flap, and in blue on front flap, back and spine.

Copies sold for 30s. a copy. *On verso of title-leaf:* '... All
rights reserved Roy Campbell's translation of Horace's The
Art of Poetry © Mary Campbell 1960 Joseph M. Lalley's Foreword
and Notes © The Bodley Head Ltd and Henry Regnery Inc 1968
This edition © Mary Campbell 1968 Printed and bound ... by
C. Tinling & Co Ltd, Liverpool, London and Prescot Set in
Monotype Ehrhardt This edition first published 1968'

Contents: Editor's Foreword [close: 'J.M.L.'], p. [9]; text
[divisional headings]: Lyrical and Love Poems, pp. 11-35;
Narrative and Allegorical Poems, pp. 37-59; The Flaming Terrapin, pp. 61-95; Epigrams, pp. 97-102; Satirical and Polemical
Poems, pp. 103-46; The Ars Poetica of Horace, pp. 147-66;
Translations from the French, Spanish and Portuguese, pp. 167-
215; Index of Titles, pp. 217-18; Index of First Lines,
pp. 219-21.

b. First American edition:

Roy Campbell | [rule] | [hollow caps:] SELECTED POETRY |
EDITED BY J.M. LALLEY | HENRY REGNERY | CHICAGO

Copies sold for $6.95. *On verso of title-leaf:* '© The Bodley
Head Limited and Henry Regnery Inc 1968 ... This edition first
published in the U.S.A. 1968'

Identical in all other respects to the first English edition.
Dust jacket not seen.

Section B

Books of Prose
by Roy Campbell

Taurine Provence

Roy Campbell

Dust jacket front and spine of *Taurine Provence* (B1b)
(Courtesy of Stanford University Libraries)

a. First edition, ordinary copies:

TAURINE PROVENCE | BY | ROY CAMPBELL | DESMOND HARMSWORTH | LONDON

79 pp. 8-1/2 x 6-5/8 in. illus. by author. Bound in orange-red cloth over boards; printed reproduction of side view of charging bull centered on front cover; spine printed across in black; sewn; flyleaves; wove, cream-colored paper. Grey dust jacket printed on front, spine, back and front flap. Illus. of bull centered on front, heraldic crest on back. Front flap provides as subtitle: 'The Philosophy, Technique and Religion of the Bullfighter'.

Copies sold for 6s. *On verso of title-leaf:* 'Taurine Provence by Roy Campbell was first published in mcmxxxii by Desmond Harmsworth Ltd., at 44 Great Russell Street W.C. 1 and was made and printed in Great Britain by Ebenezer Baylis & Son, Ltd., at the Trinity Press, Worcester and London'

Dedication, p. [5]: 'To Mary and Fiona with my love and with a cocarde each from the ganaderias of Feraud and Saurel.'

Contents: Text, with running title, pp. [11]-79, divided into three sections, concludes with author's name in large capital letters; 20 line drawings, most placed on pages with text-- one, on recto of leaf preceding text, captioned 'Defile of Toreadors: Nîmes'

b. First edition, signed copies:

Title page and collation as for the first edition, ordinary copies. 10 x 7-1/2 in.

Copies sold for 21s. *On verso of title-leaf:* below the colophon occur the author's signature and, beneath it, the

statement of limitation: 'This Edition is limited to One Hundred Signed Copies, of which this is No. [no. written in]'

Pale yellow cloth over boards; side view illus. of bull printed
on front in black; stamped in blood red across spine. Light
yellow dust jacket printed on front in red and black; heraldic crest centered on back; front flap provides as subtitle:
'The Philosophy, Technique and Religion of the Bullfighter'.

B2   BROKEN RECORD   1934

a. First edition, ordinary copies:

[ornamental rule] | [in scarlet:] BROKEN | [in scarlet:]
RECORD | [ornamental rule] | REMINISCENCES | BY | ROY CAMPBELL |
[ornamental rule] | LONDON [bullet] BORISWOOD [bullet]
MCMXXXIV

208 pp. 7-11/16 x 5-7/8 in. Light blue cloth over boards;
on front, facsimile of author's signature angled upward at
lower right stamped in bright yellow; on back at lower left
publisher's device blind stamped; stamped down spine in bright
yellow ochre; sewn; lettered [a] to n. Yellowish white dust
jacket printed in black and reddish orange on front; printed
on front flap and on back.

Published in 1934 at 7s. 6d. *On verso of title-leaf:*
'Printed ... at the Alcuin Press, Campden, Gloucestershire,
for Boriswood Ltd, 15a Harrington Road, London, S.W.7 Copyright'

Contents: Eight chapters; text of each chapter is preceded by
a part title leaf giving the chapter synopsis.

Notes: In the first state of this edition, chapter iv ended
with comments on pp. 104-05 alluding to the Scottish poet
Hugh MacDiarmid (Christopher Murray Grieve). When MacDiarmid
threatened a libel suit, the offending part of page 104 and
all of page 105 were cancelled. For details, see JII.35.
In 1936 Boriswood reissued *Broken Record* in a "cheap edition,"
priced at 3s. 6d.; not seen, but it was probably a further
printing of the first edition.
    Recorded on microforms for on-demand reprinting by Univer-
sity Microfilms International (not seen).

b. Special colonial edition:

Title-leaf and collation as in the first edition, ordinary copies; pages 104-05 cancelled. On page [1] below half title, 'SPECIAL COLONIAL EDITION' is rubber stamped. Green cloth over boards; facsimile of author's signature set at angle at lower right stamped in navy blue on front; stamped in navy blue down spine; no blind stamping of publisher's device on back.

Note: The compiler has been informed of a copy bound in green cloth that lacks the "Special Colonial Edition" stamp.

c. First deluxe edition, signed copies:

Title-leaf and collation as in the first edition, ordinary copies; pages 104-05 cancelled. On page [1] under half title occurs the statement of limitation: 'Fifty numbered copies of this special edition have been printed on hand-made paper & signed by the author. Eight presentation copies have also been printed. [number] [signature]'

Bound in white vellum; facsimile of author's signature stamped in gold down spine; pages gilt at top edges, trimmed at fore and bottom edges. No blind stamping of publisher's device on back.

d. Reprint (1971):

Not seen. Republished 1971 by Scholarly Press, 22929 Industrial Drive East, St. Clair Shores, Michigan 48080. All the other Campbell reprints by Scholarly Press are very similar. See A2b and A10c, also published in 1971, for comparison. For this title BIP 1977-78 lists the price as $15.50. Neither L.C. nor National Library of Canada can report locations.

B3   LIGHT ON A DARK HORSE   1951

a. First English edition:

LIGHT ON A | DARK HORSE | An Autobiography | (1901-1935) |
by | ROY CAMPBELL | [line drawing of herd of antelope] |
HOLLIS & CARTER

5 leaves, 347 pp.   8-11/16 x 5-5/8 in.   port., illus.   Choco-
late-brown cloth over boards; stamped in gold across spine,
decorative border at top; pages stained light blue at top;
lettered [A] to X.   Reproduction of the Augustus John portrait
facing title page; 22 line drawings by author, placed at begin-
nings or ends of chapters.   Dust jacket front is a photo-
reproduction of the author, printed over in white, yellow
and brilliant blue; back cover has illus. of horses printed
in yellow, black and brilliant blue.

Copies sold for 18s.; reissued in 1953 at 9s. 6d.   *On verso
of title-leaf:* 'Printed ... by the Chiswick Press, New South-
gate, N.11 for Hollis and Carter Ltd. 25 Ashley Place, London,
S.W.1   First published 1951'

Dedication, p. [vii]: 'Dedicated to My Mother'

Contents: Introduction, pp. 1-9, followed by 23 chapters,
each beginning under Roman numeral and with its own running
title.

b. First American edition (1952):

Same title page as for the first English edition, except at
foot: HENRY REGNERY COMPANY | CHICAGO [bullet] 1952

8 leaves, 312 pp.   8-3/4 x 5-9/16 in.   port., illus.   Blue
cloth over boards; stamped in gold down spine; sewn.

Copies sold for $4.00 a copy.   *On verso of title-leaf:* 'Copy-
right 1952 Henry Regnery Company Chicago 4, Illinois Manufactured in the United States of America'

c. Reprint (1969):

ROY CAMPBELL | Light on a Dark Horse | AN AUTOBIOGRAPHY |
1901-1935 | [line drawing of an antelope] | WITH LINE
ILLUSTRATIONS | BY THE AUTHOR | HOLLIS & CARTER | LONDON
SYDNEY | TORONTO

4 leaves, 347 pp., 2 blank leaves. 8-3/4 x 5-11/16 in.
illus. Red cloth over boards; stamped in gold across spine;
sewn; lettered [A] to Z. Glossy paper dust jacket printed
in black and red on white ground on front cover, with reproduction of photo of author centered within red border;
printed down spine in red and black and across in black;
back cover and front flap printed in black, back flap printed
in black and red.

Copies sold for 35s.; also published by Penguin Books, 1971, at
50p. *On verso of title-leaf:* 'Dedicated to My Mother ... Foreword © Laurie Lee 1969 Printed ... by Lowe & Brydone (Printers)
Ltd., London First Published 1951 Reprinted 1969'

Contents: Foreword [closing: 'Laurie Lee London, 1969'],
pp. [vi-viii]; text, pp. 1-347.

d. Paperback edition (1971):

ROY CAMPBELL | [star] | LIGHT ON A DARK HORSE | An
Autobiography | WITH LINE ILLUSTRATIONS | BY THE AUTHOR |
AND A FOREWORD BY | LAURIE LEE | [line drawing] | PENGUIN
BOOKS

351 pp. 7 x 4-1/4 in. illus. Front cover printed in orange,
black, blue and green has white lettering; printed down spine
in black, white and orange; back cover printed in white and
black on orange. Front cover design by Enzo Ragazzini from a
photograph of the author by Jane Bown; sewn.

Copies sold for 50p.; in Canada, for $2.15. *On verso of*
title-page: 'Penguin Books Ltd, Harmondsworth, Middlesex,
England Penguin Books Australia Ltd, Ringwood, Victoria,
Australia [short rule] First published by Hollis & Carter
1951 Published in Penguin Books 1971 All rights reserved
[short rule] Foreword copyright © Laurie Lee, 1969 [short
rule] Made and printed in Great Britain by Cox & Wyman Ltd,
London, Reading and Fakenham Set in Linotype Pilgrim [state-
ment of sale conditions at foot]'

Contents: Foreword, pp. 9-11; Introduction, pp. 13-21; text, pp. 23-351.

B4   LORCA   1952

a. First English edition:

LORCA | AN APPRECIATION OF HIS POETRY | BY | ROY CAMPBELL |
BOWES & BOSES | CAMBRIDGE

79 pp. 7-1/4 x 4-1/2 in. Canary yellow cloth over boards;
stamped down and across spine in gold, author's name and title
enclosed in double-lined rectangle; sewn; lettered [A] to E.
Dust jacket printed in mustard yellow with white repeat pattern;
printing on panel in white on front cover and another on
spine; flaps printed.

Copies sold for 6s.; distributed by British Book Service at
$1.25 a copy. *On verso of title-leaf:* 'First published in
1952 in the Series Studies in Modern European Literature and
Thought by Bowes & Bowes Publishers Limited Editor's Note [on
omission of quotations in the original Spanish and the use of
C's translations] Author's Note [acknowledgments; initialled
'R.C.'] Dedicated To Rob Lyle Printed in the Netherlands by
Joh. Enschede en Zonen, Haarlem'

Contents: Text, pp. 7-77: I. The Regional Poet -- II. The
Early Poems -- III. The Romancero Gitano -- IV. The Canciones
-- V. The Dramas -- VI. Cante Jondo, Poeta en Nueva York, and
Llanto por Ignacio Sánchez Mejías; Biographical Note, p. 78;
Lorca's Published Work, p. 79. The poems translated in the
text by Quevedo and by Lorca, with the notable exception of
the *Llanto*, were collected in CP60. For other appearances of
the latter, see Index. The text also contains numbers of
translated fragments.

b. First American edition:

LORCA | AN APPRECIATION OF HIS POETRY | BY | ROY CAMPBELL |
NEW HAVEN | YALE UNIVERSITY PRESS | 1952

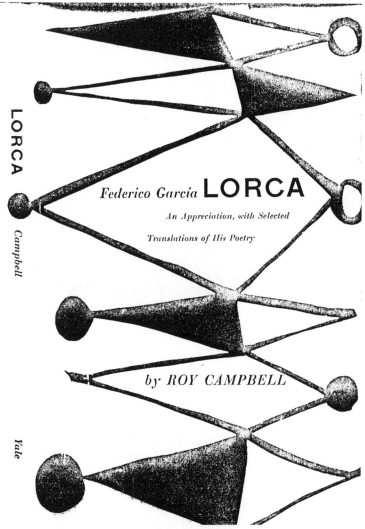

LORCA

Campbell

Yale

Federico García **LORCA**

An Appreciation, with Selected

Translations of His Poetry

by *ROY CAMPBELL*

Dust jacket front and spine of *Lorca: An Appreciation of His Poetry* (B4b)
(Courtesy of Yale University Press)

Collation as for first English edition.   8-3/4 x 5-3/4 in.
Beige cloth over boards, printed on front and down spine;
glued. Front of dust jacket has a zig-zag design in red and
is printed in black; the designer was Richard De Natale.

Published October 22, 1952; 1000 copies printed and bound;
copies sold for $2.50. *On verso of title-leaf:* 'Copyright
1952 by Yale University Press printed in the United States
of America [Editor's and Author's notes and dedication as in
English edition]'

c. First paperback edition (1959):

Title page and contents the same as for the first English edition, but reset in larger type; Editor's Note and Author's
Note placed on recto of additional leaf following title-leaf.
102 pp. 8 x 5-1/8 in. Covers printed in olive and red;
printed down and across spine in olive and red; photo of author
reproduced at top left on back.

Published September 16, 1959; 5250 copies printed and bound;
copies sold for 95¢ and were distributed in Canada by Burns &
MacEachern at $1.25 a copy. In 1960, an additional 5200
copies were printed.

d. Reprint (1961):

Identical in all respects to the first English edition, with
these differences: p. [1] under series title describes the
General Editor differently and adds the name of a second editor; title page has 'LONDON' in place of 'CAMBRIDGE', and the
same change occurs on the verso; latter also has: '... printed
by photolitho by Unwin Brothers Limited Woking and London
Reprinted 1961'

e. Reprint (1971):

LORCA | AN APPRECIATION OF HIS POETRY | BY | ROY CAMPBELL |
[publisher's device] | HASKELL HOUSE PUBLISHERS LTD. |
Publishers of Scarce Scholarly Books | New York, N.Y. 10012 |
1970

Collation as for the first English edition. 8-3/4 x 5-11/16 in. Glazed grey-blue cloth over boards; printed in gold down and across spine; sewn.

533 copies published January 1971.

B5   THE MAMBA'S PRECIPICE   1953

a. First English edition:

THE | MAMBA'S PRECIPICE | by | ROY CAMPBELL | Illustrated by Dolf Rieser | FREDERICK MULLER LTD. | LONDON

175, [1] pp. 7-7/16 x 5 in. illus. Dark red-brown cloth over boards; stamped across spine in gold; sewn; lettered [A] to K. Dust jacket printed on front in deep red, brilliant yellow and yellowish white.

Copies sold for 8s. 6d.; distributed in Canada at $2.25 Can. by S.J. Reginald Saunders. *On verso of title-leaf:* 'First published by Frederick Muller Ltd in 1953 Printed and bound ... by The Garden City Press Ltd. Letchworth, Herts.'

Dedication, p. [6]: 'To Hugh Lyle, Sandra Cox, Kerry Swift, and Michael Stuart.'

Contents: List of Illustrations [8 line drawings], p. 11; text [chapter headings used as running titles], pp. 13-175.

b. First American edition (1954):

The Mamba's Precipice | ROY CAMPBELL | THE JOHN DAY COMPANY | New York

189 pp., 1 blank leaf. 8-1/8 x 5-9/16 in. illus. Bound in shiny light blue paper over boards; printed down spine in navy blue; glued. One illus. by Dolf Rieser only: enlarged version of line drawing captioned "The Peace Cottage," p. [10].

Copies sold for $2.75. *On verso of title-leaf:* 'First American Edition, 1954 Copyright, 1953, by Roy Campbell ...

Published by the John Day Company ... and in Canada by Longmans, Green & Company, Toronto ...'

Dedication, p. [5], as in English edition.

Contents: Text, pp. 11–189. Starred footnotes as in the
English edition, except that on p. 29 "Miss" is placed in
brackets after *"inkossana"*; in the English edition, p. 29,
the word "Inkosasana" is starred for the footnote, "Miss."
Chapter headings not used as running titles as in the other
edition.

B6   PORTUGAL   1957

a. *First English edition:*

ROY CAMPBELL | [rule] | PORTUGAL | [publisher's device] |
MAX REINHARDT [bullet] LONDON

206 pp., 1 blank leaf. 8-11/16 x 5-11/16 in. illus. Gold-
brown cloth over boards; stamped in gold down and printed in
gold across spine; lettered [A] to N; sewn; stiff flyleaves.

Copies sold for 21s.; distributed in Canada by British Book
Service at $4.25 a copy. *On verso of title-leaf:* 'Published
by Max Reinhardt Ltd., 10 Earlham Street, London, W.C.2 ©
Roy Campbell 1957 This book is copyright under the Berne Con-
vention ... Set in Fournier and printed in Great Britain by
Richard Clay and Company, Ltd Bungay, Suffolk'

Contents: Table of illustrations, p. vi: thirteen sets of
photo reproductions, tipped in, facing pp. 32, 33, 48, 49,
112, 113, 128, 129; Introduction [initialled 'R.C.' at close],
pp. vii–x; ten chapters, pp. 11–206: 1 Romans and Celts --
2 Elysian Fields -- 3 On Wines -- 4 Under the Atlantic --
5 Portuguese Horsemen and Horses -- 6 Gado Bravo and the
Campinos -- 7 Portuguese Poetry -- 8 Portuguese Prose --
9 Fado: The Music of Lisbon / And the Gypsies -- 10 A Word
About Lisbon; [includes translations of Portuguese poetry,
some of them fragments, by Mindinho, Pero Meogo, Airas Nunes,
Gil Vicente, Camões, Bocage, Antero de Quental, Fernando
Pessoa, Francisco Bugalho, José Régio; there are also some
translations of prose passages].

Note: List facing title page of works under *Prose Translations* erroneously includes *The Relic* by Eça de Queiroz.

b. BIP 1977-78 records:

"*Portugal.* Roy Campbell. 1957. $15.00. Arden lib [Arden Library, Darby, Penn.]" Not recorded in LC-NUC 1957-78, nor in CBI 1970-78; not included in BM Cat. Supp. 1956-65; not listed in *The Bookseller*, 1977-78, *Book Publishing Record*, 1972-78, *International Bibliography of Reprints*, Munich, 1976. Despite several requests for information, the publisher has not responded, except to say the title is out of print. The compiler has not succeeded in obtaining a copy for examination.

c. First American edition (1958):

ROY CAMPBELL | [rule] | PORTUGAL | HENRY REGNERY COMPANY | Chicago 1958

Identical in all other aspects to the English edition, except that verso of title-leaf reads: '© Roy Campbell South African 1957. This book is copyright under the Berne Convention ... Set in Fournier and printed in Great Britain by Richard Clay and Company ...' In addition, the spine is stamped, not printed, across as well as down; among the works "By the same Author" listed on p. [ii], a translation of *The Relic* by Eça de Queiroz is not included, the titles being only those published by Regnery. Price of copies on publication not ascertained.

Section C

Books of Translations
by Roy Campbell

a. First edition:

HELGE KROG | [rule] | THREE PLAYS | HAPPILY EVER AFTER? |
TRIAD [bullet] THE COPY | translated from the Norwegian by |
ROY CAMPBELL | [rule] | BORISWOOD : LONDON

5 leaves, 185 pp. 7-9/16 x 5-1/8 in. Black cloth over boards;
stamped in red across spine, title given as: '3 Plays'; top
edges stained salmon pink, trimmed at bottom edges; sewn;
publisher's device stamped in outline at lower left on back;
lettered [A] to M.

Copies sold for 7s. 6d. *On verso of title-leaf:* 'Printed and
made ... at the Kemp Hall Press, Oxford: for Boriswood Limited
... First Published November 1934 Copyright'

Contents: Introduction [at close: 'Roy Campbell'], pp. ix-x;
Happily Ever After? a play, pp. 1-60; Triad [I: The Circle;
II: Who Knows -?; III: A Toast to Agnete], pp. 65-141; The
Copy, pp. 145-85. The text of each play is preceded by a part
title leaf, counted but unnumbered, with "Characters in the
Play" listed on verso, except that *Triad* is preceded by a
part title leaf, verso blank, and a second leaf giving the
playlet titles on recto and characters in them on verso.

b. First paperback edition, Happily Ever After?

HELGE KROG | [rule] | HAPPILY | EVER AFTER? | Translated from
the Norwegian by | ROY CAMPBELL | A PLAY | [rule] | BORISWOOD :
LONDON

1 blank leaf, 3 leaves, 60 pp., 1 blank leaf. 7-1/2 x 5 in.
Covered in beige paper printed on front and down spine in red.
Light tan dust jacket printed in black and red on front, down
spine in black with red starring; printed on back (one red

star follows printed matter) and on front flap. The front
flap has

ROY CAMPBELL writes:
        Chronologically succeeding Ibsen and Heiberg, Helge
Krog is the third and latest name in the noble dynasty of
Norwegian drama. Krog is a musician in human emotions
and in human nature. The verve and vitality of his dia-
logue is almost unparalleled on the modern stage. He is
one of those rare people who can snatch the ridiculous
from the tragic, and *vice versa*, without burning his
fingers.
        I have never seen the midnight sun, but I should
imagine that it must play over the northern landscape in
some such happy and amusing fashion as Krog's mind plays
over the loves and jealousies and antipathies of his
characters.
        I have not read any more stageworthy plays than these.
There is no local colour. The types are the same in every
European country wherever there is an upper middle class.
I look forward to the day when Krog's plays will be produced familiarly in both London and New York. So should
all sensible playgoers.

Copies sold for 2s. 6d. *On verso of title-leaf:* 'Printed and
made in Great Britain at the Kemp Hall Press, Oxford: for
Boriswood Limited ... First Published November 1934 Copyright'

Note: These actors' copies are very scarce. The compiler
has seen only a copy of *The Copy* and received information
about a copy of *Happily Ever After?* Since these match in
appearance and format, it may be reasonable to assume that
Triad does likewise.

c. First paperback edition, Triad

TRIAD | COMEDIES OF LOVE | translated from the Norwegian by |
ROY CAMPBELL

Not seen. But note similarities between *Happily Ever After?*
(see above) and *The Copy* (see below).

d. First paperback edition, The Copy

HELGE KROG | [rule] | THE COPY | translated from the Norwegian
by | ROY CAMPBELL | A COMEDY | [rule] | BORISWOOD : LONDON

1 blank leaf, 3 leaves, 41 pp., 1 blank leaf. Otherwise as
for *Happily Ever After?*

C2   POEMS OF ST JOHN OF THE CROSS   1951

a. First English edition:

THE POEMS OF | [in red:] ST JOHN OF THE CROSS | The Spanish
text | with a translation by | ROY CAMPBELL | Preface by |
M. C. D'ARCY, S.J. | [in red:] [publisher's device; incorpor-
ated at base of device:] HARVILL | 23 Lower Belgrave Street,
London

3 leaves, 90 pp. 8-1/2 x 5-1/2 in. Dull black cloth over
boards; stamped in gold down spine; sewn; lettered [A] to F;
dark cream flyleaves; laid paper. Beige dust jacket printed on
front, back and flaps in black and red, down spine in black.

Published in 1951 at 12s. 6d. Published simultaneously by
Pantheon Books, Inc., New York (see below). *On verso of
title-leaf:* '... Printed and made in Great Britain by Hague
Gill & Davey Ltd at Pigotts near High Wycombe and published
by The Harvill Press Ltd ... First published 1951 The Spanish
text of these poems is that of Padre Silverio de Santa Teresa
C.D. ('Obras de San Juan de la Cruz', Burgos, 1929-31), reprinted with his permission. It has previously appeared in
England in 'San Juan de la Cruz: Poesias', Liverpool, Institute of Hispanic Studies, 1933, and in 'Poems of St John of
the Cross', translated and edited by E. Allison Peers, London,
Burns Oates, 1947.'

Dedication, to Mary, on page [ii].

Contents: The Preface, pp. 1-8, closes with 'M. C. D'Arcy, S.J.'
The divisional title preceding the text on page 9 is 'POESÍAS --
POEMS'; however, in the table of contents only the titles in
English and the pagination for the translations are given:
twenty-two poems, beginning with "Upon a Gloomy Night," p. 11,
and ending with "Summary of perfection," p. 90. For each poem

the Spanish text occurs on the verso, the English on the recto
of facing pages, except on page 90 where both texts occur;
the text of each poem has its number superscribed in Roman
numerals.

b. *First American edition:*

This edition is identical in all respects, including dust
jacket design, to the first English edition, except for the
publishing details on title-leaf: recto has '[in red:]
[publisher's device] | PANTHEON BOOKS, INC.'; verso has
'Printed in Great Britain for Pantheon Books, Inc., 333 Sixth
Avenue, New York City First Edition 1951 [and, beneath the
statement giving the history of the text:] Printed by Hague
Gill & Davey Ltd, Pigotts, High Wycombe'

The edition sold for $2.75 a copy, and was distributed in
Canada by McClelland & Stewart at $3.75 Can. a copy.

Notes: A copy of the fourth edition was examined. This "edition" is identical in all respects to the first except *on the
verso of title-leaf:* '... First Edition, 1951 Second Edition,
1952 Third Edition, 1953 Fourth Edition, 1956 ... Printed by
Barnicotts Ltd. at Taunton, Somerset.' Black pebbled cloth
over boards; glued.
    LC-NUC records: "The poems of St. John of the Cross ...
London, Harvill 1956 90 p." From this one might suppose that
there were all four like English editions, but the compiler
has not been able to confirm this. Concerning publication
data for their editions of *Poems of St John of the Cross* and
Poems of Baudelaire (see C3b), a note from Pantheon's editorial department states: "I'm terribly sorry but I'm afraid
this information is simply not available."
    Subsequently, the compiler has learned from R.S.
Speck, M.D., bibliophile, of a later, undated edition not
recorded either by NUC or CBI, which differs from the preceding editions in the following respects:

. . . D'ARCY, S.J. | PANTHEON BOOKS | A Division of Random
House | NEW YORK [no publisher's device; all lettering in
black]

Leaves slightly shorter (by 1/16 to 2/16 in.). Black simulated-
cloth-textured paper over boards. Dust jacket deeper tan,
printed in brown and black; spine lettered 'ST JOHN OF THE
CROSS ROY CAMPBELL [CAMPBELL only on dust jackets of earlier
editions]'. The back wrapper advertises *Belief and Faith* by

Joseph Pieper (published 1963) and *The Humanity of Christ* by
Romano Guardini (published 1964). A new note appears on the
front inside flap under a rule: 'Roy Campbell was awarded the
1951 William Foyle Poetry Prize for this translation'

Imprint at foot of verso of title page: 'Printed in Great
Britain for Pantheon Books Inc., a Division of Random House';
the title leaf is not a cancellans.

c. *Paperback reprint of first American edition:*

The POEMS of | ST. JOHN of the CROSS | The Spanish text |
with a translation by | ROY CAMPBELL | Preface by | M. C.
D'ARCY, S.J. | [publisher's device] | The Universal Library |
GROSSET & DUNLAP | NEW YORK

Collation the same as for the first U.S. edition. 8 x 5-3/8 in.
Bound in stiff, shiny off-white paper; printed on front in
white, blues, browns and black; printed down spine and on back;
insides of covers have repeat pattern in grey-green and white
on grey; glued. On front and on spine coded "UL216."

Copies sold for $1.95; $2.50 in Canada. *On verso of title-*
leaf: the history of the text is given at the top of the page,
with the following sentence added: 'It is based on the Sanlúcar
MS.' Beneath: 'Universal Library Edition, 1967 By arrangement
with Pantheon Books, A Division of Random House, Inc. Printed
in the United States of America'

d. *Privately printed deluxe edition (1959):*

The Poems of | [in red:] ST JOHN | [in red:] OF THE CROSS |
The Spanish text with a translation by | ROY CAMPBELL |
Preface by M. C. D'ARCY, S.J. | With the kind permission of |
THE HARVILL PRESS LTD. [bullet] LONDON, ENGLAND

1 blank leaf, 5 leaves, 189 pp., 1 leaf (colophon), 1 blank
leaf. 8-5/8 x 6-7/8 in. illus. Half brown suèded leather
with sides of dark brown paper over boards; gilt cross on
each of upper and lower corners; spine gilt lettered; sewn;
gatherings unmarked; paper unwatermarked. Dust jacket of the
same brown paper as the binding; also with gilt lettering and
crosses.

Colophon: 'Twenty five copies were printed privately on hand-
made paper from Hamilton Farms Mill at Gladstone, New Jersey.
None are for sale.   The drawings are by Elsa Schmid.   The
type is 12 point Palatino, set at Huxley House, New York.
The book was printed at Olsen Press, Newark, New Jersey, and
bound by Master Bookbinding Company, Inc., of New York.'

Illustrations: frontispiece, p. [2], half-length figure of
the saint in robe and cowl, intersected by a large cross,
small tree form crossing his proper left arm, large crowned
Sacred Heart above, connected by lines to smaller hearts in
each of the saint's hands, another on his breast; p. [6],
facing "Contents," full-length figure of the saint overlaid
by a large cross, suspended against a landscape with town
rooftops at his feet, mountains behind, apparently rising to
a tall peak surmounted by a chapel (?) above his head; p. [10],
facing preface, head of the saint, cowled, with indication of
tree form at right; tailpiece below colophon, full-length
figure of the saint with repeat of the Sacred Heart motif
used in the frontispiece.   (For the descriptions of these
illustrations and the rest of the information on this edition,
the compiler is indebted to Mr. Joseph T. Rankin, Curator,
Spencer Collection, New York Public Library.)

Note: Not seen.   LC-NUC records: "The poems of St. John of
the Cross ... Newark, N.J., Privately printed at Olsen press
for Mrs. Suydam Cutting ... [1959]...."   Mr. Joseph T. Rankin
states, concerning the copy in the Spencer Collection: "Neither
Mrs. Cutting's name nor the publication date is actually
printed in the book.   On the back free endpaper, a note in
the handwriting of the then curator reads 'Gift of Mrs. C.
Suydam Cutting.   New York, Feb. 1960.'"

e. First paperback edition (1960):

ST JOHN OF THE CROSS | POEMS | WITH A TRANSLATION BY | ROY
CAMPBELL | [thick-thin rule] | Penguin Books

109 pp., 1 leaf.   7-3/16 x 4-7/16 in.   Stiff paper covers;
turquoise, peacock-green and black on front and back, spine
printed down in black and green; sewn; lettered [A] to E.

Copies sold for 2s. 6d.   *On verso of title-leaf:* 'Penguin
Books Ltd, Harmondsworth, Middlesex U.S.A.: Penguin Books Inc.,
3300 Clipper Mill Road, Baltimore 11, Md Australia: Penguin
Books Pty Ltd, 762 Whitehorse Road, Mitcham, Victoria [short

rule] This translation first published by Harvill 1951
Published in Penguin Books 1960 Made and printed in Great
Britain by Unwin Brothers Ltd, Woking and London'

Dedication, p. [5]: 'These translations are dedicated TO
MARY'

Contents: Preface, pp. 9-15 [at end, on right: 'Mary Campbell';
at left: 'Linho, September, 1957']; Introduction, pp. 17-24
[at end: 'M.C. D'Arcy, S.J.']; on page 25: 'POEMS The Spanish
text of these poems is that of Padre Silverio de Santa Teresa,
C.D. (Obras de San Juan de la Cruz, Burgos, 1929-31), reprinted
with his permission. It has previously appeared in England in
San Juan de la Cruz: Poesías, Liverpool (Institute of Hispanic
Studies), 1933, and in Poems of St John of the Cross, translated by E. Allison Peers, London (Burns Oates), 1934-5.'
Text, pp. 26-109, with Spanish on versos, English on rectos.

On page [1]: 'The Penguin Classics ... L101'

f. Reprint of first paperback edition (1968):

ST JOHN OF THE CROSS | POEMS | WITH A TRANSLATION BY | ROY
CAMPBELL | [publisher's device] | [thick-thin rule] | Penguin
Books | BALTIMORE [bullet] MARYLAND

Collation as in C2e. Stiff shiny paper covers, grey-green and
sepia on front, black on spine and back; front printed in
black, spine and back in white. The front cover shows a
detail of "Burial of Jesus," a fresco by Giotto in Florence,
as photographed by Germano Facetti; glued; lettered [A] to E.

Copies sold for $1.25. *On verso of title-leaf:* 'Penguin Books
Ltd, Harmondsworth, Middlesex, England Penguin Books Inc.,
3300 Clipper Mill Road, Baltimore, Md 21211, U.S.A. Penguin
Books Australia Ltd, Ringwood, Victoria, Australia [short rule]
This translation first published by Harvill 1951 Published in
Penguin Books 1960 Reprinted 1968 [short rule] Made and
printed in Great Britain by Cox and Wyman Ltd, London, Reading
and Fakenham Set in Monotype Fournier [statement of sale conditions at foot]'

C3   POEMS OF BAUDELAIRE   1952

a. First English edition:

[First two lines in red:] POEMS OF | BAUDELAIRE | A translation
of | LES FLEURS DU MAL | by | ROY CAMPBELL | [publisher's
device] | THE HARVILL PRESS

8 leaves, 228 pp.   8-5/8 x 5-3/4 in.   Mid-brown cloth over
boards; spine stamped across in gold; sewn; gatherings numbered [1] to 9.   White dust jacket overprinted in deep red
with white lettering.

Published in 1952 at 21s.; simultaneously published by Pantheon
Books, Inc., New York (see below).   *On verso of title-leaf:*
'First published in 1952 Printed and made by Hague Gill &
Davey Ltd. and published by the Harvill Press Ltd. 23 Lower
Belgrave Street, S.W.1'

Dedication, p. [viii]: 'This translation is dedicated to ROB
AND FELICIA LYLE'

Contents: Pp. [v-vi], Translator's Note [at close: 'ROY
CAMPBELL']; p. [vii]: Editorial Note; order of textual con-
tents as indicated by divisional headings and subheadings:
'LES FLEURS DU MAL 1861' ["To the Reader"], pp. 1-2; Spleen et
Ideal, pp. 3-111; Tableaux parisiens, pp. 112-40; Le Vin,
pp. 141-60; La Revolte, pp. 161-76; 'LES EPAVES 1866', pp.
179-92; Galanteries, pp. 193-99; Epigraphes, pp. 200-02;
Pieces diverses, pp. 203-05; [divisional heading, p. 208:]
SUPPLEMENT AUX FLEURS DU MAL 1866-68; Nouvelles Fleurs du
Mal, pp. 209-20; Poemes ajoutes a l'edition posthume, pp. 221-
23; Conclusion ["The Unforeseen"], pp. 227-28.   [Accents not
supplied in Lable of contents.]

Editorial Note, p. [vii], reads in part: 'The poems have
been arranged in the order followed by Y.G. Le Dantec in
Baudelaire, Oeuvres, Bibliotheque de la Pleiade, N.R.F., Paris,
1934, except for the poem 'L'Imprevu': by Mr. Campbell's request this has been placed as the concluding poem....'

b. First American edition:

This edition is identical in all respects to the first English
edition, except for the publishing details on the title-leaf:

POEMS
of
BAUDELAIRE

Les Fleurs du Mal

Translated by
Roy Campbell

Dust jacket front and spine of *Poems of Baudelaire* (C3a)
(Courtesy of Poetry/Rare Books Collection,
State University of New York at Buffalo)

recto has: '[American publisher's device] | PANTHEON BOOKS
INC.'; verso has: 'Printed in Great Britain for Pantheon
Books, Inc., 333 Sixth Avenue, New York City First Edition
1952 Printed by Hague Gill & Davey Ltd, Pigotts, High Wycombe'

This edition sold for $3.50 a copy and was distributed in
Canada by McClelland & Stewart at $5.00 Can. a copy.

See note to C2b.

c. First edition, selections (1960):

[Thick-thin ruled border, ornamental border within:] | THE
POCKET POETS | [rule] | BAUDELAIRE | [publisher's device] |
TRANSLATED | BY ROY CAMPBELL | [rule] | LONDON : VISTA BOOKS

48 pp. 7-1/4 x 4-1/2 in. Paper with purple repeat pattern on
magenta ground over cardboard; two panels printed in black
and white on front: the upper, 2-1/2 x 2 in., the lower, 2-1/2 x
5/8 in.; printed down spine; sewn; lettered [A] to C; laid
paper; flyleaves.

Sold for 2s. 6d. *On verso of title-leaf:* 'First published in
1960 by Vista Books: Longacre Press Limited 161/166 Fleet
Street London E.C.4 Made and printed in Great Britain by Pur-
nell and Sons, Ltd. Paulton (Somerset) and London © Mary
Campbell 1960'; *on verso of p. 5:* 'This selection from *Les
Fleurs du Mal* (1861, 1866) in Roy Campbell's translation is
published by courtesy of the Harvill Press, publishers of the
complete translation of the poems of Baudelaire by Roy Campbell, and also by the Bodley Head, publishers of the *Collected
Poems* of Roy Campbell.'

Contents: To the Reader -- The Albatross -- Elevation -- *I
love the thought of those old naked days* -- Ill Luck --
Gipsies on the Road -- Man and the Sea -- The Giantess -- Her
Hair -- Sed non Satiata -- *With waving opalescence in her gown*
-- Duel -- The Balcony -- The Possessed -- The Living Torch --
Reversibility -- The Cat -- The Splendid Ship -- Song of
Afternoon -- Sorrow of the Moon -- The Owls -- The Cask of
Hate -- Spleen -- The Red-haired Beggar Girl -- The Seven Old
Men -- The Little Old Women -- The Skeleton Navvy -- The Dance
of Death -- Meditation

C4   COUSIN BAZILIO (by José Maria de Eça de Queiroz)   1953

a. *First English edition:*

COUSIN | BAZILIO | [rule] | by EÇA DE QUEIROS [sic] |
Translated by | ROY CAMPBELL | LONDON | MAX REINHARDT

295, [1] pp. 8 x 5-1/2 in. Pink cloth over boards; printed
across spine in gold, title and author's name ('De Queiroz')
enclosed within gold rectangle on blue square; sewn; lettered
[A] to K. Dust jacket printed on white ground in light blue,
black and pink on front and spine; back printed in black and
pink on white; flaps printed.

Copies sold for 12s. 6d.; distributed in Canada by British
Book Service at $3.00 Can. a copy. *On verso of title-leaf:*
'First published in 1953 ... Printed at the St. Ann's Press
Park Road, Altrincham'

Contents: Fifteen chapters numbered I to XV, each numeral in
heavy type centered at head of chapter; text on page [296]
closes with 'FINIS'.

b. *First American edition:*

COUSIN | BAZILIO | Eça de | Queiroz | [at left: publisher's
device; at right:] THE NOONDAY PRESS, New York 1953

On page [iii]: 'translated by Roy Campbell with an introduction by Federico de Onís'

4 leaves, 343 pp. 8-1/4 x 5-1/2 in. Light ochre cloth over
boards; ornament stamped in purple on front; stamped in purple
down spine; sewn. Dust jacket of rough, flecked beige paper
printed in light blue and orange on front, in light blue and
olive on spine and in light blue on back and flaps.

Copies sold for $4.00 a copy; distributed in Canada by Longmans
(Toronto) at $4.50 Can. Colophon, p. [iv]: 'Copyright 1953
by The Noonday Press Manufactured in the United States Designed
by Alvin Lustig'

Contents: Introduction by Federico de Onís, pp. v-viii; text,
pp. 1-343, ending 'FINIS'; fifteen chapters, openings indicated
by Roman numerals, each centered at chapter head.

c. First paperback edition (1956):

Not seen. CBI, 1953-56 records: "... pa. $1.25 Noonday '56."
It is most likely that this was just a paperbound reprint of
the above.

C5   THE CITY AND THE MOUNTAINS (by Eça de Queiroz)   1955

a. First English edition:

THE CITY | AND | THE MOUNTAINS | BY | EÇA DE QUEIROZ |
Translated from the Portuguese by | ROY CAMPBELL | [publisher's
device] | MAX REINHARDT | LONDON

217, [1] pp., 1 blank leaf. 7-1/2 x 5 in. Bound in black cloth
over boards; on spine decorative gold border encloses title
and author's name in gold, all stamped, at foot publisher's
name stamped across in gold; sewn; lettered [A] to O. Dust
jacket printed on front in yellow, black and white on faint
pink ground; back and flaps printed.

Copies sold for 12s. 6d.; distributed by British Book Service
at $2.75. *On verso of title-leaf:* 'First published 1955 Eça
de Queiroz, generally considered as Portugal's greatest modern
novelist, was born in Povoa de Varzim in 1843, and in 1866
went to live in Lisbon. Much of his later life was spent in
the Portuguese diplomatic service, travelling in Egypt, Pales-
tine, France and England, and at the same time writing
letters, stories, essays and novels. Composed in Pilgrim type
and printed at the St. Ann's Press Park Road, Altrincham'

Text: pp. 5-[217], chapters One to Sixteen; numbers centered
above chapter openings in larger, heavy type.

Note: On page [2], under 'By the same author', *The Relic*
translated by Aubrey F.G. Bell [sic] is listed.

b. Reprint (1962):

THE CITY | AND | THE MOUNTAINS | BY | EÇA DE QUEIROZ |
Translated from the Portuguese by | ROY CAMPBELL | DUFOUR
EDITIONS | Philadelphia | 1962

Collation as for the first English edition. *On verso of title-leaf:* 'First published 1955 ... Printed in Great Britain for Dufour Editions'. Red cloth over boards; stamped across spine in gold. Buff dust jacket with brown edging at top and bottom; printed in red and black on front, back and spine; printed on front flap.

c. First American edition (1967):

The City & | the Mountains | Eça de Queiroz | Translated from the Portuguese | by Roy Campbell | Ohio University Press | Athens, Ohio | [publisher's device]

2 leaves, 216, [1] pp., 1 blank leaf. 8-1/2 x 5-1/2 in. Covered in light brown charcoal cloth over boards; initials 'E De Q' stamped in silver on front; stamped down spine in silver and mid-green; tops of pages stained pink; sewn. Glossy white stiff paper dust jacket printed on front and spine in black, magenta and green; on back printed in black with pen and ink portrait of Eça de Queiroz reproduced.

Published July 19, 1967; 1585 copies printed; originally priced at $4.50. *On verso of title-leaf:* 'Copyright ⓒ 1967 by Ohio University Press ... Manufactured ... by H. Wolff Book Manufacturing Company, New York'

Page [1] has biographical and critical note on Eça de Queiroz, with comment by Frederico [sic] de Onis, 'former head of the Hispanic Institute of Columbia University'.

C6   COLLECTED POEMS, VOLUME 3 (TRANSLATIONS)   1960

a. First English edition:

The | Collected Poems of | ROY CAMPBELL | VOLUME 3 | [in square brackets] TRANSLATIONS | with a Foreword by Edith Sitwell | THE BODLEY HEAD | LONDON

144 pp. 8-3/4 x 5-11/16 in. Red cloth over boards; printed across spine in gold, author's name and title near top in black panel enclosed by double gold rule; sewn; lettered [A] to H; flyleaves. Beige dust jacket printed in dark blue.

Copies sold for 18s. each; distributed by British Book Service
at $4.25 a copy. *On verso of title-leaf:* 'Roy Campbell's
translations of Horace's *The Art of Poetry*, three poems by
Rafael Morales, and two poems by J. Paco d'Arcos © Mary Campbell 1960 Foreword © Edith Sitwell 1960 Printed in Great Britain for The Bodley Head ... by William Clowes and Sons Ltd,
London and Beccles Set in Monotype Centaur First Published
1960'

Contents: Foreword by Edith Sitwell, pp. 5-7; Preface [close:
'MARY CAMPBELL'], p. 13; text [with divisional headings:]
'Part One / Four French Poems', pp. 17-22; 'Part Two / Horace
-- The Art of Poetry', pp. 25-43; 'Part Three / St. John of
the Cross', pp. 47-57; 'Part Four / Federico García Lorca',
pp. 61-80; 'Part Five / Other Spanish Poems', pp. 83-92;
'Part Six / From Baudelaire's *Les Fleurs du Mal*', pp. 95-115;
'Part Seven / Portuguese Poems', pp. 119-44.

b. *First American edition:*

Title-leaf, collation and binding identical to those of the
first English edition, except that at foot of title page is
'HENRY REGNERY COMPANY | CHICAGO' and on verso of title-leaf,
Henry Regnery Company replaces The Bodley Head, as on spine;
on page [2] only titles published by Regnery are listed.
Copies sold on publication for $6.50.

C7   NOSTALGIA   1960

First edition:

NOSTALGIA | [rule] | a Collection of poems by | J. PAÇO
D'ARCOS | Translated from the Portuguese and introduced by |
ROY CAMPBELL | Sylvan Press

48 pp., 2 leaves. 7-1/2 x 5 in. Beige paper over boards, printed
in rust red on front and up spine; stitched. Dust jacket of
heavy beige paper printed in rust red on front, back, flaps
and up spine.

Copies sold for 12s. 6d. *On verso of title-leaf:* 'First
published in 1960 by Sylvan Press London Printed at The Curwen
Press, Plaistow ...'

Contents: Roy Campbell on J. Paço D'Arcos [author's preface], pp. 5-6; text, pp. 8-48: First Glimpse of African Shores -- The Harbour Master of the Wild Island -- Fear -- The Murmur of the Rain in the Gutter [São Paulo] 1929 -- Regrets for What I Was, What I Am Not and What I Am to Be! [Pau February] 1931 -- Febrile City between the Mountains and the Sea [Rio de Janeiro] 1932 -- Negress from Your Straw Hut -- It Was in a Distant Town on the Shores of China -- When the Writer had Finished His First Novel 1940 -- Philadelphia, by Night, Without Moonlight [Philadelphia] 1941 -- Lost in the City of Infinite Lives [New York] 1941 -- My Dress of Velvet with White Lace -- Castles in Spain -- Those who Remained Wandering about the World -- The Dead Queen [Glasgow-London July] 1946 -- The Shade of the Cathedral Covers the City of Riches [Antwerp] 1946 -- Lucerne beside the Lakes [Lucerne April] 1948 -- One Half of Me Fights the Other Half [Vichy September] 1948 -- All the Verses which I Keep in my Memory 1950 -- The Doubt and Uncertainty which Paralyse Me [At Sea] 1950 -- Reencounter [Moçamedes 8 December] 1950 -- Yearning for Other Captivities [Bay of Saint Tomé December] 1950 -- Portrait of Madame Gautreau in the Tate Gallery [London April] 1951 -- The City with Towers Higher than Heaven [New York April] 1952 -- I Do Not Wish to Miss the Boat at New Orleans [New Orleans 30 April] 1952 -- This is the Land of Texas Jack [Texas on the way to New Mexico, May] 1952 -- It Was Twenty, Thirty, a Thousand Years Ago? [23 May] 1952 -- To Write is to Conquer Death [All preceding matter in brackets supplied in text at ends of poems.]

C8   THE SURGEON OF HIS HONOUR (Calderón)   1960

a. First edition:

Calderón de la Barca | The Surgeon of His Honour | Translated by Roy Campbell | [decorative rule] | With an Introduction by Everett W. Hesse | The University of Wisconsin Press | Madison, 1960

15 leaves, 82 pp. 8-11/16 x 5-11/16 in. Light brown cloth over boards; spine printed down and across in black; glued; beige flyleaves.

Colophon, p. iv: 'Published by the University of Wisconsin Press ... Copyright © 1960, by the Regents of the University

of Wisconsin Printed ... by The William Byrd Press, Inc.,
Richmond, Va.'

Contents: Introduction, pp. vii-xxiv; Selective Bibliography,
pp. xxiv-xxvi; 'The Spanish Dramatists: A Note | Roy Campbell',
pp. xxvii-xxx; *Dramatis Personae*, p. 2; text, pp. 3-82: Act I,
pp. 3-28 -- Act II, pp. 29-56 -- Act III, pp. 57-82.

Note: For the particulars of publication, the compiler was
referred by the University of Wisconsin Press ("no longer our
publication") to Greenwood Press (see below). The latter gave
some details about its publication of the reprint, but nothing
on the earlier history of the title.

b. Reprint (1978):

Identical to the first edition, except that the device, name
and address of Greenwood Press, the publisher, appear on the
title page in place of the original publishing details; it is
bound in light blue cloth over boards, printed in white down
and across spine, sewn, and has stiff grey flyleaves.

Published February 24, 1978, at $11.00 a copy; 172 copies
printed. *On verso of title-leaf:* 'Copyright © 1960 by the
Regents of the University of Wisconsin Reprinted with the
permission of the University of Wisconsin Press ...'

Section D

Prefaces or Other Contributions
by Roy Campbell to Books
by Other Writers

WATLINGIA, or a symposium of views on the much lamented departure of GEORGE & IVY WATLING of the Hog-in-the-Pound, Oxford Street, London.

Written by their friends and Hand-set by
Tambimuttu at THE HOG IN THE POUND PRESS

40, Crawford Street, London W.1

1947

D1 Lewis, Wyndham. *Satire and Fiction. Preceded by The History of a Rejected Review by Roy Campbell.* (Enemy Pamphlets No. 1.) London: The Arthur Press, 1930. [Facsimile editions of *Satire and Fiction* were reprinted by Folcroft Press, Folcroft, Pennsylvania, in 1967, 1974 (Folcroft Library Edition), and by Norwood Press, Norwood, Pennsylvania, 1975.] "Reviewer's Preface," by Campbell, pp. 13-14; "The Rejected Review," pp. 15-16.

D2 Campbell, Margaret W[ylie]. *Paper Toy Making.* Foreword by R.R. Tomlinson. London: Sir Isaac Pitman and Sons, [1937]. Rpt. by C.T. Branford Co., Newton, Mass., 1960, 1963, and by Dover Publications, New York, 1975. The author of this title was C's mother. [Not seen.] Preface by Roy Campbell, p. v.

D3 *Watlingia, or a symposium of views on the much lamented departure of George & Ivy Watling of the Hog-in-the-Pound, Oxford Street, London.* Written by their friends and hand-set by Tambimuttu at the Hog in the Pound Press, 1947. [Among the sixteen contributors: Nicholas Moore, G.S. Fraser, John Waller.] Quatrain, p. [v].

D4 *South African Poetry: A New Anthology.* Compiled by Roy MacNab and Charles Gulston. London: Collins, 1948. Foreword [so called on title page; called "Introduction" at head of text], pp. xxi-xxiii.

D5 *First Words: A Miscellany of Verse and Prose.* Compiled and edited by Clifford Dobb, Jack Hobbs and J.M. Russell. [A periodical miscellany by members of the Makers Society of St. Edmund Hall.] [Oxford], 1949-50. Introduction, pp. 5-7.

D6 *Il Paradiso di Dante.* An English Version by T.W. Ramsey. Aldington, Kent: The Hand and Flower Press, 1952. Foreword, pp. v-vii.

D7   Anon. *On the Four Quartets of T.S. Eliot.* London:
     Vincent Stuart, 1953. [On the title page of the Second
     Impression, 1965, the author is identified as Constance
     De Masirevich.]
     Foreword, pp. 7-8.

D8   Cope, Joan Penelope [Lady Grant], translator. *Arabic
     Andalusian Casidas.* Tunbridge Wells, Kent: Peter
     Russell (The Pound Press), 1953.
     Preface, pp. 7-8.

D9   Dutton, Geoffrey. *Africa in Black and White.* London:
     Chapman and Hall, 1956.
     Preface, pp. v-viii.

D10 Plumb, Charles. *Toward the Sun: Three Poems.* With a
     Preface by Roy Campbell and illustrations by John
     Peppiatt. London: Parry Jackman, 1956.
     Preface, pp. 7-8.

D11 Slater, Francis Carey. *The Collected Poems.* Edinburgh
     and Cape Town: William Blackwood and C.N.A., 1957.
     Preface, p. vii.

D12 "'The Trickster of Seville,' by Tirso de Molina, trans-
     lated by Roy Campbell." [Version for radio.] *Master-
     pieces of the Spanish Golden Age.* Edited by Angel
     Flores. New York: Rinehart, 1957. Pp. 287-367.
     [Differences from version coll. in Bentley (see below):
     Act I has 25 or so minor variants; Act II contains
     three major passages differing in lines and some 40
     minor variants; Act III gives five main passages dif-
     fering either through addition or omission and about
     35 minor variants. Sometimes needs of the aural medium
     are the evident cause of alterations.]

D13 Tschiffely, A.F. *Little Princess Turtle Dove.* Illus.
     by Alfons Purtscher. London: Muller [also Blackie],
     1957.
     Preface, pp. 5-6.

D14 Bentley, Eric, ed. *The Classic Theatre. Volume Three:
     Six Spanish Plays.* Garden City, N.Y.: Doubleday
     (Anchor Books), 1959.
     Contents: *Celestina, or the Tragic Comedy of Calisto and
     Melibea*, by Fernando de Rojas, translated by James
     Mabbe and adapted by Eric Bentley; the remaining five
     plays translated by Roy Campbell--*The Siege of*

Numantia, by Miguel de Cervantes, pp. [97]-160;
Fuente Ovejuna, by Lope de Vega, pp. [161]-231; *The
Trickster of Seville and His Guest of Stone*, by Tirso
de Molina, pp. [233]-314; *Love After Death*, by Calderón
de la Barca, pp. [315]-405; *Life's A Dream*, by Calderón
de la Barca, pp. [407]-80. In addition, an appendix
provides Shelley's translation of the first three
scenes of Calderón's *The Wonder-Working Magician*. The
translations of *The Trickster of Seville* and *Life is a
Dream* were rpt. in *World Masterpieces*, Rev. Ed., Vol.
1, ed. by Maynard Mack *et al.*, New York: Norton, 1965.

D15 *Lament for the Death of a Matador*. Four Paintings by
John Fulton Short. Based on the Poem Llanto Por
Ignacio Sánchez Mejías by Federico García Lorca.
Printed by private subscription - copyright John Fulton
Short - Sevilla, 1964.
Campbell's contributions [all taken from his *Lorca: An
Appreciation of His Poetry*]: "Biographical note on
Federico García Lorca," p. 27; "Lorca--an appreciation
of his poetry," p. 28; translation, with connecting
commentary, of the four parts of the *Llanto*, pp. 28-35.

Section E
First Publication in Periodicals
of Individual Poems
by Roy Campbell

E1 "Bongwi, the Baboon." *Coterie*, 4 (Easter 1920), 23-24.

E2 "Gigue Macabre." *Coterie*, 4 (Easter 1920), 23-24.

E3 "Absinthe." By Royston Dunnachie Campbell. *Oxford and Cambridge Miscellany*, June 1920, p. 30.

E4 "The Theology of Bongwi, the Baboon." *Oxford and Cambridge Miscellany*, June 1920, p. 2.

E5 "The Porpoise." *Oxford Poetry, 1920*. Oxford: Blackwell, 1920. P. 10.

E6 "Canal." *Coterie*, 6 & 7 (Winter 1920-21), 23-24.

E7 "The Head." *Coterie*, 6 & 7 (Winter 1920-21), 23-24.

E8 "The Sleepers." *Coterie*, 6 & 7 (Winter 1920-21), 23-24.

E8a "Abracadabratesque." *Sackbut*, 1.9 (March 1921), 411.

E8b "A Formal Parting at Dawn." *Sackbut*, 1.9 (March 1921), 412.

E8c "Thirst." *Sackbut*, 1.9 (March 1921), 413.

E9 "The Theology of Bonave." *The First Edition and Book Collector*, 1.2 (September-October 1924), 87.

E10 "To a Young Man with Pink Eyes." *Voorslag*, 1.2 (July 1926), 62.

E11 "L'albatross - (Charles Baudelaire)." By Lewis Marston [pseud., identified as C's by William Plomer in "Voorslag Days," *London Magazine*, 6 (July 1959), 48]. *Voorslag*, 1.3 (August 1926), 46.

E12 "The Burial of a Poet - (Charles Buadelaire)." By Lewis Marston [pseud.]. *Voorslag*, 1.3 (August 1926), 46-47.

E13   "Les Chercheuses de Poux - (after Rimbaud)." By Lewis
      Marston [pseud.]. *Voorslag*, 1.3 (August 1926), 46.

E14   "Don Juan in Hell - (Charles Baudelaire)." By Lewis
      Marston [pseud.]. *Voorslag*, 1.3 (August 1926), 46-47.

E15   "The Serf." *The Nation* (London), 40 (November 6, 1926),
      183.

E16   "The Zulu Girl." *The New Statesman*, 28 (November 27,
      1926), 206.

E17   "From thee, Goddess,...." *The South African Nation*,
      December 31, 1926, pp. 7-8.

E18   "Tristan da Cunha." *The Waste Paper Basket of the Owl
      Club*. Cape Town: Hortors, 1926. Pp. 6-7. [Annual.]

E19   "The Sleeping Woman." *The South African Nation*,
      January 29, 1927, p. 11.

E20   "The Festivals of Flight." *The Calendar*, 4.1 (April
      1927), 1-3.

E21   "The Making of a Poet." *The New Statesman*, 29 (August 20,
      1927), 597.

E22   "The Sisters." *The New Statesman*, 29 (August 27, 1927),
      619.

E23   "African Moonrise." *The New Statesman*, 29 (September 10,
      1927), 679.

E24   "The Zebras." *The New Statesman*, 30 (February 18, 1928),
      593.

E25   "The Palm." *Life and Letters*, 1.4 (1928), 42.   [Prose
      translations in French by Georges Limbour of "The Palm"
      and "The Gum Trees" appeared in *Commerce*, 18 (1928),
      68-85.]

E26   "Garden." *The New Statesman*, 33 (January 22, 1929), 337.

E27   "The Albatross" ["Stretching white wings in strenuous
      repose ..."]. *The Enemy*, 1 (First Quarter, 1929), 85.

E28   "Horses on the Camargue." *The New Statesman*, 33 (July 13,
      1929), 437.

E29 "Open Windows" ["An Open Window"]. *The New Statesman*, 33 (September 21, 1929), 709.

E30 "Autumn." *The New Statesman*, 34 (November 9, 1929), 157.

E31 "The Sleeper." *The New Statesman*, 34 (December 14, 1929), 330. [Had previously appeared in *The Cape Times*, October 23, 1929, and was to appear in the *Montreal Star*, December 1929.]

E32 "Mass at Dawn." *The New Statesman*, 24 (January 18, 1930), 468.

E33 "A Veld Eclogue: The Pioneers." *The New Statesman*, 34 (March 1, 1930), 664-65.

E34 "Mazeppa." *The New Statesman*, 34 (March 15, 1930), suppl., viii-ix.

E35 "Buffel's Kop: Olive Schreiner's Grave." *The New Statesman*, 34 (March 15, 1930), 739.

E36 "Wings." *The New Statesman*, 4 (September 3, 1932), 259.

E37 "Lescot's Horses" ["Jousé's Horses"]. *The New Statesman*, 4 (September 24, 1932), 345.

E38 "The Road to Arles." *The New Statesman*, 4 (October 29, 1932), 513.

E39 "Autumn Plane." *The New Statesman*, 4 (November 19, 1932), 625.

E40 "On the Top of the Caderau." *The New Statesman*, 5 (January 28, 1933), 100.

E41 "The Shell." *The New Statesman*, 5 (March 4, 1933), 254.

E42 "Vespers on the Nile." *The New Statesman*, 5 (March 4, 1933), 254.

E43 "Stanzas from 'The Swords.'" [3 sonnets, coll. with minor differences as "The Third Sword," "The Second Sword," and "The First Sword" of "Mithraic Frieze" in *Mithraic Emblems*.] *The New Statesman*, 5 (April 8, 1933), 445.

E44   "From 'The Swords.'" [Coll. with minor differences as
      "The Fourth Sword" of "Mithraic Frieze" in *Mithraic
      Emblems*.] *The New Statesman*, 5 (July 29, 1933), 134.

E45   "From 'The Swords.'" [The earlier version of "The Sixth
      Sword" of "Mithraic Frieze" in *Mithraic Emblems*.] *The
      New Statesman*, 5 (August 26, 1933), 237.

E46   "Toril." *The Listener*, August 1, 1934, p. 209.

E47   "Overtime." *The New Statesman*, 4 (August 27, 1934), 232.

E48   "Familiar Daemon." *Outspan*, 16 (September 30, 1934), 33.
      [Also in *Virginia Quarterly Review*, 11 (January 1935),
      34.] [Not seen.]

E49   "A Good Resolution." *Outspan*, 16 (September 30, 1934),
      33. [Also in *Virginia Quarterly Review*, 11 (January
      1935), 34.] [Not seen.]

E50   "Rust." *Outspan*, 16 (September 30, 1934), 34. [Also
      in *Time and Tide*, 16 (May 11, 1935), 690.] [Not seen.]

E51   "Vaquero to His Wife." *Outspan*, 16 (September 30, 1934),
      33. [Also in *Virginia Quarterly Review*, 11 (January
      1935), 34.] [Not seen.]

E52   "Autograph (to C.J. Sibbett – an apology for having
      neglected to thank him for gifts and letters)." *The
      Waste Paper Basket of the Owl Club*. Cape Town: Hortors,
      1934. [Annual.]

E53   "The Mocking Bird." *Virginia Quarterly Review*, 11
      (January 1935), 34-36.

E54   "To the Survivors." *Time and Tide*, 16 (March 2, 1935),
      304.

E55   "The Fight." *Time and Tide*, November 9, 1935, p. 1608.

E56   "Hard Lines, Azaña!" *The British Union Quarterly*, 1.1
      (January-April 1937), 104. [Published under the gene-
      ral title, "Three Poems from Toledo"; the other two
      poems, "The Alcazar" and "The Fight," had appeared in
      Mithraic Emblems.]

E57   "The Carmelites of Toledo." *The Tablet*, January 1, 1938,
      p. 7. [Also in *Spain*, 5.65 (December 22, 1938), 245-
      46, 248.]

E58 "The Loaves and Fishes / (Answered by a legionary to
Mr. Atlee)." [Later, part of *Flowering Rifle*.] *The
Tablet*, January 1, 1938, p. 7.

E59 "A Legionary Speaks." [Later, part of *Flowering Rifle*.]
The Tablet, January 15, 1938, pp. 69–71.

E60 "La Mancha." *The Tablet*, June 25, 1938, p. 826.

E61 "Not Against Flesh and Blood (a Poem from Spain)."
[Later, part of *Flowering Rifle*.] *The Tablet*,
October 29, 1938, pp. 549–50.

E62 "The Singer." *Right Review* 8 (April 1939), [20].

E63 "The People's Army." *Right Review*, 8 (June 1939), [6].

E64 "Dreaming Spires." *Outspan*, 35 (June 9, 1944), 27.

E65 "Heartbreak Camp." *Outspan*, 35 (June 9, 1944), 35.

E66 "One Transport Lost." *Outspan*, 35 (June 9, 1944), 27.

E67 "The Skull in the Desert." *African World*, May 1946,
p. 23. [Also in *Northern Review*, 6 (April–May 1953),
2–7.]

E68 "The Volunteer's Reply to the Poet." *Lilliput* (June
1946), 83. [Not seen.]

E69 "'Reyerta' / (brawl of Spanish gypsies). / Translated from
the Spanish of Federico Garcia Lorca." *The Poetry Review*, 38.6 (November–December 1947), 407.

E70 "'Songs between the Soul and the Bridegroom' / by
St. John of the Cross. Translated by Roy Campbell."
The Changing World, 3 (Winter 1947–48), 62–68.

E71 "The Gypsy Woman." [Translation of a poem by Georges
Ribement Dessaignes.] *Poesie 39–45: An Anthology*.
Edited by Pierre Seghers. London: Editions Poetry
London, 1947.

E72 "The Death of Antonio Torres Heredia, known as 'El Cam-
borio' / Translated from the poem by Federico Garcia
Lorca." *The Poetry Review*, 39.2 (April–May 1948),
106–07.

E73   "Kwa-Heri." *Harvest. Vol. I: Travel.* London: Vincent
      Stuart, 1948. ["Kwa-Heri" is not in *Talking Bronco*
      (London, 1946), though listed with poems from that
      volume in CP49.]

E74   "Ska-hawtch wha hae!" *The Catacomb*, Old Series, 1
      (April 1949), 6-7.

E75   "'Guitar' / Translation of a Poem by Federico Garcia
      Lorca." *The Poetry Review*, 40 (April-May 1949), 101.

E76   "Spooring an Angel." *The Catacomb*, Old Series, 3 (June
      1949), 59-60.

E77   "'Ballad of Three Rivers' / Translation of a Poem by
      Federico Garcia Lorca." *The Poetry Review*, 40 (June-
      July 1949), 173-74.

E78   "Drunken Boat." [Translation of *Le Bateau ivre* by
      Rimbaud.] *The Catacomb*, Old Series, 4 (July 1949), 75.

E79   "Ballad of Don Juan Tenorio." *The Catacomb*, Old Series,
      5 (August 1949), 102.

E80   "Lament for the Matador, Part 3: 'the Wake!" / Translated
      by Roy and Mary Campbell from the poem by Federico
      García Lorca, in 'Federico García Lorca' by Roy Camp-
      bell." *The Catacomb*, Old Series, 7 (October 1949),
      160-66. [Also in *Forum: Stories and Poems*, 1.2 (1949),
      30.]

E81   "A Prayer to St. Christopher." [Translated from *La Ruta
      de San Cristobal* by Aurelio Valls.] *The Catacomb*, Old
      Series, 8 (November 1949), 170.

E82   "The Rodeo of the Centaurs." *The Catacomb*, Old Series,
      8 (November 1949), 187.

E83   "'The Flame of Living Love' / Translation from a Poem by
      St. John of the Cross." *The Month*, New Series, 2.6
      (December 1949), 365.

E84   "Saint Gabriel (Seville)." [Translation of a poem by
      Federico Garcia Lorca.] *The Catacomb*, Old Series, 11
      (February 1950), 221.

E85   "Elevation - after Baudelaire." *The Catacomb*, Old
      Series, 13 (April 1950), 316.

E86 "Meditation - after Baudelaire." *The Catacomb*, Old
Series, 13 (April 1950), 316.

E87 "On the Architect's Designs for the Escorial." *Nine*,
2 (Summer 1950), 113.

E88 "Rhapsody of the Man in Hospital Blues and the Hyde
Park Lancers." *The Catacomb*, New Series, 1.1 (Summer
1950), 410-11.

E89 "Ballad of the Moon, the Moon." [Translation under
heading, "Five Romanceros of Lorca," pp. 209-16.]
Nine, 2.3 (August 1950).

E90 "He died of love." [Translation under heading, "Five
Romanceros of Lorca," pp. 209-16.] *Nine*, 2.3 (August
1950).

E91 "The Martyrdom of Saint Eulalia - I. Panorama of
Mérida -- II. The Martyrdom - III. Hell and Glory."
[Translation under heading, "Five Romanceros of
Lorca," pp. 209-16.] *Nine*, 2.3 (August 1950).

E92 "Oriental Song." [Translation under heading, "Five
Romanceros of Lorca," pp. 209-16.] *Nine*, 2.3
(August 1950).

E93 "Preciosa and the Wind." [Translation under heading,
"Five Romanceros of Lorca," pp. 209-16.] *Nine*, 2.3
(August 1950).

E94 "Sorrow of a Star." [Translated from Guillaume Apollinaire.] *The Catacomb*, New Series, 1.2 (Autumn 1950),
478-79.

E95 "Adam." [Translation under heading, "Five Poems of
Lorca," pp. 54-58.] *Nine*, 3.1 (December 1950).

E96 "Ballad of the Unfaithful Wife." [Translation under
heading, "Five Poems of Lorca," pp. 54-58.] *Nine*, 3.1
(December 1950).

E97 "Norms." [Translation under heading, "Five Poems of
Lorca," pp. 54-58.] *Nine*, 3.1 (December 1950).

E98 "Saint Raphael (Córdoba)." [Translation under heading,
"Five Poems of Lorca," pp. 54-58.] *Nine*, 3.1 (December
1950).

E99   "Sonnet" ["Tall silver ghost, the wind of midnight
       sighing"]. [Translation under heading, "Five Poems
       of Lorca," pp. 54-58.] *Nine*, 3.1 (December 1950).

E100   "Preface to 'Les Fleurs du Mal.'" [Translated from
       Baudelaire.] *Nine*, 3.1 (December 1950), 9-10.

E101   "Bestiary." [Translated from Cuillaume Apollinaire.]
       The Catacomb, New Series, 1.2 (Winter 1950-51), 478.

E102   "Sorrow of the Moon." [Translated from Baudelaire.]
       The Catacomb, New Series, 1.3 (Winter 1950-51), 547.

E103   "The Splendid Ship." [Translated from Baudelaire.]
       The Catacomb, New Series, 1.3 (Winter 1950-51), 546.

E104   "The Family Lumber-Chest." [Contains variants from the
       coll. version, "The Lumber-Chest."] *National and
       English Review*, 136 (January 1951), 28.

E105   "'Owls' - (by Charles Baudelaire)." *Poetry-London*,
       6.22 (Summer 1951), 6.

E106   "To a Millstone on the Ground." [Translation from a
       poem by Dionisio Ridruejo.] *The Catacomb*, New Series,
       2.2 (Summer 1951), 116.

E107   "To a Young Diana." [Translation of "A una joven
       Diana," by Juan Ramon Jimenez.] *The Catacomb*, New
       Series, 2.2 (Summer 1951), 127.

E108   "Jan Smuts." *Sunday Express* (Johannesburg), September 9,
       1951, p. 2. [Not seen.]

E109   Mahoney, R. [pseud.]. "Cancao VIII [sic]: Junto de un
       esteril, duro monte" ["There is a mountain, sterile,
       stark and dry,...." Translation from Camões; see
       translation from Canto IX of *The Lusiads*, CP60.]
       Nine, 3.2 (Autumn 1951), 173-74.

E110   "The Drummer Boy's Catechism (an essay on Hopkinese)."
       The Catacomb, New Series, 2.3 (Autumn 1951), 182-83.

E111   "On Lisi's Golden Hair." [Translation of a poem by
       Francisco de Quevedo.] *Nine*, 3.2 (Autumn 1951), 187.

E112   "Other Verses with a Divine Meaning by the same author."
       [Translation of a poem by St. John of the Cross.]
       Nine, 3.2 (Autumn 1951), 184.

E113 "The Sailor Girl." [Translation of a poem by Luis de
   Camões.] *Nine*, 3.2 (Autumn 1951), 173.

E114 "Song of the Soul that is glad to know God by faith."
   [Translation of a poem by St. John of the Cross.]
   Nine, 3.2 (Autumn 1951), 183-84.

E115 "Spectre of the Rose." [Translation of a poem by Luis
   de Góngora.] *Nine*, 3.2 (Autumn 1951), 185-86.

E116 "L'Avertisseur." [Translation under heading, "Three
   Translations from Baudelaire," pp. 259-60.] *Nine*,
   3.3 (April 1952).

E117 "Cats." [Translation under heading, "Three Translations
   from Baudelaire," pp. 259-60.] *Nine*, 3.3 (April 1952).

E118 "The Clock." [Translation under heading, "Three Translations from Baudelaire," pp. 259-60.] *Nine*, 3.3
   (April 1952).

E119 "Inscape of Skyte-Hawks on the Cookhouse Roof." *Nine*,
   3.3 (April 1952), 272.

E120 "'Bullfight in Ronda' (from Dona Rosita la Soltera)."
   [Translated from Federico García Lorca.] *Atlante*,
   1.1 (1953), 27.

E121 "Reflections." *Northern Review*, 6 (April-May 1953),
   2-7.

E122 "Twin Reflections" [here titled simply "Poem"]. *The
   Times Literary Supplement*, October 9, 1953, p. 638.

E123 "The Singing Hawk." *London Magazine*, 2.6 (1955), 254.

E124 "'The Chief of the Wild Island' Translated from the
   Portuguese of Joaquim Paço d'Arcos." *Adam International Review*, 23 (1955), 251.

E125 "To Frédéric Mistral (Neveu)." *National Review*, 1
   (January 11, 1956), 21.

E126 "Dawn on the Sierra of Gredos." *The Month*, New Series,
   15.1 (January 1956), 5-8.

E127 "Liscot's [sic] Horses." *National Review*, 1 (February
   1956), 8.

E128   "A Trip Underground with C.M. Doughty." *Nine*, 4.2
       (April 1956), 26-27.

E129   "Vision of Our Lady Over Toledo / (For Edith Sitwell)."
       [Finale of Book V, the revised *Flowering Rifle*.]
       Nine, 4.2 (April 1956), 11-14.

E130   "Don Juan Tenorio and the Man of Stone." *National
       Review*, 2 (May 30, 1956), 11.

E131   "Soci dou Felibrige / (à Frederic Mistral, Neveu)."
       The Times Literary Supplement, October 26, 1956,
       p. 626.

E132   "Autobiography in Fifty Kicks." *The Poetry Review*, 48
       (June-July 1957), 133-34.

Section F
Published Letters

F1 About an attack on William Plomer's *Turbott Wolfe*.
    Voorslag, 1.2 (July 1926), 10.

F2 A riposte, consisting in part of verse squibs, to two
    attacks on Plomer's *Turbott Wolfe*. *Voorslag*, 1.3
    (August 1926), 51–52.

F3 To Wyndham Lewis about *The New Statesman*'s rejection of
    his review of *The Apes of God. Satire and Fiction*.
    London: The Arthur Press, 1930. P. 9.

F4 On a review of *Flowering Rifle*. *The Times Literary
    Supplement*, February 25, 1939, p. 121.

F5 On a review in an earlier issue attacking *Flowering
    Rifle*. *Blackfriars*, 20.232 (July 1939), 546.

F6 About a review of *The Complete Poems of Richard Aldington*.
    The Times Literary Supplement, February 26, 1949,
    p. 139.

F7 A reply to a letter by Howard Parsons in the preceding
    issue attacking C's "scathing remarks about rhyme and
    metre" in his review of Richard Aldington's *Complete
    Poems*. *The Poetry Review*, 40.4 (August–September 1949),
    298.

F8 In reply to E.H.W. Meyerstein's objections to his review
    of Meyerstein's translation of Rimbaud. *The Poetry
    Review*, 41.1 (January–February 1950), 50.

F9 A reply to a further letter by Howard Parsons on C's
    views on rhyme and metre. *The Poetry Review*, 41.2
    (March–April 1950), 109.

F10 In defense of Edith Sitwell. *The European*, 15 (May
    1954), 62–63.

F11 Four extracts from letters to Francis Carey Slater.
    Francis Carey Slater, *Settlers' Heritage*. [Lovedale?]:

Lovedale Press, 1954. Pp. 256-57.

a. From Martigues (no date) on Jan Van Arond's *Drought*.
b. From London (no date) thanking him for a copy of
   the new edition of his anthology, with comments on
   some of the contents.
c. From London (February 17, 1946) welcoming forthcoming appearance of Slater's *Selected Poems*.
d. From 17 Campden Grove [London] (no date) congratulating Slater on the appearance of *Selected Poems*
   and its good review in the *TLS*.

F12 On Dylan Thomas after his death.   *Poetry London-New York*,
     1.1 (March-April 1956), 33-36.

Section G
Broadcasts

Roy Campbell's broadcasts were more numerous than
the following list suggests. However, it has
been possible to obtain information only on those
listed. All but those subsequently printed, G4
and the participation in the panel discussion
(there is a note on this in the University of
Texas collection) are available in typescript
either at the Killie Campbell Africana Library
(see below: 1, 10, 11, 12) or at the National
English Documentation Centre, Rhodes University
(see below: 2, 5, 8, 9). A phono disc of G4 is
held by the South African Library, Cape Town.
Campbell did some broadcasting for the B.B.C.
during the War and afterwards became a talks producer for the Third Programme; his broadcasting
of his own work encompassed poetry readings,
having the translations of at least two classical
Spanish plays produced, and talks on a variety
of subjects. But evidence for much of this activity is indirect--references in letters and the
memoir on Dylan Thomas, with whom he worked in
radio. Some of his talks were rebroadcast by
the South African Broadcasting Corporation, for
which he also made several broadcasts.

G1 "Calling South Africa." B.B.C. talk, February 10,
1942; repeated, April 16, 1942.

G2 "With the Askaris in East Africa." B.B.C. talk, n.d.
[1942?] [Not seen.]

G3 "Where Everyone is a Bullfighter." B.B.C. talk, printed
in *The Listener*, 34 (October 18, 1945), 431-32.
[See H20.]

G4 "The Reader Takes Over." No. 13 in the B.B.C. series;
made on August 18, 1947. Rebroadcast by S.A.B.C. in
1949.

G5   "The Spaniards and Their Olives." In B.B.C. series
      "Travel Talks," January 1950. [Not seen.]

G6   "Poetic Licence." Took part in a panel discussion on
      this subject with Dylan Thomas, George Barker and W.R.
      Rogers, broadcast by the B.B.C., December 13, 1950.

G7   "The Poetry of Edith Sitwell." B.B.C. talk, later pub.
      in *Trek* (Johannesburg C.N.A. Monthly), 15.5 (June–
      July 1951), 11–13. [See H44.]

G8   "'Personal Anthology No. 1,' Chosen by Roy Campbell."
      B.B.C. talk, October 1951. [Not seen.]

G9   "St. John of the Cross." B.B.C. talk, June 1952. [Not
      seen.]

G10   "A South African Poet in Portugal." 15-minute broadcast.
      S.A.B.C., March 19, 1954. Printed in S.A.B.C. bulletin,
      July 1954, pp. 6ff. [See also H53.]

G11   "Some South African Writers." S.A.B.C. broadcast,
      March 26, 1954. Rebroadcast by B.B.C., April 26, 1954.

G12   "The English-Speaking South Africans." S.A.B.C. broad-
      cast, circa May 15, 1954.

Section H

Incidental Prose Writings
by Roy Campbell

H1   "Modern Poetry and Contemporary History." *The Natal Witness*, March 19, March 26, April 2, April 16 and April 23, 1925.

H2   "How I Began to Write." *The Cape Argus*, October 1925. [Not seen.]

H3   Hughes, Mary Ann [pseud.]. "Tolstoy and Dostoevsky." *Voorslag*, 1.1 (June 1926), 46-52. [Hughes was identified as being C by William Plomer—see E11.]

H4   Review of the "Collected Works" of T.S. Eliot. *Voorslag*, 1.1 (June 1926), 59-62.

H5   Review of *The Worship of Nature*, by Sir James Frazer. *Voorslag*, 1.1 (June 1926), 62-63.

H6   "The Significance of 'Turbott Wolfe.'" *Voorslag*, 1.1 (June 1926), 39-45.

H7   "Fetish Worship in South Africa." *Voorslag*, 1.2 (July 1926), 3-19.

H8   Marston, Lewis [pseud.]. "'Eunuch Arden' and 'Kynoch Arden.'" *Voorslag*, 1.2 (July 1926), 32-38. [Identified as by C by Plomer. See E11.]

H9   Reviews of *The Three Sitwells*, by R.L. Mégroz, and *Rustic Elegies*, by Edith Sitwell. *The Calendar*, 4.1 (April 1927), 74-76.

H10   "The Mental Traveller": review of *Blake's Poetry and Prose*, by Geoffrey Keynes. *The New Statesman*, 29 (August 27, 1927), 623.

H11   "The Emotional Cyclops": review of *Time and Western Man*, by Wyndham Lewis. *The New Statesman*, 29 (December 3, 1927), suppl. p. x.

H12   "Rossetti": review of *Rossetti: His Life and Works*, by Evelyn Waugh. *The Nation & the Athenaeum* (May 19, 1928), p. 212.

H13   "François Villon": review of *François Villon*, by D.B.
      Wyndham Lewis. *The New Statesman*, 30 (March 24, 1928),
      765-66.

H14   "Contemporary Poetry." *Scrutinies by Various Writers.*
      Collected by Edgell Rickword. 2 vols. London: Wishart,
      1928, 1931. Vol. I, pp. 162-79.

H15   "White Laughter": review of *Paleface*, by Wyndham Lewis.
      The New Statesman, 34 (July 20, 1929), 473-74.

H16   "The Death of the Sanglier." *Natal Week-end Advertiser*
      (Durban, Natal, South Africa), September 16, 1933.
      [Not seen.]

H17   "Answer to an Inquiry." *New Verse*, 11 (October 1934),
      14.

H18   "Uys Krige (a Portrait)." *The Critic* (Rondebosch, Cape
      Province, South Africa), 3.2 (January 1935), 61-67.

H19   "British Bullfighter Trapped by Rival Armies." *Daily
      Express* (Johannesburg), August 13, 1936. [Not seen.]

H20   "Where Everyone is a Bullfighter." *The Listener*, 34
      (October 18, 1945), 431-32. [See G3.]

H21   "Dylan Thomas." *Vandag*, 1.7 (December 1946), 18-20.

H22   "Wellington": review of *Wellington*, by Richard Aldington.
      The Windmill, 2.1 (1947), 83.

H23   "The Literary Loss to South Africa of Writers Who Gravi-
      tate Oversea." *The Sunday Times* (Johannesburg),
      March 16, 1947.

H24   "The Poetry of Francis Carey Slater": review of *The
      Selected Poems of Francis Carey Slater. British Africa
      Monthly*, 1.7 (March 26, 1948). [Not seen.]

H25   "Richard Aldington: Happy Pagan": review of *The Complete
      Poems of Richard Aldington. The Poetry Review*, 40
      (April-May 1949), 115-19. Reprinted in *Richard
      Aldington: An Intimate Portrait*, edited by Alister
      Kershaw and F.-J. Temple. Carbondale, Ill.: Southern
      Illinois University Press, 1965.

H26   "Rimbaud--and Two Homely Muses": reviews of *Four Poems
       by Rimbaud*, translated by Ben Belitt, and *Rimbaud's
       Le Bateau Ivre, Done into English Rhyme and Latin
       Hexameters*, by E.H.W. Meyerstein. *The Poetry Review*,
       40 (June-July 1949), 199-201.

H27   "The Mahatma of Misanthropy": review of Aldous Huxley's
       Ape and Essence. Enquiry, 2.1 (July 1949), 54-57.

H28   "The Poet and the Free Man": review of *The Collected
       Poems of John Gawsworth. Enquiry*, 2.2 (August 1949),
       55-59. Reprinted in *A Review of The Collected Poems
       of John Gawsworth*, edited by Iyengar K.R. Srinivasa.
       [A leaflet of 8 sides. With appreciations by Campbell,
       Austin Clarke, Lawrence Durrell and others. Not seen.]

H29   "Tendencias de la Literatura Inglesa Contemporanea."
       Escorial; Revista de cultura y letras (Segunda época)
       (Madrid), tomo XX (Agosto 1949), 1021-37. This trans-
       lation into Spanish of a lecture C gave at the Ateneo
       in Barcelona, October 14, 1948, was printed in *Escorial*
       with an introduction by José Maria Alonso Gamo, who also
       provided a translation of C's poem "San Juan de la Cruz"
       that follows the text. The translation of C's "ensayo"
       is attributed to J.M. Blasco Gamo. In the preliminaries
       to CP57 to CP60 this essay is listed among C's prose
       works and the publisher given as "Spanish Government,"
       but it is not recorded in NUC or elsewhere. It may be
       that the fact that it also appeared as a "separate,"
       or offprint, led to the supposition that it was an inde-
       pendent publication. [*Note:* Information supplied by
       Teresa Campbell, who also kindly lent the compiler her
       copy of the offprint.]

H30   "Moo, moo! Or ye olde new awareness": review of *Poetry
       of the Present: An Anthology of the Thirties and After*,
       edited by Geoffrey Grigson. *The Poetry Review*, 40.4
       (August-September 1949), 287-91.

H31   "Federico Garcia Lorca." *The Catacomb*, Old Series, 7
       (October 1949), 160-66.

H32   Campbell, Roy, and Rob Lyle. "Editorial." *The Catacomb*,
       Old Series, 8 (November 1949), 169.

H33   Rob Roy [Roy Campbell and Rob Lyle]. "On to Methuselah."
       The Catacomb, Old Series, 8 (November 1949), 171-73.

H34 "Persecution of Spanish Communists in Russia." *The
     Catacomb*, Old Series, 9 (December 1949), 219-21.

H35 "A Screw-tapey Letter." *The Catacomb*, Old Series, 10
     (January 1950), 245-49.

H36 "A Decade in Retrospect." *The Month*, New Series, 3.5
     (May 1950), 319-33. [Other contributors to the series
     of retrospects were Denis Johnston, Jacquetta Hawkes,
     F.A. Voigt and André L. Simon.]

H37 Review of Sacheverell Sitwell's *Spain*. *The Catacomb*,
     New Series, 1.1 (Summer 1950), 421-23.

H38 "Epitaph on the Thirties": review of *The Collected
     Shorter Poems* of W.H. Auden. *Nine*, 2.4 (November
     1950), 344-46.

H39 "The Message of Don Quixote." *John O'London's Weekly*,
     59 (November 24, 1950), 629.

H40 "The Secret of Modern Gaiety": review of *Selected
     Writings by Guillaume Apollinaire*, translated, with a
     critical introduction, by Roger Shattuck. *Nine*, 3.1
     (December 1950), 76-77. [The same review, under the
     heading, "Apollinaire Trismegistus," appeared in *The
     Catacomb*, New Series, 1.3 (Winter 1950-51), 548-52.]

H41 "The Prisoner, the Snow Queen and the Naturalist": re-
     views of *A Book of the Winter*, by Edith Sitwell; *The
     Victorians: An Anthology*, edited by Geoffrey Grigson;
     and *Ezra Pound*, edited by Peter Russell. *The Poetry
     Review*, 52.1 (January-February 1951), 31-32.

H42 Review of *Veld Patriarch and Other Poems*, by F.C. Slater.
     African Affairs, 50.199 (April 1951), 168-69. [Not
     seen.]

H43 Review of Charles Causley's *Farewell, Aggie Weston*.
     The Catacomb, New Series, 2.1 (Spring 1951), 64.

H44 "The Poetry of Edith Sitwell." *Trek* (Johannesburg C.N.A.
     Monthly), 15.5 (June-July 1951), 11-13. [See G7.]

H45 "Wyndham Lewis." *Time and Tide*, July 7, 1951, p. 650.

H46 Review of *Fifty Spanish Poems*, by Juan Ramon Jimenez,
     with English translations by J.B. Trend, and two other
     books. *The Catacomb*, New Series, 2.2 (Summer 1951), 126-
     28. [Under "Jimenez" the review of *Fifty Spanish Poems*

was reprinted, with attached explanatory editor's note, in *Nine*, 3.4 (Summer-Autumn 1952), 361-63.]

H47 "Born Story-Teller." *John O'London's Weekly*, 61 (April 18, 1952), 385-86. [On Masefield as narrative poet.]

H48 Reviews of *No Time for Cowards*, by Phoebe Hesketh, and *A Change of World*, by Adrienne Rich. *The Poetry Review*, 44.3 (July-September 1953), 397-98.

H49 "A Note on W.L." *Shenandoah* ("Wyndham Lewis Number"), 4. 2-3 (Summer-Autumn 1953), 74-76.

H50 "I Banderillas de Fuego!": review of *Lament for the Death of a Bull Fighter, and other Poems*, by Federico García Lorca, translated by A.L. Floyd. *The Poetry Review*, 44.4 (October-December 1953), 449-51.

H51 Tribute, in French, under general heading, "Une Larme Pour Adonais." *Adam International Review* ("Dylan Thomas Memorial Number"), 238 (1953), 13.

H52 "Dylan Thomas--The War Years." *Shenandoah* ("Dylan Thomas Number"), 5.1 (Spring 1954), 26-27.

H53 "A Poet in Portugal." *Courier*, 22.5 (May 1954), 66-68. [See G10.]

H54 "Poetry and Experience." *Theoria*, 6 (1954), 37-44.

H55 "The Road to Dead's Town." *Explorations: Studies in Culture and Communication* (Toronto; edited by E.S. Carpenter), 5 (June 5, 1955), 45-50.

H56 "Memories of Dylan Thomas at the B.B.C." *Poetry*, 87.2 (November 1955), 111-14. Reprinted in *Dylan Thomas: The Legend and the Poet*, edited by E.W. Tedlock. London: Heinemann, 1960.

H57 "Formidable Weapon": review of *The Problem of Jesus: A Freethinker's Diary*, by Jean Guitton. *National Review*, 1 (December 14, 1955), 29-30.

H58 "Trial of a Trial": review of *The Retrial of Joan of Arc*, by Régine Pernoud, translated by J.M. Cohen. *National Review*, 1 (February 15, 1956), 28-29.

H59 "Worthy Crown": review of *The Castle and the Ring*, by C.C. Martingale, S.J. *National Review*, 1 (February 29, 1956), 29.

H60   "All Too Seldom": review of *Guerrilla Days in Ireland*,
      by Tom Barry. *National Review*, 1 (April 11, 1956),
      29-30.

H61   "Tauromachy": review of *Bull Fever*, by Kenneth Tynan.
      National Review, 1 (April 25, 1956), 21.

H62   "Train-Window Insight": review of *Background to Bitter-
      ness*, by Henry Gibbs. *National Review*, 2 (June 27,
      1956), 19-20.

H63   "Passion for Bach": review of *Beyond Desire*, by Pierre
      de la Mure. *National Review*, 2 (December 1, 1956), 21.

H64   "Valor Rooted in Faith": review of *Garlic for Pegasus*,
      by Wilfred P. Schoenberg, S.J. *National Review*, 2
      (December 22, 1956), 20-21.

H65   "Spanish Mission": review of *The Treasure of Mission
      Santa Inés*, by Kurt Baer. *National Review*, 3 (May 11,
      1957), 456-57.

H66   "Overseas Comments on Australian Literature." *Austral-
      ian Letters*, 1.1 (June 1957), 18.

H67   "Roy Campbell's Free Speech." *The Poetry Review*, 48
      (June-July 1957), 134. [Slightly revised version of
      part of review of *The Complete Poems of Richard
      Aldington*.] [See H25.]

H68   "The Poetry of Luiz de Camões." *London Magazine*, 4.8
      (August 1957), 23-33.

Section I
Appearances in Anthologies

I1   *Eighty Poems: An Anthology.* Edited by L.A.G. Strong.
      Oxford: Basil Blackwood, 1924.
      "Bongwi's Theology," p. 14.

I2   *The Centenary Book of South African Verse (1820 to 1925).*
      Chosen and arranged by Francis Carey Slater. London:
      Longmans, Green, 1925.
      "Hialmar and the Aasvogel" [coll. as "Hialmar"], pp. 36-
      37; "The Theology of Bongwi," pp. 37-38; "The Dark
      Champion," pp. 38-40. [Under biographical and biblio-
      graphical notes: "... Author of 'The Flaming Terrapin,'
      a work of great power and beauty...."]

I3   *A South African Literary Reader.* Edited by Miss E.M.
      Thompson, B.A. Cape Town: Juta, 1926. [School text.]
      Extracts from *The Flaming Terrapin*, pp. 34-39. [From
      introductory note by the editor: "Mr. Roy Campbell gives
      his consent to the extracts ... with the following reser-
      vation:- 'But I must stipulate one condition which I
      hope will not seem too severe. I cannot have my work
      inflicted on students as memory-training, either for
      purposes of recitation or for examination.'"]

I4   *New Paths on Helicon.* Compiled by Henry Newbolt. London:
      Nelson, n.d. [1927?].
      "From The Flaming Terrapin / Part I" ["Maternal Earth
      stirs redly ... Red thunderbolts to purify the world"],
      pp. 61-66.

I5   *The Best Poems of 1928.* Selected by Thomas Moult. New
      York: Harcourt, Brace, 1928.
      "'Tristan da Cunha' - New Statesman, London, October,"
      pp. 33-36.

I6   *Twentieth Century Poetry.* An anthology chosen by Harold
      Monro. (The Phoenix Library.) London: Chatto and
      Windus, 1929.
      "The Sisters," p. 169; "Tristan da Cunha," pp. 197-200.

I7   *A Broadcast Anthology of Modern Poetry.* Edited by
     Dorothy Wellesley. (Hogarth Living Poets, No. 17.)
     London: The Hogarth Press, 1930.
     "The Garden," pp. 29-30; "Tristan da Cunha," pp. 49-53;
     "The Zebras," p. 83; "Horses on the Camargue," pp. 129-
     30; "Dedication to Adamastor / (To Mary Campbell),"
     pp. 141-43; "The Sisters," p. 144; "The Zulu Girl,"
     p. 149; "The Sleeper," p. 217.

I8   *Modern British Poetry: A Critical Anthology.* Edited by
     Louis Untermeyer. 3rd revised edition. New York:
     Harcourt, Brace, 1930.
     Bio-critical introduction, pp. 749-50; "Tristan da Cunha,"
     pp. 750-53; "From 'The Flaming Terrapin': Part I"
     ["Maternal Earth stirs redly ... Red thunderbolts to
     purify the world"], pp. 753-57; "The Palm," pp. 758-59.

I9   *The Best Poems of 1930.* Selected by Thomas Moult. New
     York: Harcourt, Brace, 1930.
     "'Horses on the Camargue' - New Statesman, London, July,"
     pp. 2-3.

I10 *Younger Poets of Today.* Selected by J.C. Squire.
     London: Martin Secker, 1932.
     "Autumn," p. 87; "Horses on the Camargue," pp. 88-90;
     "The Sisters," pp. 91-92; "The Zulu Girl," pp. 93-94;
     "Tristan da Cunha," pp. 95-99.

I11 *Whips and Scorpions: Specimens of Modern Satiric Verse,
     1914-1931.* Collected by Sherard Vines. London:
     Wishart, 1932.
     "Description of a Colony" [extract from *The Wayzgoose*:
     "Attend my fable if your ears be clean ... Where all
     the *acres* in the land are *wise!*"], pp. 43-45; "On the
     Golden Mean" [extract from *The Georgiad*: "Hail, Medio-
     crity, beneath whose spell ... A benefit it could well
     do without."], pp. 45-53.

I12 *Recent Poetry, 1923-1933.* Edited with an introduction
     by Alida Monro. London: Gerald Howe Ltd. & The Poetry
     Bookshop, 1933.
     "Horses on the Camargue," pp. 24-25; "The Zebras," p. 26;
     "Choosing a Mast," pp. 27-28.

I13 *Modern Poetry, 1922-1934: An Anthology.* Compiled by
     Maurice Wollman. London: Macmillan, 1934.
     "Choosing a Mast," pp. 74-76; "Dedication / (To Mary
     Campbell)," pp. 106-08; "Horses on the Camargue," pp.
     161-63; "The Sleeper," pp. 114-15; "The Zebras," p. 168.

I14 *The Year's Poetry: 1934.* A representative selection
compiled by Denys Kilham Roberts, Gerald Gould and
John Lehmann. London: The Bodley Head, 1934.
"Toril." [Not seen.]

I15 *The Modern Muse: Poems of Today British and American.*
London: Published for the English Association by the
Oxford University Press, 1934.
"Tristan da Cunha," pp. 56-59; "From 'The Flaming Terrapin'" ["For when the winds have ceased their ghostly
speech ... Rasping starved teeth against an old dry
bone."], pp. 59-60.

I16 *The Best Poems of 1935.* Selected by Thomas Moult &
decorated by Agnes Miller Parker. New York: Harcourt,
Brace, 1935.
"'The Mocking Bird' - Virginia Quarterly Review, January,"
p. 75.

I17 *The Year's Poetry: 1935.* A representative selection
compiled by Denys Kilham Roberts, Gerald Gould and
John Lehmann. London: The Bodley Head, 1935.
"The Mocking Bird"; "To the Survivors." [Not seen.]

I18 *Poems of Tomorrow.* Edited by Janet Adam Smith. London:
Chatto and Windus, 1935.
"Toril," pp. 29-30.

I19 *The Oxford Book of Modern Verse, 1892-1935.* Chosen by
W.B. Yeats. Oxford: Clarendon Press, 1936.
"The Serf," p. 393; "The Zulu Girl," p. 394; "The Sis-
ters," pp. 394-95; "Autumn," pp. 395-96.

I20 *A Treasury of Modern Poetry: An Anthology of the Last
Forty Years.* Edited by R.L. Megroz. London: Pitman,
1936.
"The Palm," pp. 34-35; "The Zulu Girl," pp. 35-36; "Mass
at Dawn," p. 36; "African Moonrise," pp. 36-37; "Tristan da Cunha," pp. 37-40.

I21 *Edwardian Poetry: Book One, 1936.* London: Richards,
1936.
"Dedication of a Tree / (To 'Peter Warlock')," p. 38.

I22 *Modern American Poetry / Modern British Poetry: A
Critical Anthology.* Edited by Louis Untermeyer. The
Combined Edition (Fifth Revised Edition of *Modern
American Poetry*; Fourth Revised Edition of *Modern
British Poetry*). New York: Harcourt, Brace, 1936.

Introduction, full of biographical inaccuracies, p. 497;
"The Zebras," pp. 497-98; "Tristan da Cunha," pp. 498-
500; "The Flaming Terrapin, Part I" ["Maternal Earth
stirs redly ... Red thunderbolts to purify the world."],
pp. 500-04; "The Palm," pp. 504-05; "Autumn," pp. 505-06.

123 *A New Anthology of Modern Poetry*. Edited, with an intro-
duction, by Selden Rodman. New York: Random House (The
Literary Guild of America Inc.), 1938.
"The Serf," p. 212.

124 *The Poets' Harvest*. Compiled by E.W. Parker. London:
Longmans, 1939.
"Horses on the Camargue," pp. 20-22; "Choosing a Mast,"
pp. 37-39.

125 *The Viking Book of Poetry of the English-Speaking World*.
Chosen and edited by Richard Aldington. New York: The
Viking Press, 1941.
"The Zebras," p. 1198.

126 *The Faber Book of Comic Verse*. Compiled by Michael
Roberts. London: Faber, 1942.
"A Veld Eclogue: The Pioneers," pp. 358-62; "On Some
South African Novelists," p. 362; "On Professor
Drennan's Verse," p. 362.

127 *A Treasury of Great Poems*. Edited by Louis Untermeyer.
New York, 1942.
Introduction, pp. 1205-06; "Autumn," p. 1206; "The
Serf," p. 1207.

128 *Thudding Drums: An Anthology` of English and South
African Poetry*. Compiled by G.M. Miller. London:
University of London Press, 1942. Reprinted 1944,
1946.
"To a Pet Cobra," pp. 25-26; "Rounding the Cape," pp.
45-46; "The Serf," pp. 58-59; "The Zulu Girl," pp. 60-
61; "Out of the Ark" [from *The Flaming Terrapin*: "Out
of the Ark's grim hold ... With the fierce wind foaming in their manes"], pp. 71-72; "The Albatross" [from
The Flaming Terrapin: "Now far along the skyline, like
a white / Signal of triumph through the muffled light, /
An Albatross ..."], p. 81; "Horses on the Camargue,"
pp. 81-82; "To the Springboks in England, 1932,"
pp. 116-17.

I29 *Soldiers' Verse.* Verses chosen by Patric Dickinson with
original lithographs by William Scott. (New Excur-
sions into English Poetry; Editors: W.J. Turner and
Sheila Shannon.) London: Frederick Muller, 1945.
"Hialmar," pp. 47-48.

I30 *The Week-End Book.* Edited by Francis and Vera Meynell.
(Service Edition.) London: The Nonesuch Press, 1945.
"On Some South African Novelists," p. 175.

I31 *The New Centenary Book of South African Verse.* Revised
and abridged edition of *The Centenary Book of South
African Verse*, with many new poems added thereto.
Chosen and arranged by Francis Carey Slater. London:
Longmans, 1945.
"African Moonrise"; "Autumn"; "The Secret Muse"; "The
Palm"; "The Hat"; "Luis de Camões"; "The Raven I";
"The Raven II"; "The Gum Trees"; "The Serf"; "Horses
on the Camargue"; "Hot Rifles"; "The Olive Tree I";
"A Jug of Water"; "Rounding the Cape"; "San Juan de la
Cruz"; "Tristan da Cunha." [Not seen.]

I32 *An Anthology of Recent Poetry.* Compiled by L. D'O.
Walters and A.E.M. Bayliss. New and Enlarged Edition.
London: Harrap, 1945.
"Autumn," p. 80.

I33 *Twentieth Century Verse: An Anthology.* Chosen by Ira
Dilworth. Toronto: Clarke, Irwin, 1945.
"Choosing a Mast," pp. 83-85; "Tristan da Cunha,"
pp. 85-89; "From 'The Flaming Terrapin'" ["For when
the winds have ceased their ghostly speech ... Rasping
starved teeth against an old dry bone."], pp. 89-90.

I34 *Collected English Verse.* Chosen by Margaret and Ronald
Bottrall. London: Sidgewick, 1946.
"Tristan da Cunha," pp. 554-58.

I35 *A Little Treasury of Great Poetry English and American
from Chaucer to the Present Day.* Edited by Oscar
Williams. New York: Scribner's, 1947.
"The Death of Polybius Jubb," p. 736.

I36 *Translation. Second Series.* Edited by Neville Braybrooke
and Elizabeth King. London: Phoenix Press, 1947.
"Federico Garcia Lorca (1899-1936) 'Somnambulistic
Ballad.' Translated by Roy and Mary Campbell," pp.
29-30.

137 *Spirit of the Trees: An Anthology of Poetry Inspired by*
     Trees. Compiled by Ruth Alston Cresswell. With a
     foreword by V. Sackville-West. Abbotsbury, Dorset:
     Society of the Men of the Trees, 1947.
     "The Mountain Pine or Choosing a Mast," p. 64.

138 *Readings in South African English Prose.* Selected and
     arranged by A.C. Partridge. 2nd and revised edition.
     Pretoria: J.L. Van Schaik, 1948.
     "Memories of Natal" [Ed.'s heading: extracts from *Broken*
     Record], pp. 185-94; biographical note, p. 288.

139 *Turnstile One: A Literary Miscellany from The New*
     Statesman and Nation. Edited by V.S. Pritchett.
     London: Turnstile Press, 1948.
     "The Zulu Girl," p. 143.

140 *South African Poetry. A New Anthology.* Compiled by Roy
     MacNab with Charles Gulston. With a foreword by Roy
     Campbell. London: Collins, 1948.
     "Luis De Camões," p. 33; "After Rubén," pp. 33-34; "The
     Zulu Girl," p. 34; "Dreaming Spires," pp. 35-38;
     "Rounding the Cape," p. 39; "Autumn," pp. 39-40; "The
     Serf," p. 40.

141 *First Time in America.* A selection of poems never before
     published in the U.S.A., collected and introduced by
     John Arlott. New York: Duell, Sloan and Pearce, 1948.
     "Familiar Daemon," p. 46; "Pomegranates," pp. 46-48;
     "The Gum Trees," pp. 48-50; "Choosing a Mast," pp. 50-
     52; "'Si Kulu Lez' Isiswe,' (Translated from the Zulu
     War-Song during the 1906 Rebellion)," pp. 52-53 [at
     end: " - from MS."].

142 *The Charm of Poetry.* Edited by J.D. Bevington. London:
     Ginn, 1949.
     "Choosing a Mast" [extract], p. 184; "Autumn" [extract],
     pp. 187-88.

143 *The Voice of Poetry (1930-1950).* Edited by Hermann
     Peschmann. London: Evans, 1950.
     "Horses on the Camargue," pp. 31-32; "Autumn," p. 32;
     "The Zulu Girl," pp. 32-33.

144 *A Little Treasury of British Poetry: The Chief Poets*
     from 1500 to 1950. Edited by Oscar Williams. New
     York: Scribner's, 1951.
     "The Serf," pp. 728-29; "The Zebras," p. 729.

I45 *The Worldly Muse: An Anthology of Serious Light Verse.*
Edited and with an introduction by A.J.M. Smith. New
York: Abelard Press, 1951.
"On Some South African Novelists," p. 263.

I46 *New Poems 1953: A P.E.N. Anthology.* Edited by Robert
Conquest, Michael Hamburger and Howard Sergeant.
Introduction by C.V. Wedgwood. London: Michael Joseph,
1953.
"Ballad of Don Juan Tenorio and the Statue of the
Comendador," pp. 32-34.

I47 *A Pocket Book of Modern Verse: English and American
Poetry of the Last 100 Years, from Walt Whitman to
Dylan Thomas.* Edited by Oscar Williams. Revised Edition.
New York: Washington Square Press, 1954.
"The Zebras," pp. 454-55; "Choosing a Mast," pp. 455-57.

I48 *Joyce Kilmer's Anthology of Catholic Poets.* With a new
supplement by James Edward Tobin. New York: Liveright,
1955; 1st edition, 1939. [Campbell not in 1st ed.]
"Autumn," p. 248; "Familiar Daemon," p. 249; "A Good
Resolution," p. 249; "The Zulu Girl," p. 250.

I49 *Ten Centuries of Spanish Poetry. An Anthology in English
Verse with Original Texts, from the Eleventh Century
to the Generation of 1898.* Edited by Eleanor L. Turn-
bull. Baltimore: Johns Hopkins Press, 1955.
"'Lisi's Golden Hair,' translated from the Spanish of
Francisco de Quevedo." [Not seen.]

I50 *Selected Poems of Federico García Lorca.* Edited by
Francisco García Lorca and Donald M. Allen. (The New
Classics Series.) Norfolk, Conn.: New Directions,
1955.
[Two translations:] "Adan" - "Adam," pp. 28-29; "Fabula"
- "Fable," pp. 32-33.

I51 Charles Baudelaire. *The Flowers of Evil.* Selected and
edited by Marthiel and Jackson Mathews. New York: New
Directions, 1955.
[The translations by Campbell included were:] "III Ele-
vation"; "V I Love the Thought ..."; "XXXIX The
Possessed"; "XL Ill Luck"; "XLV The Living Torch";
"XLVI To One Who is Too Gay"; "LIII Misty Sky"; "LIV
The Cat" ["A fine strong gentle cat ..."]; "LV The
Splendid Ship"; "LXIII Praises of My Frances"; "LXX
The Owls"; "LXXIII Burial"; "LXXIV Fantastic Engraving";

"LXXVI The Cask of Hate"; "LXXXII Obsession"; "LXXXV
Sympathetic Horror"; "LXXXVIII The Clock"; "XCI The
Red-Haired Beggar Girl"; "XCIII The Seven Old Men";
"XCIV The Little Old Women"; "XCVII Skeletons Digging
I" [II trans. by Yvor Winters]; "C The Dance of Death";
"CXIII The Martyr"; "CXVI Lesbians" ["Like pensive
cattle ..."]; "CXVII The Two Good Sisters"; "CXXIV The
Denial of Saint Peter"; "CXXXI Dream of a Curious
Person." [From "Further Poems":] "I Epigraph for a
Condemned Book"; "XII The Unforeseen"; "XIX Hymn";
"XXIV On Delacroix's Picture of Tasso in Prison."

152 *Modern Verse 1900-1950.* Chosen by Phyllis M. Jones.
     2nd edition enlarged. London: Oxford University
     Press, 1955; first pub., 1940.
     "The Serf," pp. 177-78; "Choosing a Mast," pp. 178-80.

153 *The Chatto Book of Modern Poetry 1915-1955.* Edited by
     C. Day Lewis and John Lehmann. London: Chatto and
     Windus, 1956.
     "The Sisters," p. 129; "Buffel's Kop / (Olive Schreiner's
     Grave)," p. 129; "The Zulu Girl," p. 130; "On Some
     South African Novelists," p. 130.

154 *The Silver Treasury of Light Verse from Geoffrey Chaucer
     to Ogden Nash.* Edited by Oscar Williams. New York:
     New American Library, 1957.
     "The Death of Polybius Jubb," p. 92; "On Some South
     African Novelists," p. 100.

155 *The Guinness Book of Poetry 1956/57.* Foreword by Lord
     Moyne. London: Putnam, 1958.
     "Félibre," p. 46.

156 *Poets in South Africa.* Edited by Roy MacNab. Cape Town:
     Maskew Miller, 1958. [Dedicated to the Memory of Roy
     Campbell 1901-1957.]
     "Rounding the Cape," p. 13; "The Zulu Girl," pp. 13-14;
     "The Dreaming Spires (An Extract)," pp. 14-15; "The
     Serf," p. 15; "Autumn," pp. 15-16; "The Secret Muse,"
     p. 16; "Félibre (to Fréderic Mistral, Neveu)," pp.
     16-17.

157 *An Anthology of Spanish Literature in English Transla-
     tion.* Edited by Seymour Resnick and Jeanne Pasmantier.
     London: John Calder, 1958.
     "'Verses written after an ecstasy of high exaltation,'
     translated from St. John of the Cross," p. 102.
     [Not seen.]

158 *The Atlantic Book of British and American Poetry*.
Edited by Edith Sitwell. Boston: Little, Brown, 1958.
"To a Pet Cobra," pp. 924-25; "The Zulu Girl / To F.C.
Slater," pp. 925-26; "Pomegranates / To Thomas Earp,"
pp. 926-27; "The Snake," pp. 927-30; "Horses on the
Camargue / To A.F. Tschiffely," pp. 930-31; "On Lisa's
[sic] Golden Hair / Translated from Francisco de
Quevedo, 1580-1645," p. 931; "Upon a Gloomy Night /
Translated from St. John of the Cross," pp. 932-33.

159 *Modern Verse in English*. Edited by David Cecil and
Allen Tate. London: Eyre and Spottiswoode, 1958.
"The Sisters," p. 465; "Tristan da Cunha / (to Robert
Lyle)," pp. 465-68; "The Zulu Girl / (to F.C. Slater),"
pp. 468-69; "On Some South African Novelists," p. 469.

160 *The Viking Book of Poetry of the English-Speaking World*.
Chosen and edited by Richard Aldington. 2 vols. Re-
vised edition. New York: The Viking Press, 1958.
[In Vol. 2:] "The Zebras," p. 1222; "From *Talking Bronco*:
'The Volunteer's Reply to the Poet' ('Will It be So
Again?')," pp. 1222-24.

161 *A Book of South African Verse*. Selected and introduced
by Guy Butler. London: Oxford University Press, 1959.
[Dedication: To Roy Campbell 1901-1957]
"From *The Flaming Terrapin*: i. Invocation to the African
Muse ['Far be the bookish Muses! ... Salute with me
the advent of the Ark.'], ii. The Fall of Satan ['Like
a stone toppled from an endless hill, ... To nurse the
mangled relics of his bones.'], iii. Noah ["High on
the top of Ararat alone ... Smiled on the proud irre-
verence of Man."], pp. 33-36; "The Serf," p. 37; "The
Zulu Girl / To F.C. Slater," pp. 37-38; "The Zebras /
To Chips Rafferty," pp. 38-39; "From *The Wayzgoose*"
["Attend my fable if your ears be clean ... And turnips
into Parliament are voted?"], pp. 39-40; "On Some
South African Novelists," p. 40; "On the Same," p. 41;
"From 'A Veld Eclogue: The Pioneers'" ["... But 'name-
less somethings' and 'unbounded spaces' ... Blame only
the traditions I pursue."], pp. 41-43; "Rounding the
Cape," pp. 43-44; "The Sling," pp. 44-48; "Luis de
Camoes," pp. 48-49; "Dreaming Spires," pp. 49-53.
[Included are C's notes to the parts of *The Wayzgoose*
and "A Veld Eclogue: The Pioneers"; "Rounding the Cape"
and "The Sling" have editorial notes.]

162 *The Sheldon Book of Verse.*   Compiled by P.G. Smith and
      J.F. Wilkins.   4 vols.   London: Oxford University
      Press, 1959.
      [In Vol. III:] "Horses on the Camargue," pp. 132-34;
      [in Vol. IV:] "The Zebras," p. 59.

163 *Poems of Our Time 1900-1960.*   Original edition chosen
      by Richard Church, C.B.E., and Mildred Bozman; modern
      supplement chosen by Dame Edith Sitwell, D. Litt.
      Enlarged edition.   New York: Dutton, 1959; last re-
      print, 1961; first pub., London: Dent (Everyman),
      1945.
      "Autumn," p. 218; "The Zulu Girl," p. 230; "Horses on
      the Camargue," pp. 231-32.

164 *Collins Albatross Book of Verse: English and American
      Poetry from the Thirteenth Century to the Present Day.*
      Edited by Louis Untermeyer.   Revised and enlarged
      edition.   London: Collins, 1960.
      "The Zulu Girl," pp. 610-11.

165 *Seven Centuries of Poetry: Chaucer to Dylan Thomas.*
      Edited by A.N. Jeffares.   New edition.   London: Long-
      mans, Green, 1960; first published, 1955.
      "Horses on the Camargue," pp. 401-02.

166 *The Winchester Book of Verse.*   Edited by H.D.P. Lee.
      London: Harrap, 1960.
      "Horses on the Camargue," p. 271.

167 *The Harrap Book of Sea Verse.*   Arranged and edited by
      Ronald Hope.   London: Harrap (in co-operation with the
      Seafarers' Education Service), 1960.
      "Choosing a Mast," pp. 16-18.

168 *An Anthology of Spanish Poetry from Garcilaso to García
      Lorca in English Translation with Spanish Originals.*
      Edited by Angel Flores.   Garden City, N.Y.: Doubleday
      (Anchor Books), 1961.
      "*Alegoria de la brevedad de las cosas humanas*' / 'Allegory
      of the Brevity of Things Human' by Luis de Góngora,
      translated by Roy Campbell," pp. 90-92; "'*En crespa
      tempestad del oro undoso*' / 'When You Shake Loose Your
      Hair ...' by Francisco de Quevedo, translated by Roy
      Campbell," p. 137.

169 *Music in Their Dreams.*   Compiled by J.W. Laubser.
      Johannesburg: Juta, 1961.   [School anthology.]

"To a Pet Cobra"; "Out of the Ark" from *The Flaming Terrapin*; "The Serf"; "The Zulu Girl." [Not seen.]

I70 *An Anthology of Modern Verse 1940-1960.* Chosen and with an introduction by Elizabeth Jennings. London: Methuen, 1961.
"Nativity," pp. 58-59; "Luis de Camões," p. 59; "San Juan de la Cruz / For Eve Kirk," pp. 59-60.

I71 *Modern British Poetry: A Critical Anthology.* Edited by Louis Untermeyer. New and enlarged edition. New York: Harcourt, Brace & World, 1962.
Bio-critical introduction, p. 410; "The Zebras," pp. 410-11; "Tristan da Cunha," pp. 411-13; "From 'The Flaming Terrapin': Part I" ["Maternal Earth stirs redly ... Red thunderbolts to purify the world."], pp. 413-17; "The Palm," pp. 417-18; "Autumn," p. 418; "On Some South African Novelists," p. 419; "Toledo / July, 1936," p. 419; "From 'The Georgiad'" [Part 2], ["Hail, Mediocrity, beneath whose spell ... To dwarf the ox he envies for his size."], p. 419; "The Serf," p. 419. [Poems by C did not appear in Untermeyer's *Modern American and British Poetry*, Revised Shorter Edition, New York, 1955.]

I72 *Modern Poems: An Anthology for Students of English.* Edited by Michael Thorpe. London: Oxford University Press, 1963.
"The Zulu Girl," pp. 2-3; "Horses on the Camargue," pp. 69-70.

I73 *Dawn and Dusk: Poems of Our Time.* Chosen and introduced to boys and girls by Charles Causley, with designs by Gerald Wilkinson. New York: Franklin Watts, 1963.
"Horses on the Camargue / To A.F. Tschiffely," pp. 88-89.

I74 *Anthology of Modern Poetry.* Edited by John Wain. London: Hutchinson, 1963.
"Autumn," pp. 80-81; "The Zulu Girl," pp. 93-94.

I75 *An Anthology of Commonwealth Verse.* Edited by Margaret J. O'Donnell. London: Blackie, 1963.
"Poets in Africa / To William Plomer," pp. 320-22.

I76 *Roofs of Gold: Poems to Read Aloud.* Edited and with an introduction by Padraic Colum. New York: Macmillan, 1964.
"Tristan da Cunha," pp. 52-55.

177 *The Mid Century English Poetry 1940-1960.* Introduced
     and edited by David Wright. Harmondsworth, Middlesex:
     Penguin Books, 1965.
     "Luis de Camões," p. 43; "'En Una Noche Oscura' / Trans-
     lated from St John of the Cross," pp. 43-44; "November
     Nights," p. 45.

178 *Poets and Poetry. Book Four.* Chosen by M.L. Cherry.
     Croyden, Victoria: Longmans of Australia, 1966.
     "Horses on the Camargue," pp. 63-64.

179 *The Penguin Book of Modern Verse Translation.* Intro-
     duced and edited by George Steiner. Harmondsworth,
     Middlesex: Penguin Books, 1966.
     "The Albatross (From the French of Charles Baudelaire),"
     p. 157; "Ill Luck (Baudelaire)," pp. 157-58; "The
     Giantess (Baudelaire)," p. 158; "'With waving opales-
     cence in her gown' (Baudelaire)," pp. 158-59; "The
     Carcase (Baudelaire)," pp. 159-60; "Meditation (Baude-
     laire)," pp. 160-61; "'Upon a gloomy night' (From the
     Spanish of St John of the Cross)," pp. 161-62; "Song
     of the soul that is glad to know God by faith (St John
     of the Cross)," pp. 162-63; "Romance of the Civil Guard
     of Spain (From the Spanish of Federico Garcia Lorca),"
     pp. 164-65; "Reyerta (Lorca)," pp. 165-66; "Somnambu-
     listic Ballad (Lorca)," pp. 166-68; "Song of the Horse-
     man (Lorca)," pp. 168-69; "On a Shipmate, Pero Moniz,
     dying at sea (From the Portuguese of Luis de Camões),"
     p. 169; "Yes, I sing Fado Cançao (From the Portuguese
     of José Régio)," pp. 169-70; "Fear (From the Portuguese
     of Paço d'Arcos)," pp. 170-71; "Febrile City between
     the Mountain and the Sea - Rio de Janeiro (Paço
     d'Arcos)," pp. 171-72.

180 *Poetry of the 1930's.* Edited by Allan Rodway. (Long-
     man's English Series.) London: Longmans, 1967.
     "The Theology of Bongwi, the Baboon," p. 131; "A Song
     for the People," pp. 131-33; "The Zulu Girl," pp. 133-
     34; "The Zebras," p. 134; "Horses on the Camargue,"
     pp. 135-36; "On Some South African Novelists," p. 136;
     "A Sleeping Woman," pp. 136-37; "Familiar Daemon,"
     p. 137; "Toril," pp. 138-39; "Christ in Uniform,"
     p. 139; "Posada," p. 140.

181 *Poets' Choice: An Anthology of English Poetry from
     Spenser to the Present Day.* Compiled by Patric Dickin-
     son and Sheila Shannon. London: Evans, 1967.
     "Dreaming Spires," pp. 382-86; "Mass at Dawn," pp. 386-87.

182 *The Penguin Book of South African Verse.* Compiled and
introduced by Jack Cope and Uys Krige. Harmondsworth,
Middlesex: Penguin Books, 1968.
"The Theology of Bongwi, the Baboon," p. 25; "Buffel's
Kop (Olive Schreiner's Grave)," p. 25; "Rounding the
Cape," p. 26; "Tristan da Cunha," pp. 26-30; "Mass at
Dawn," p. 30; "Horses on the Camargue," pp. 30-31;
"Choosing a Mast," pp. 32-33; "The Secret Muse," p. 34;
"Driving Cattle to Casas Buenas," pp. 34-35; "Luis de
Camões," p. 35; "Ballad of Don Juan Tenorio and the
Statue of the Comendador," pp. 35-37; "Fishing Boats
in Martigues," p. 38; "'Upon a Gloomy Night' *St. John
of the Cross* / Translation by Roy Campbell," pp. 38-39.

183 *Inscapes: A Collection of Relevant Verse.* Compiled by
Robin Malan. Cape Town: Oxford University Press, 1969.
"The Serf," p. 82; "The Zulu Girl," p. 83; "Horses on
the Camargue," pp. 83-84; "Tristan da Cunha," pp. 85-87.

184 *Poems of Spirit and Action.* Compiled by W.M. Smyth.
Second edition. London: Arnold, 1971.
"Out of the Ark: From 'The Flaming Terrapin' by Roy
Campbell" ["Out of the Ark's grim hold ... With the
fierce wind foaming in their manes."], pp. 38-39.

185 *The Oxford Book of Twentieth Century English Verse.*
Chosen by Philip Larkin. Oxford: The Clarendon Press,
1973.
"Heartbreak Camp," pp. 334-35; "Autumn," p. 336; "From
'The Golden Shower'" ["Here, where returned by changing
seasons, burn ... We think the world a beetle on its
stalk."], pp. 336-38; "On Some South African Novelists,"
p. 338; "On the Same," p. 338; "From *The Georgiad*"
["Next him Jack Squire ... Walk sadly up and down to
kill the time."], p. 339.

186 *Poetry for Pleasure. A Choice of Poetry & Verse on a
Variety of Themes.* Made by Ian Parsons & illustrated
by John Ward, R.A. New York: Norton, 1977; first
American edition, 1978.
"The Zebras," p. 45; "Horses on the Camargue," pp.
167-68.

187 *The New Oxford Book of English Light Verse.* Chosen by
Kingsley Amis. New York: Oxford University Press,
1978.
"On Some South African Novelists," p. 240.

Section J
Works about Roy Campbell

I. EXTENSIVE STUDIES

JI.1   Tate, Allen. "Roy Campbell's Poetry." *New Republic*,
March 18, 1931, p. 133.

Sees *Adamastor* as a great improvement over *The Flaming
Terrapin*. "The new poems are intelligently conceived,
and the imagery is not decorative but inherent ... the
best poems range from fifteen to forty lines ... 'Rounding the Cape,' 'The Zulu Girl,' 'African Moonrise' and
notably 'The Sisters' are unsurpassed by anything like
them since the War ... unless by Hart Crane's 'Black
Tambourine.'" Illustrates some of the faults and
characteristics of *The Flaming Terrapin* and concludes
that it resembles more the work of Sir Richard Blackmore
and Ambrose Philips than that of Rimbaud.

JI.2   Watkin-Jones, A. "South African Bard and English Reviewers. Byron and Campbell: a Study in Satire."
The Critic (Rondebosch, Cape Province, South Africa),
1.3 (March 1933), 133-45.

A comparison based mainly on *English Bards and Scotch
Reviewers* and *The Georgiad*. C's hatred of Bloomsbury-
ians recalls Byron's of the Reviewers. Both attacked
individuals because of what they represented. As a foe
J.C. Squire for C stood for what Jeffrey did for Byron.
"'The loud gushings of the Georgian Spring' is the kind
of diabolic phrase that Byron would have used to describe
the 'Lakers'....'' In assessing C's development as a
satirist, takes account of his essay in *Scrutinies* ...
[see H13] and the influence and example of Wyndham
Lewis.

JI.3   Bonnerot, Louis. "Un poète pécheur d'images: Roy
Campbell." *Revue Anglo-Américaine*, 11 (October 1933),
43-48.

Discusses *Adamastor* and *Flowering Reeds*. In the
former, "Son meilleurs vers ont l'élan, le crépitement
d'un galop." In the latter, especially "Choosing a
Mast," "... il préfère aux éclats cuivrés les mélodies

modulées de la flute." Calls C "le plus prestigieux
rhéteur au sens noble du mot, que connaisse la poésie
moderne." Praises particularly the imagery of "The
Albatross," "The Festivals of Flight" and "The Gum
Trees." Makes on the whole a favorable comparison with
Rimbaud, a generally unfavorable one with Valéry.

JI.4 O'Brien, Justin. "Poet on Horseback." *Kenyon Review*,
      4 (Winter 1942), 75-86.

      Attempts to show that C's better poetry derives from
      the French. "When one takes from Roy Campbell's produc-
      tion the poems he owes to his French models, one greatly
      diminishes his value as a poet since most of his best
      and universally interesting work turns out to be but
      copybook exercises." Serious claims of dependence are
      made about "Dedication" and "The Albatross," in
      Adamastor; about "Hialmar," "An Open Window," "The
      Palm," "The Garden," "The Gum Trees," "The Secret Muse"
      and "Wings." Most borrowing is seen to be from Valéry
      rather than Rimbaud or Baudelaire.

JI.5 Campbell, Ethel. *The Life of Sam Campbell Told in Verse
      (and Lettered by His Daughter Ethel)*. Durban:
      published privately (John Singleton and Williams,
      printers), 1946. [First written in 1933, with After-
      word, 1935; postscripts, 1938 and 1944.]

      Detailed and picturesque account of C's forebears,
      their settlement in Durban, the life and character of
      his father, his family life and youth. Provides a use-
      ful guide to all the family connections and evokes the
      places of C's youth: Durban home, uncle's house at
      Mt. Edgecombe, Peace Cottage, Rhodesian holidays. Many
      echoes to be found in the autobiographies and *The
      Mamba's Precipice*. Attached correspondence includes
      revealing letters by the youthful C.

JI.6 Gray, Cecil. *Musical Chairs, or Between Two Stools:
      Being the Life and Memoirs of Cecil Gray*. London:
      Home & Van Thal, 1948.

      Treats from another perspective some of the events
      and many of the people figuring in *Light on a Dark
      Horse*: among others, T.E. Lawrence, William Walton,
      Philip Heseltine, Bernard van Dieren, Nina Hamnett,
      Jacob Epstein, Wyndham Lewis and, in particular, Thomas
      Earp. Recounts the antics of his eccentric cousin,
      Stewart Gray, including his encounter with the starving

Lascar who died of ptomaine poisoning and his amour
with the policewoman, so corroborating several of the
more improbable episodes.

JI.7   Scott, Tom. "Impressions of Roy Campbell's Poetry."
       Western Review (State U. of Iowa, Iowa City), 14.3
       (Spring 1950), 214-22.

       Concentrates on *Adamastor* and *Talking Bronco*. Con-
       tains inaccuracies, especially in titles. Comparisons
       with Burns. Changing use of language extensively dis-
       cussed, and the effects on his poetry of C's personality
       and South African background. "... early poems are
       poems of discovery, of unveiling a mystery. In
       'Mazeppa' he discovers the pain and majesty of his gift.
       In 'The Albatross' he surveys in verse superbly vitalized
       by a profusion of detonating verbs, the range, power,
       ethics, and possible end of that gift. In 'Rounding
       the Cape' he takes leave of the spirit of Africa....
       Campbell's experience of the war strikes more chords in
       me than that recorded by any other poet, though he
       treats it rather as Kipling might have done, bluster-
       ingly."

JI.8   Russell, Peter. "The Poetry of Roy Campbell." *Nine*, 2
       (May 1950), 81-86.

       "The most subtle and complex influences of our time
       are implicit in his work--Rimbaud and Valery, Lorca and
       Yeats, Chesterton and Wyndham Lewis.... The healthy
       masculinity, the absence of morbid introspection and
       the rough honest humour are essential characteristics
       of a man who is at once bullfighter and poet, cattleman
       and painter." Praises the force and economy of poems
       like "The Zulu Girl" and "The Fight," but notes limita-
       tions. Discusses the religious poetry and thinks
       Mithraic Emblems the best imaginatively.

JI.9   Harvey, C.J.D. "The Poetry of Roy Campbell." *Stand-*
       punte, 5 (October 1950), 53-59.

       Argues C "is one of those writers ... impossible to
       discuss on literary grounds without including a great
       deal about his personality, his philosophy, his poli-
       tics...." Believes the strength of C's personality has
       made critics lose sight of the poetry. Instances forms
       of condemnation on artistic grounds and asserts these
       often based on antipathy towards C's attitudes. Queries,
       "We accept Hardy's atheism, Hopkins's Catholicism--even

without sharing them--why do we find it impossible to
make that discrimination in Roy Campbell's case?"

JI.10   Fraser, G.S. *The Modern Writer and His World: Con-
         tinuity and Innovation in Twentieth-Century Litera-
         ture.* London: Derek Verschoyle, 1953.

         General comments, including biographical. Takes
         pains to place C among literary contemporaries of Left
         and Right. "The word 'Fascist' ... in its looser
         senses ... could probably be applied to Campbell, but
         he used himself to insist he was not a Fascist, but
         rather a strong traditionalist ... with an instinctive
         dislike for political interference with what he thought
         of as healthy local habits and customs.... Campbell
         never sufficiently chastened his irascible appetite,
         or his taste for over-acting, to make the tenor of his
         thoughts and feelings a sufficiently noble content for
         the grandly sonorous vehicle of his verse."

JI.11   Opperman, D.J. "Roy Campbell en die Suid-Afrikaanse
         Poësie." *Standpunte*, 31 (March 1954), 4-15. [Re-
         printed in his *Wiggelstok*. Cape Town: Nasionale B.P.,
         1959.]

         Discusses South African poetry, both English and
         Afrikaans, before C, C's poetry and its influence,
         before ending with a comparison of C with van Wyk Louw.
         Except for Pringle, deals scathingly with C's prede-
         cessors. Sees C as major influence upon the "digters
         van dertig"--I.D. du Plessis, C.M. van den Heever,
         N.P. van Wyk Louw, Uys Krige and W.E.G. Louw. C "ver-
         los die Suid-Afrikaanse poësie van koloniale knegskap.
         Verder het Campbell deur die gaafheid van sy verse en
         hulle beeldende kwaliteit en deur die oorsese erkenning
         wat hy geniet het, beseel tot groter inspanning en tot
         die begeerte dat die Suid-Afrikaanse vers moet kan
         meeding met die poësie van oorsee. Kortom, Campbell
         word vir die Suid-Afrikaanse poësie maatstaf." Cites
         Guy Butler and Anthony Delius as current disciples
         among the English-speaking poets. Gives high praise
         to *Light on a Dark Horse* and compares Spender's *World
         Within World* to it disparagingly.

JI.12   Delius, Anthony. "Slater and Campbell." *Standpunte*,
         New Series, 9 (1954), 64-70.

         Takes issue with Opperman (see JI.11) for slighting
         F.C. Slater and for "hasty and shaky comparison between

Campbell and van Wyk Louw." Disagrees *Raka* and *The Flaming Terrapin* are comparable and thinks C would never have wished to write poems such as *Ballade van die Bose*. "To suggest that Campbell has a slightly empty magnificence is, to my mind, as wrong as to say that van Wyk Louw's greatest virture ... is a slightly narrow intellectual penetration."

JI.13 Davis, Valerie. *Bibliography of the Works of Ignatius Roy Dunnachie Campbell*. Cape Town: University School of Librarianship, 1954. [2 leaves, 17 pp.] [unpub.]

A checklist, with some brief annotations. Lists collected and separate works, translations, some articles and reviews by C; a number of articles on C appearing in South African, English and American periodicals; books, including general reference works, containing biographical material; miscellanea. Appendices supply further references, a chronological list of C's books; indexes of authors, titles.

JI.14 Grobler, P. du P. "Campbell en Van Wyk Louw." *Standpunte*, New Series, 9.5 (1955), 73-76.

Agrees with Delius (see JI.12) that Opperman was hasty in seeing likenesses between C and van Wyk Louw. Otherwise assertively attacks point by point what is for him Delius's over-estimation of C and undervaluing misrepresentation of van Wyk Louw. Feels the real value of Opperman's essay, missed he says by Delius, is its seeing S.A. literature as one phenomenon.

JI.15 Joost, Nicholas. "The Poetry of Roy Campbell." *Renascence*, 8 (Spring 1956), 115-20.

Reviews state of C's reputation prior to and following appearance of *Selected Poems*; essay partly inspired by Randall Jarrell's attack (see JIII.XIX.1) on latter. While admitting weaknesses in this collection, Joost asserts, "... just as Lorca survives in spite of his own bad taste, so no doubt will Roy Campbell." Numbers C among the great scholar-adventurers and sees him as "a poet who has conserved and transmitted the Christian tradition of the West," notably in his translating. Dwells on C's technique, especially in satire and use of imagery. C is "several kinds of poet--the Churchillian satirist [refers to Charles Churchill] ..., the neo-symbolist disciple of Baudelaire and Rimbaud, the political poet, the religious poet, the activist of the great open spaces of Africa and the Mediterranean."

JI.16 Abrahams, Lionel. "Roy Campbell: Conquistador, Refu-
       gee." *Theoria*, 8 (1956), 46-65.

       Castigates C for leaving South Africa: might have
       led movement to mature S.A. idiom. Argues "Maternal
       Earth" imagery of *The Flaming Terrapin* abandoned for
       desert-adversity symbolism and stress on sky and air,
       as in "The Palm." In "Choosing a Mast" the tree set
       free and the poem's flight motif are made to relate
       to C's no longer being rooted in his native soil.

JI.17 Dutton, Geoffrey. "In Natal With Roy," *Africa in
       Black and White*. London: Chapman and Hall, 1956.
       Pp. 27-35.

       Describes C's return visit to South Africa in 1954
       to receive an honorary D.Litt. from the University of
       Natal and impressions of members of his family and
       some of the places celebrated in his writings.

JI.18 Seymour-Smith, Martin. "Zero and the Impossible."
       Encounter, 9.5 (November 1957), 38-51. [Last ten
       pages on other figures.]

       Says comparison of C with Wyndham Lewis and Henri de
       Montherlant possible only in part. Lewis solved the
       problem of language much more effectively; de Monther-
       lant possessed stylistic genius and dramatic ability.
       C wrote his best early, before becoming infected by
       narcissism. Quotes T.E. Lawrence: "Roy Campbell ...
       is sick, not strong." Asks one to compare the "coarse,
       long-winded and monotonous hymn of self-praise"
       "Orpheus" with the shorter, more truthful "Tristan da
       Cunha." C's career illustrates the consequences of
       "allowing a rhetorical and descriptive energy ... to
       remain unattached." Finds C did rediscover his old
       self in the St. John of the Cross translations, but is
       critical of the Lorca.

JI.19 Paton, Alan. "Roy Campbell: Poet and Man." *Theoria*,
       9 (1957), 19-31.

       Very much a tribute. Nearly all of the anthology
       poems come in for praise or approving mention. Gives
       glimpses of C's unpredictability and variety by quoting
       from or referring to contents of *Broken Record* and
       Light on a Dark Horse. Treats such matters as C's
       earlier admiration for Hitler and Mussolini mildly and
       with touches of indulgent humor; quotes some of the
       more extraordinary statements in *BR*. Calls this work
       as a whole "provocative, boastful, and fascinating."

JI.20 Sergeant, Howard. "Restive Steer: A Study of the
       Poetry of Roy Campbell." *Essays and Studies* (1957),
       pp. 105-22.

       Quotes passages from C's writing in *Voorslag* and
       analyzes *The Flaming Terrapin* to determine the philo-
       sophy animating C's poetry. "Danger, hardship, beauty
       and love, filling every moment with their particular
       excitements--these are the attributes of the life he
       extols." Certain figures in the poetry represent re-
       curring oppositions: equestrian-pedestrian; cattleman-
       shopkeeper; Sons of Cain-Sons of Abel; cowboys, toreros,
       vaqueros-Charlies, Tommies, Pommies, wowsers. Besides
       discussing poems like "Mass at Dawn," "Mazeppa,"
       "Tristan da Cunha" and "The Albatross (after Baude-
       laire)," concludes concerning C's satire in *The Geor-
       giad*, "He has the Byronic flow, but not the Byronic
       relevance."

JI.21 MacDiarmid, Hugh (Christopher Murray Grieve). *The
       Battle Continues*. Edinburgh: Castle Wynd Printers,
       1957.

       An attack in verse on *Flowering Rifle* and a spirited,
       lengthy assertion of the eventual triumph in Spain of
       the Republican cause and of "the people" everywhere.
       This matching answer to C's poem consists of 107 pp.
       in three parts, with notes. Sample:

           The young lives wrecked and high hopes blasted
           Move this "poet" to no just indignation,
           No pity or noble passion,
           But only to barrack-room bestiality
           And nose-thumbing wit as though
           It were not Roy Campbell we heard
           But Quiepo [sic] de Llano broadcasting.

JI.22 Davis, R.V. *Roy Campbell--A Critical Survey*.
       Potchefstroom: University of Potchefstroom, 1957.
       [Unpub. M.A. thesis.]

       Contains much useful biographical detail over and
       above that provided in the autobiographies, particu-
       larly as related to C's early illnesses and injuries,
       his lifelong fascination with military life and his
       first sojourns--including the stints as a comic bull-
       fighter--in France. Also details the circumstances of
       the composition and publication of *The Wayzgoose* and
       the key role played by Mistral's poems in inducing C
       to return to writing and publishing poetry in 1930.
       Provides analyses of parody in *The Georgiad* and of

verse form and of the Mithraic background in *Mithraic
Emblems*. Deals somewhat astringently with C's autobiographical inconsistencies and untenable views in
Flowering Rifle, but sees his last work as a supreme
effort to regain greater temperateness and better
discipline.

JI.23   Gardner, W.H. "Voltage of Delight: An Appraisal of
        Roy Campbell." [In 2 parts.] *The Month*, 19, New
        Series, 1 (January 1958), 5-17; 19, New Series, 3
        (March 1958), 133-47.

        Part I of the essay centers on *The Flaming Terrapin*
        and *The Wayzgoose*. Terms the former "one of the most
        accomplished and exhilarating first poems ever written."
        Speaks of C's "passionate contemplation of wild ani-
        mals" in it and the *Adamastor* poems and maintains C,
        though influenced by Nietzsche, sought a more natural,
        organic fusion of mind-body-spirit. Stresses the
        Baroque qualities of C's earlier style, including his
        gaiety and humor and invokes Crashaw, Coleridge, the
        Elizabethans, and Gongorism. Discusses the genesis of
        C's satire in his *Voorslag* experience. Part II traces
        C's subsequent development "from a disillusioned
        Shavian liberalism to a staunch, bucolic and even fiery
        Catholicism," and concludes: "... in spite of his
        superb achievement he failed to fulfil the high expec-
        tations raised by *The Flaming Terrapin* and *Adamastor*--
        a failure due either to a definite intellectual limita-
        tion or to his not having extended his knowledge and
        deepened his insight by wide reading and many-sided
        thought."

JI.24   Payn, Bill. "Roy Campbell." *Durban High School
        Magazine*, February 1958, pp. 21-30.

        Former teacher and lifelong friend recollects C
        when he matriculated. Marvels at C's ability to mingle
        with all sorts and change his language accordingly.
        Notes C always fascinated by language. Says he was
        like Dylan Thomas in his love of a party, like Pepys
        in his inexhaustible curiosity about others and the
        unusual. To illustrate this last, quotes a number of
        ebullient and arresting passages from C's letters
        written to him from Portugal.

JI.25   Plomer, William. "'Voorslag' Days." *Standpunte*, 12.3
        (1958), 1-6. [Also in *London Magazine*, 6 (July
        1959), 46-52.]

A lively re-creation of the circumstances of the
founding and running of the Durban magazine *Voorslag*,
edited by Campbell, Plomer and Laurens van der Post;
extends treatment already given in *Double Lives* [see
JII.36], notably in depicting C's way of life, sur-
roundings and outlook. Takes credit for influencing
C, especially on the race question, but acknowledges C
the leader in defense of *Turbott Wolfe* and objection
to attempts to muzzle *Voorslag*. Traces the beginning
of his estrangement from C: "His native land had got
on his nerves. 'The whole of this country,' he said
one day, 'has an acid smell, and all the white people
have khaki faces.' It is the function of a poet to
say things for effect ... but when he remarked, on the
18th August, 1926, 'One must be theatrical at all
costs,' I felt a sudden chill." With a glance at
Talking Bronco, gives his version of the break-up of
the *Voorslag* partnership, when he took ship to Japan.

JI.26   Krige, Uys. "Roy Campbell as Lyrical Poet: some quieter
aspects." *English Studies in Africa*, 1.2 (September
1958), 81-94.

Adamastor, *Flowering Reeds* and French influence:
latter helped to temper earlier excessiveness. "In
Flowering Reeds, the 'savage,' the barbarian that the
South African was in the best sense ... has become
'civilized,' a Provencal, without losing anything of
his ... South African identity." Considers "Choosing
a Mast" and "Mass at Dawn" great poems. Specifies
links between numbers of C's poems and various French
poets, and refers also to Rubén Dario's and Lorca's
influence.

JI.27   *Hommage à Roy Campbell*. Montpellier: Editions de
La Licorne, 1958.

A collection of tributes chosen by Armand Guibert,
who translated those originally in English into French.
Tributes by F.-J. Temple, Rob Lyle, Richard Aldington,
Lawrence Durrell, Alan Paton, Edith Sitwell, Maurice
Ohana, Alister Kershaw, Cilette Ofaire, Armand Guibert,
Uys Krige, Wyndham Lewis, Henri Chabrol, Charles de
Richter, Frédéric Mistral, Neveu, Catherine Aldington
and F. de Fréminville. Also, poems by C translated by
Armand Guibert: "Dedicace / A Mary Campbell," "En
Doublant le Cap," "A Un Cobra Favori," "Buffel's Kop,"
"Tristan da Cunha," "Les Soeurs," "Saint-Pierre-des-
Trois-Canaux," "La Flamme," "La Fleur," "Chevaux en

Camargue," "Les Zèbres," "Le Choix d'un Mat"; biographical note, bibliography. Reproductions of five photos
of C, one of them being of de Fréminville's bust of
him. [Apparently a version in English exists--not
seen.]

JI.28   Aldington, Richard. "A Note on Roy Campbell." *The*
          European, 12.5 (January 1959), 292-97. [English
          version of tribute in above collection.]

        "... English poetry has lost the one man of genius
who had the strength to maintain and to extend its
ancient and arduous tradition." Elaborates on the
politico-critical "bureaucratizing" reasons for the
undue neglect and "spiteful denigration" during their
lifetimes of writers like D.H. Lawrence and C.
Sketches C's career and character as poet, man of
action and soldier, and asserts, "Campbell is at his
best, as poet, as prose-writer and as a person, when
he is in touch with the virility and vitality of the
'outer' world--the world of South African hunters and
natives, of the fishermen and *jouteurs* and *razeteurs*
of Provence, of cattle-men and bull-fighters of Provence
and Spain and Portugal, of seamen before the mast. When
he is in England, among the Oxford or London intellectuals and artists, he loses strength and virtue like
Antaeus...." This is owing to the fact that his art
derives above all from experience. "In Roy Campbell
was a poet who at first hand had experienced War,
Love, and Religion and ... Nature, which to the pave-
ment artists and critics appeared not only unfair but
untrue." Takes notice of C's satiric talent by finding
in the *Talking Bronco* poems a mastery equal to Dryden's
and of his translations by referring not only to those
of St. John of the Cross and Baudelaire, but to that
of Horace. [See also JII.123.]

JI.29   Krige, Uys. "First Meeting with Roy Campbell."
          Theoria, 12 (1959), 24-28. [Reprinted. See JI.48.]

        Account of C's life at Martigues in 1930-31 and de-
tails of his exuberant enthusiasm for specific poems
of Rimbaud, Baudelaire, Valéry, Apollinaire and Cor-
bière, and equally for particular French rugby players
and Spanish bullfighters.

JI.30   Guibert, Armand. "Roy Campbell (1901-1957)."
          Preuves, 98 (April 1959), 28-31.

A tribute covering familiar, mostly biographical ground; does allude, though, to own rare translation of *Adamastor* and provides other fresh detail, as in comparison of C and Fernando Pessoa and in description of the circumstances of the composition of *Flowering Rifle*.

JI.31 Plomer, William. "'Voorslag' Days." *London Magazine*, 6 (July 1959), 46-52.

[See JI.25.]

JI.32 Pujals, Esteban. *España y la Guerra de 1936 en la Poesia de Roy Campbell*. Madrid: Ateneo, 1959.

Considers C under following heads: Roy Campbell and Spain, Poet and Man of Action, His Poetical Works, Spain and the Poetry of Campbell, Conclusion. Gives a detailed commentary on "Dawn on the Sierra of Gredos." Supplies some further details on C's escape from Toledo; also, on his reasons for fighting for the Allies in the Second World War. Comments on his sympathy for cripples. Sees C as a bard in the Byron-Whitman mold and his poems specifically on Spain as representative of his range: "... la colección de poemas de asunto o ambiente español de Roy Campbell no es un producto secundario o circunstancia de su ingenio, sino que constituye una selección original perfectamente representiva de su poesía." Translates some of *Mithraic Emblems* and CP57 bearing on Spain to show how naturally and successfully the poems go into Spanish. Comments on the influence of El Greco and the role of the bull in C's poetry. Finds *Flowering Rifle* "difficult to synthesize" and in analyzing it manages to avoid all political references!

JI.33 Campbell, Mary. Preface to Roy Campbell's translation of St. John of the Cross, *Poems*. Harmondsworth, Middlesex: Penguin Books, 1960. Pp. 9-15.

Suggests closeness to world of St. John and Teresa of Avila C achieved when living in Toledo in 1936 and influence upon him of Carmelites. "He knew the Carmelite writers Crisogono, Silverio, and Evaristo, who have done such valuable research work on the lives and texts of St. John and St. Teresa." Retells the story of the murder of Fr. Eusebio, C's chief friend in Toledo, and of C's saving of the Carmelite archives from the Republican mob and sums up: "Through [Fr. Eusebio] and his death [C] came to understand the

spirit, not only of St. John, but of the Cross...."
States that C was much more of a mystic than is realized. "The violent side of his character was used as
a cloak for a vulnerable contemplative spirit." Discusses C's knowledge of theology and the stages of his
translating St. John.

JI.34 Collins, Harold R. "Roy Campbell: The Talking Bronco."
       Boston University Studies in English, 4.1 (Spring
       1960), 49-63.

       Characterizes C as embodying "the warrior spirit."
       "Campbell's sense of style in conduct is quite alien
       to the industrial spirit." Dwells on imagery of "the
       sun, the female form, and the horse" in C's poetry.
       Views C's satiric and aficionado personae positively
       and in other ways defends him from detractors: he must
       be seen as primarily a poet of the senses; it is unfair
       to call him a plagiarist; though old-fashioned his
       poetry has Miltonic expansiveness and clarity, and its
       rhythms and images are generally effective if at times
       overdone. Quotes largely from critics enthusiastic
       about C, notably Louis Bonnerot and Geoffrey Stone,
       and counters findings of Hugh Kenner and Justin O'Brien.

JI.35 Elliott, Robert C. *The Power of Satire: Magic, Ritual,
       Art*. Princeton: Princeton University Press, 1960.
       Chapter V, pp. 223-56.

       As satirist C, "strenuously Byronic, presents an
       image of himself as a lonely, alienated bard, gifted
       with strange knowledge and strange power...." Associa-
       tion with Wyndham Lewis and the latter's theories seen
       as harmful to C's satire. "Many of the opinions [in
       C's work as a whole] must be loathsome to any civilized
       mind.... however, we must face the extraordinary fact
       ... Campbell has written ... some excellent poetry....
       The *Georgiad* is a more successful poem than the
       Wayzgoose, in part, no doubt, because of its subject
       matter and locale, but in good measure because the
       verse here is more assured, more controlled, and the
       incidence of wit is high." Discusses merits and
       defects of both poems. Goes on to analyze *Flowering
       Rifle* and *Talking Bronco*; can see some merits only in
       the latter. Regards C's decline as satirist as result-
       ing mainly from his obsessive belief in the magical,
       prophetic efficacy of his art.

JI.36 Krige, Uys. "The Poetry of Roy Campbell: A Few
Aspects," *Poems of Roy Campbell*. Cape Town: Maskew
Miller, 1960. [Introduction], pp. 1-32.

Conclusion: "Of his poetry I should like to say
finally, that whatever its faults ... when all the
cliques, claques and coteries of our time have settled
into their rightful little grooves, Roy Campbell will
stand out as one of the finest lyric voices of his
generation."

JI.37 Miller, Fey. *First Line and Title Index to the Poetry
of Roy Campbell*. [Johannesburg]: University of
Witwatersrand, School of Librarianship, 1961.
[56 pp.]

Prelims include brief biographical notes, list of
references used, explanatory notes and bibliographical
key. Following the code numbered index are two appendix listings of C's poems--"Poems Written under Roy
Campbell's African Muse" and "Foreign Poets and Their
Translated Works." The Index gives the locations of
C's poems in his own works and in journals and anthologies mainly British and South African. It is acknowledged that the compiler did not have access to numbers
of relevant journals; anthologies listed in *Granger's
Index to Poetry* (New York, 1953, 1957) are not
included.

JI.38 Wright, David. *Roy Campbell* (Pamphlet No. 137 of
Writers and Their Work series). London: Longmans,
Green, 1961.

Brief, incisive, sympathetic overview of the main
aspects of C's life, character and work, together with
some personal impressions; in ten sections followed by
a bibliography. Counters the view of C as a vengeful
isolate and contends, "a profound, even a perverse,
humility ... led Campbell to cyclopean bragging of
qualities and talents ... not specifically his or, if
they were, of small importance compared to his true
gift."

JI.39 Armstrong, Robert. "On My Right, Roy Campbell." *The
Critic* (St. Thomas More Association, Chicago), 20.4
(February-March 1962), 18-21.

Circumstantial account of C's physical assault in
1949 upon Stephen Spender when Spender was reading his
poetry at a meeting of the Contemporary Music and

Poetry Circle of the Progressive League. "To their
eternal credit, not a single person out of those hundred
or so present so much as phoned or sent in an account
for which the papers would have given their eye teeth.
In fact the newspapers were blissfully unaware until
Roy Campbell impatiently sent in his own version several months later." Concluding, states that in 1957
"I received a note from him of apology and serenity
with words of friendship and remembrance."

JI.40   Hamm, Victor M. "Roy Campbell: Satirist." *Thought*,
            37 (Summer 1962), 194-210.

Appraises *The Wayzgoose*, *The Georgiad* and *Flowering
Rifle* after brief discussion of earlier short poems
like "To a Pet Cobra." *Talking Bronco* merely alluded
to. "The *Wayzgoose* is the poet's initial attempt at
a *Dunciad*; the full-fledged thing was to come with the
Georgiad...." Cites Popean parallels in *The Wayzgoose*
but sees it as "Rabelaisian and good-tempered in spite
of the hard knocks it deals out"; in *The Georgiad* "the
robust wit never falters," and the poem is even more
Rabelaisian, but besides echoing Pope at points, it
evinces the spirit of Dryden and, here and there, of
Byron. Considers *Flowering Rifle* a "tragic satire"
and a poem demanding "evaluation as a report as much
as a satire." "A Letter from the San Mateo Front" is
more succinct and much better--has more shape, is a
less monotonous and fatiguing tirade. However,
Flowering Rifle is full of "Cervantesque description";
at times it possesses "incandescent fervor" and better
parts once more echo Pope and Dryden and, interestingly,
Butler's *Hudibras*. Despite the "towering egotism" of
some, C's footnotes can remind one of Swift's.

JI.41   Sitwell, Edith. "Roy Campbell and Dylan Thomas,"
            Taken Care Of: An Autobiography. London: Hutchinson,
            1965. Chapter 20, pp. 162-66.

Most adulatory; praises "The Palm" especially.
Illustrates the strength, "pure fire," virtuosity of
technique and language in many poems. Furnishes a
number of good anecdotes and defends C's espousal of
Franco's cause.

JI.42   Jurgens, Heather L. "Behind the Poetry of Roy Camp-
            bell." *Lantern*, 14 (June 1965), 27-35.

Often dependent in estimate on *Light on a Dark
Horse*. Uses "Rounding the Cape" and "In the Town
Square" (*Adamastor* poems) and more extensively *The
Flaming Terrapin* to argue that C's worship of action
and direct experience underlie his poems. Discusses
his view of progress and compares and contrasts him
with Kipling. Interestingly analyzes "The Serf."
Summarizes C's pronouncements on the vocation of the
poet. Fairly lengthily considers poems in *Mithraic
Emblems*. "Above all, it is light that fascinates
Campbell. Gleaming reflections in water, in a woman's
dark hair, in red wine; the blaze of firelight, the
setting sun ... the glare of the veld, the desert,
the bullring.... Sunlight is everywhere in Campbell's poetry, expressing his delight in the natural
world and his sense of the value and meaningfulness
of life. It is the symbol of clear vision, of truth
itself, of renewal and permanence." Accompanied by
reproductions of six photos of C, reproductions of
holograph pages of a ms and letters and reproductions
of drawings by C.

JI.43 Van der Post, Laurens. Introduction, William Plomer,
       Turbott Wolfe. London: The Hogarth Press, 1965;
       reprint of the 1926 ed. Pp. 9-55.

Contrasts the receptions of Plomer's novel in
S. Africa and England. Says C "was not exaggerating
... when he wrote ...: 'Plomer, 'twas you who, though
a boy in age, / Awoke a sleepy continent to rage,'"
but appeals for consideration of the human complexities
of the S. African response. Relates the fortunes of
Voorslag, the journal jointly edited by Plomer, Campbell and himself, in the aftermath of *Turbott Wolfe*'s
publication, and provides much insight into C's life
and work then and later. The latter part of the
Introduction deals extensively with *Turbott Wolfe* and
Plomer's and C's place in S. African literature after
Olive Schreiner. Laments over continued S. African
racialism despite efforts such as Plomer's novel, but
concludes: "... what I have called 'the growing forces
of emancipation' in my country are those forces inspired
by the conviction that South Africa, as has been proved
by the world's past, cannot forever swim against the
main stream of history."

JI.44   Ford, Hugh D. "Roy Campbell: The Voice of the Insur-
        gents," *A Poets' War: British Poets and the Spanish
        Civil War.* Philadelphia: University of Pennsylvania
        Press, 1965. Chapter 7, pp. 177-201.

        Discusses the poems in CP57, above all, *Flowering
        Rifle*, relevant to the Spanish Civil War, with emphasis
        on the magical and prophetic claims C makes concerning
        them. Deals unsparingly with the simplism, shapeless-
        ness, vicious scurrility and reckless bias of the
        longer poems, but attempts a balanced view by, for
        instance, crediting C with success in exposing the
        weaknesses of the literary Left Wing and with still
        being able to write good poetry when not overcome by
        hate.

JI.45   Povey, John F. "A Lyre of Savage Thunder: A Study of
        the Poetry of Roy Campbell." *Wisconsin Studies in
        Contemporary Literature*, 7.1 (Winter-Spring 1966),
        85-102.

        Expresses viewpoint developed in his book [see
        JI.63]: "The intellectual South African has a unique
        position in the world of letters. He is torn between
        an England he admires and resents and an Africa that
        moves his heart even while he despises it." C "rejec-
        ted Plomer's solution" [of "assimilating himself into
        English literary society"]. "The resulting strain of
        rejection, without any compensatory discovery, tore
        his poetry apart.... Campbell's work is a sad declen-
        sion, signaled by a virile and exotic talent dissipated
        in a pointless fruitless exile." Discusses excellences
        of "The Zulu Girl" and "The Zebras," while in some of
        the other S. African poems seeing evidences of coming
        decline. "His delight in attack was to be as dangerous
        to his writing as his lack of verbal and emotional dis-
        crimination. Both derived from a nature that preferred
        the quick and flamboyant effect to mature balance."
        Makes much of the sense of being separated, alien,
        exiled C felt as displaced colonial; discusses *The
        Wayzgoose* and *The Georgiad* in these terms. Hate and
        bitterness increasingly warped C's creativity, along
        with a spirit of sheer defiance; reached crescendo in
        Flowering Rifle. However, in "Hot Rifles" and "Posada"
        Spain could bring out good poems. But, finally, only
        the St. John of the Cross translations can offset the
        tiresome reiterations of the *Talking Bronco* poems.

JI.46   Robinson, Ruth. "Roy Campbell, 1901-1957," *Five*
        Catholic Poets. London: Burns & Oates; Macmillan,
        1966. (Pp. 113-41.)

        An admiring, succinct summary of C's life and career;
        depends for the most part on *Light on a Dark Horse.*
        The later years are covered only briefly. Uncritical,
        but attractive vignette.

JI.47   Bergonzi, Bernard. "Roy Campbell: Outsider on the
        Right." *Journal of Contemporary History,* 2 (April
        1967), 133-47.

        Regards C as somewhat a right-wing Hemingway, only
        more deeply ideological. C's solitary, disdainful,
        anachronistic temper--which shared the feudal outlook
        of D.H. Lawrence and Yeats--made him adopt the French
        cult of neo-classicism and "an idiosyncratic ... Cath-
        olicism ... mingled with Mithraic and other pagan elements."
        C expressed admiration for fascism in *Broken Record*
        but later modified views, though chagrined by Wyndham
        Lewis's more profound turnabout. Deals with C's
        Spanish Civil War involvement and commitment to the
        "authoritarian, Latin traditionalism ... acquired in
        Provence and Spain," as shown in editorship of *The*
        Catacomb.

JI.48   Krige, Uys. *Orphan of the Desert.* Cape Town: John
        Malherbe, 1967.

        Contains three sections on C: "First Meeting with
        Roy Campbell," pp. 28-37 (dated 1951 in text; pre-
        viously had appeared in *Theoria,* 12 (1959)--see JI.29);
        "The Man and His Humour," pp. 38-45: anecdotes to
        illustrate C's Dionysiac quality and self-created myth
        of being a turbulent, trouble-seeking person; and
        "Roy's Castles in Spain," pp. 46-53: C as lover of
        Spain, raconteur and drinker; his side-stepping of
        academic contacts.

JI.49   Paço d'Arcos, J. "Roy Campbell, O Homem e o Poeta."
        Ocidente (Lisboa), 74 (1968). [Translated adapta-
        tion appeared as "Roy Campbell: The Man and the Poet"
        in *Modern Age,* 13.4 (Fall 1969), 353-62, and in
        Contrast (Cape Town), 7.1 (February 1971), 76-89.]

        An admiring compilation of familiar biographical
        details and critical appreciations; interesting mainly
        on account of the emphases on C's Iberian sympathies
        and friendship with the author, whom he knew in

Portugal and translated. The text, as originally
printed, is of an address to the Sociedade de Lingua
Portuguesa. States that after C wrote his book on
Lorca, "Neste ensaio recorda Campbell uma vez mais
Camões, que quase poderíamos considerar seu patrono no
sono, na aventura e no estro poético."

JI.50 Weintraub, Stanley. *The Last Great Cause: The Intel-*
       lectuals and the Spanish Civil War. New York:
       Weybright & Talley, 1968. (Pp. 160-67.)

       Points to and is itself guilty of errors of fact in
       dealing with C's life and Spanish Civil War experience.
       Analyzes C's right-wing views in the thirties, includ-
       ing his contributions to the *British Union Quarterly*;
       compares him with Wyndham Lewis, especially in their
       anti-communism. Attacks *Flowering Rifle* passionately
       but fairly. "Through ... *Flowering Rifle* one learns
       that the destruction of Guernica was a Red hoax, that
       General Quiepo de Llano's voice was 'like a sunbeam,'
       that the murdered Garcia Lorca was a literary light-
       weight and a 'coward,' ... 'Red' volunteers outnumbered
       Franco's foreign troops four to one ... sexual license
       was widespread in the Republican areas ...nothing but
       sanctity and bliss in the Nationalist sectors." Con-
       cedes that amid the poem's "rubbish" are "satirical
       and descriptive gems ... here and there the excitement
       and pageantry on the surface of the war rise ... in
       vivid, powerful images."

JI.51 Paço d'Arcos, J. "Roy Campbell: The Man and the Poet."
       Modern Age, 13.4 (Fall 1969), 353-62.

       [See JI.49.]

JI.52 Cunard, Nancy. "Roy Campbell," *These Were the Hours:*
       Memories of My Hours Press, Réanville and Paris,
       1928-31, edited with a foreword by Hugh Ford.
       Carbondale and Edwardsville: Southern Illinois Uni-
       versity Press, 1969. Pp. 133-40.

       Gives some detail on T.W. Earp's friendship with C;
       refers also to relationships with Spender, MacDiarmid,
       Gawsworth and Nina Hamnett. Records bewilderment over
       C's espousal of Franco's cause and reports account of his
       being with the rebels at Toledo: had found the young
       C free of racial prejudice and of a generous nature;
       yet he wrote that "collection of diatribes against
       Jews and Marxists," *Flowering Rifle*. Concludes by

describing publication and reception of C's *Poems* by
her press and the nature of C's life at Martigues at
the time.

JI.53 Heath-Stubbs, John. *The Verse Satire.* London: Oxford
University, 1969. (Pp. 109-11.)

C, disciple of Wyndham Lewis, "published ... satirical verse throughout his career. Some of it ... is
marked by violence and personal animosity. His targets
are mostly left-wing writers and intellectuals. His
two earlier satires, *The Wayzgoose* and *The Georgiad*,
still retain a good deal of vitality, though the
literary quarrels from which they took their rise are
now largely a matter of history." Illustrates the
attacks on Smuts and South African racialism in *The
Wayzgoose* and those on Georgians and neo-Georgians,
including their sexual irregularities and deviations
and "the current fashion for the New Psychology," in
The Georgiad.

JI.54 Smith, Rowland. "Roy Campbell and His French Sources."
Comparative Literature, 22 (Winter 1970), 1-18.

Establishes C's lifelong immersion in the French
Symbolists and discusses the influence of Rimbaud on
The Flaming Terrapin, of Valéry on *Flowering Reeds*
and *The Gum Trees* and of Baudelaire and Rimbaud on the
early poems and those in *Adamastor*. "In some cases
Campbell merely borrows from a Romance poem a mood,
and the pattern of imagery which created that mood.
In other cases he molds a poem by another poet into an
original work which becomes distinctly his.... consistently the more intangible Gallic material becomes
direct and concrete...."

JI.55 Paço d'Arcos, J. "Roy Campbell: The Man and the Poet."
Contrast (Cape Town), 7.1 (February 1971), 76-89.

[See JI.49.]

JI.56 Smith, Rowland. "The Spanish Civil War and the British
Literary Right." *The Dalhousie Review*, 51.1 (Spring
1971), 60-76.

Summarizes the positions taken and roles played by
British literary figures in relation to the Spanish
Civil War and outlines main features of the conflict
before focusing on Wyndham Lewis and C. Lewis's books
on Hitler and Mussolini and his views on Spain are

surveyed in order to compare and contrast his outlook
with C's, especially as expressed in *Flowering Rifle*.
Finds them most alike in being strongly anti-Soviet
and naive about Franco; otherwise, C's much more
pronounced fascistic bias prevented him from attaining
Lewis's detachment and later ability to dissociate
himself clearly from approval of totalitarianism.

JI.57   Parsons, D.S.J. "Roy Campbell and Wyndham Lewis."
        Papers on Language and Literature, 7.4 (Fall 1971),
        406-21.

Explores the association between C and Lewis and the
influence of Lewis's non-fiction on C, notably *Time
and Western Man*, *The Art of Being Ruled* and *Paleface*,
and recalls C's fictional appearances in novels by
Lewis in order to assess the significance of C's
collaboration with Lewis in *Satire and Fiction* in
defense of the latter's *Apes of God*. Maintains that
from this collaboration derive many of the emphases
and characteristics of *The Georgiad*. "... Campbell's
coming to Lewis's defense over *The Apes of God* con-
firmed him as his follower. Thereafter both his prose
and his poetry bear many marks of the effect of Lewis's
ideas.... What indeed may be demonstrated is that
Campbell's *Georgiad* is his *Apes of God*."

JI.57a Roberts, Gildas. "'Great Bombs of Laughter': a Tenta-
        tive Reappraisal of 'The Wayzgoose,'" in Gildas
        Roberts, ed. *Seven Studies in English for Dorothy
        Cavers*. Cape Town: Purnell, 1971. Pp. 44-63.

Perceives analogies between parts of the poem and
several Graeco-Roman pastoral and satiric forms.

JI.58   Smith, Rowland. *Lyric and Polemic: The Literary
        Personality of Roy Campbell*. Montreal and London:
        McGill-Queen's University Press, 1972. [249 pp.]

The major critical study. C's more prominent poems
and, in passing, his prose works as they are informed
by his aristocratism, his Byronic isolationism and
his succession of personae attesting to his desire to
be identified with certain groups are analyzed so as
to reveal limitations and strengths. Though treatment
of the main translations is not attempted, connections between C's own poetry and sources are explored
thoroughly; also, the influences upon C of Nietzsche,
Plomer, the Sitwell group and Wyndham Lewis are
defined. Quotations from early, unpublished letters

greatly assist portrayal of the effects of C's up-
bringing. In particular, fuller discussion than is
found in other studies is given to the Provencal poems
and to *Mithraic Emblems*, that on the latter involving
an assessment of the role of C's conversion in his
poetry. This book is the published version of Smith's
Ph.D. thesis (University of Natal, 1967).

JI.59 Paton, Alan. "Thoughts on Roy Campbell." *Contrast*
(Cape Town), 37 (September 1975, Volume 10, Number 1
[sic]), 64-78. Printed abridged version of the
public lecture, April 4, 1975, opening the conference
of the Centre for Southern African Studies at the
University of York, England. The full text, entitled
"Roy Campbell," appears in *Aspects of South African
Literature*, edited by Christopher Heywood (London:
Heinemann, 1976), pp. 3-23.

After expressing reservations about C's satire and
autobiographical prose, illustrates from lyrics and
some prose passages how C "had in his verse that gift,
so closely allied to wit and so essential to imagery,
of seeing the concealed relation...." Some analysis
of *The Wayzgoose* and *The Georgiad* is then bound in
with a lengthy biographical and psychological discourse
based on research done by Paton for a biography which,
he says, he decided not to try to publish, in order to
try to spare others from pain. In this text he more
than intimates what it was that deterred him from publication. Sees three great events in C's life--his
marriage, his and his wife's experience as house guests
of Harold Nicolson and V. Sackville-West and his conversion. Most of the latter part of this treatment,
however, merely essays a series of destructive points
and ends by chronicling sadly C's last years and
death.

JI.60 Van der Post, Laurens. "More Light on a Dark Horse."
Contrast (Cape Town), 38 (January 1976, Volume 10,
Number 2 [sic]), 69-76.

A letter in response to Paton's essay in the preceding issue (see JI.59). Says purpose is to correct
errors. As one who knew and worked with C in Durban
and who visited C when he was staying with the Nicol-
sons, van der Post sets about to correct Paton's
account in some eight particulars, being especially
corrective of his version of events following the break-
up of the *Voorslag* partnership. [For other responses
prompted by Paton's essay, see JII.141, 143.]

JI.61   Parsons, D.S.J. "Roy Campbell: A Bibliography."
        Four Decades of Poetry 1890-1930, 1 (July 1976),
        151-67.

        A checklist organized in a preliminary way much
        like this present bibliography.

JI.62   Paton, Alan. "Roy Campbell," *Aspects of South African
        Literature*, edited by Christopher Heywood. London:
        Heinemann, 1976. Pp. 3-23.

        [See JI.59.]

JI.63   Povey, John. *Roy Campbell*. (Twayne World Authors
        Series 439.) Boston: G.K. Hall (Twayne Publishers),
        1977. [233 pp.]

        Provides a useful chronology and deals in some degree
        with all aspects of C, including his translations, but
        more especially analyzes and assesses the early poems
        and *Adamastor*, and *Flowering Rifle* ("A thoroughly bad
        poem") and *Talking Bronco*. These analyses of the
        earlier as against the later poetry lead to the con-
        clusion that C's "poetic career is a declension from
        the virtues, the poetic skills of his earlier work....
        There are occasional flashes of brilliance, sometimes
        a mere line, sometimes brief poems ... remind us of
        the old skill, the old poetic strength. Sadly, such
        flashes also serve to show the weakness of the dross
        in which these occasional poetic gems are set. One
        tentatively advances the thesis that the type of life
        he chose to live, the type of beliefs which he brought
        to his later years, were factors which pressed upon
        his intellectual attitude and his humane concern in
        such a way that they precluded the production of sig-
        nificant poetry." All bibliographical data in this
        study are to be treated with reserve.

JI.64   Alexander, Peter. "Roy Campbell: Towards a Reassess-
        ment," *Centre for Southern African Studies, Col-
        lected Papers: 3*. Ed. by Anne V. Akeroyd and C.R.
        Hill. York: University of York, 1978. [Not seen.]

II. BRIEF DISCUSSIONS

JII.1 Letter by T.S. Eliot on "Tristan da Cunha." *The New Statesman*, 30 (October 22, 1927), 44.

Congratulates C on the poem--"language stronger and less flamboyant than in some of his earlier work." Notes resemblances "in rhythm and in general spirit" of his poem to Johannes Th. Kuhlemann's *Tristan da Cunha*, which he says he once tried to translate himself, and wonders if C knows German--"... if he does, he might make a very brilliant translation."

JII.2 Newbolt, Henry [comp.]. *New Paths on Helicon*. London: Nelson, n.d. [1927?] (Pp. 410-11.)

In this anthology the compiler provides commentaries on the poems collected. From that on *The Flaming Terrapin*: "... the faults of this poem are its essential qualities, they make it what it is, a breathless battering transit across a vast sea in a gale so high that one cannot live in ordered thought but only in gusts of sensation with sudden lulls and glimpses between." [See I.4.]

JII.3 Lindsay, Jack. "The Modern Consciousness." *The London Aphrodite*, 1 (August 1928), 3-24.

On p. 16 makes a brief comparison between W.J. Turner and C. Of their poetry states, "The result at its best is a new sharp excitement which uses all the dark storminess of 'romanticism' to get at some closer kernel of imagery, and which packs as much colour as possible within the phrase while preserving the integrity of the intellectual statement and the curve of emotion." Quotes from *The Flaming Terrapin*.

JII.4 Riding, Laura. *Contemporaries and Snobs*. London: Cape, 1928. (P. 48.)

The Flaming Terrapin is listed among other contemporary poems which are "attempts to make the poetic absolute consist in sheer structural impressiveness."

JII.5 Lamont, H.P. "A South African Poet of Genius." *Outspan*, January 9, 1931, pp. 9, 55.

A brief appreciation, consisting largely of quotations from *Adamastor*.

JII.6   A.S.P. [Alan Paton]. "Roy Campbell." *Natal University
         College Magazine*, 24 (May 1931), 13-15.

         Calls C "the first of African poets"--he is neither
         nationalistic nor provincial--but goes on to suggest
         dangers in his poetry: it contains too few human
         figures and demonstrates an "unreasonable hatred of
         the traditions of the South African soil." Other than
         "On Some South African Novelists" the *Adamastor* frag-
         ments are so much wastepaper; when he writes of the
         vultures of Bull Hoek "he is below notice"; and in a
         poem like "The Town Square," when influenced by a
         venomous spirit, "he is often unworthy of his name."
         None but a Durban poet, however, one accustomed to the
         Durban soil, could write that the surf grooves "crim-
         son furrows" or that in the sun "the red hot acres
         smoulder." In general, C has outdone other moderns
         in amalgamating the "sordid" and the commonplace with
         the majestic in reaction to Victorian decorum.

JII.7   Wolfe, Humbert. "The Ranciad." *The New Statesman*, 1
         (June 27, 1931), 646.

         For a recognition of this poem as a reply in kind to
         The Georgiad, see Rowland Smith, *Lyric and Polemic:
         The Literary Personality of Roy Campbell* (Montreal and
         London: McGill-Queen's Press, 1972), p. 70.

JII.8   Lewis, Wyndham. *The Apes of God*. London: Grayson,
         1931.

         On p. 244 of *Light on a Dark Horse* (London, 1951),
         C identifies himself as the model for "Zulu" Blades in
         Lewis's novel. For corroboration, see W.K. Rose,
         The Letters of Wyndham Lewis (London, 1963), p. 205,
         and Geoffrey Wagner, *Wyndham Lewis: A Portrait of the
         Artist as Enemy* (New Haven, Conn., 1957), p. 45n.

JII.9   Translation into French of "Tristan da Cunha," by
         Henri Chabrol. *Les Cahiers du Sud* (Août-Septembre
         1932). [Not seen.]

JII.10   Colton, Arthur. "By Accident of Alphabet." *The
         Bookman* (New York), 75.8 (December 1932), 769-74.

         Discusses poems from *Adamastor* and *The Flaming
         Terrapin*. "*The Flaming Terrapin*, like Keats's
         Endymion, is structurally nothing. Its magnificent
         robes are draped over a shapeless figure.... The
         only real unity of effect ... he is really after ...

[is] a roused sense of the universe as power." Says *The Flaming Terrapin* has "the Elizabethan trick ... [of] the juxtaposition of the incongruous, or the jolt of contrast," and "Alexander Pope himself might have noted with respect a disdain of contemporaries so vigorous and so true to the tradition of English satire as *Georgian Spring*." Adds, "Roy Campbell is the first figure of distinction in South African letters since Olive Schreiner, and on his work too is the stamp of the veldt and the same tension of revolt, the same parallelism of grim fact and the soul's frustrate pilgrimage, the same brutality cheek by jowl with vision, the same emphasis on the discordance between them." Is unsure whether "Tristan da Cunha" represents humanity's bleak endurance or the poet's own posture.

JII.11 Hamnett, Nina. *Laughing Torso: Reminiscences*. London: Constable, 1932.

John Flanagan, who painted a portrait of C [see reproduction tipped in between pp. 56-57, *The First Edition and Book Collector*, 1.2 (September-October 1924)], referred to on p. 46. Provides an evocation of C at Oxford in company with T.W. Earp, Aldous Huxley, J.B.S. Haldane and Marie Beerbohm, pp. 106-07.

JII.12 Lewis, Wyndham. *Snooty Baronet*. London: Cassell, 1932. (Pp. 176-215.)

Contains an account of Lewis's sojourn with the Campbells in Provence, suitably fictionalized. C appears as Rob McPhail. To underline his mockery of Mithraism and dislike of bullfighting, Lewis spoofs C's bullfighting efforts. The two chapters featuring McPhail are headed "The Lord of Language and His Boat" and "Bull-Fight--Bouches du Rhône." In the opening chapter of *Broken Record* C acknowledges his portrayal in Rob McPhail. For a discussion of the connections, see Geoffrey Wagner, *Wyndham Lewis* (New Haven, 1957), pp. 256-57.

JII.13 Ikarus [pseud. of Professor I.J. Rousseau, Grahamstown, S. Africa]. "Roy Campbell, the South African Poet." *NUSAS* (the official organ of the National Union of South African Students, Pretoria), 3 (June 1933), 9-14.

Reminisces about C at Oxford, where they shared
lodgings, and briefly discusses *Voorslag*, offering
the opinion that C should not have singled out
Totius's *Die Os* for "uninformed and unfair criticism."

JII.14   Lewis, Wyndham. *One-Way Song*. London: Faber, 1933.

The Enemy in poem no. 30 (part of the section
headed "The Enemy Interlude") lists the "all too few
laurelled heads" of the "little age"--Eliot, Pound,
T.W. Earp, Campbell, Sturge Moore, Joyce, Herbert
Read, Sacheverell Sitwell, Yeats, Aldington, Graves,
Osbert Sitwell, Sassoon, Auden and MacDiarmid. The
couplet on C goes, "And there's Roy Campbell, stiff-
chested and slim, / Posed for veronicas before wild
terrapim."

JII.15   Block, Andrew. *Key Books of British Authors 1600-
1932*. London: Denis Archer, 1933. (P. 71.)

Lists *The Flaming Terrapin* and quotes from AE's
review of it in *The Irish Statesman* and from that in
the *TLS*.

JII.16   King, Charles. "Roy Campbell: A New Poet." *Great
Thoughts*, 11th Series, 6 (March 1934), 273-74.

A general appreciation of *The Flaming Terrapin*,
Adamastor and *Flowering Reeds*.

JII.17   Lewis, Wyndham. *Men Without Art*. London, 1934.

"... satire is a very *live* issue today, about that
there can be little mistake. The most brilliant and
interesting of the youngest poets, of the 'new signa-
tures,' Auden, is above all a satirist. Mr. Roy
Campbell, in his *Georgiad* has produced a masterpiece
of the satiric art, which may be placed beside the
eighteenth-century pieces without its suffering by
that proximity" [from chapter V: "Virginia Woolf"].

JII.18   Spender, Stephen. "One-Way Song." [Rev. of Lewis's
Men Without Art.] *The Spectator*, October 19,
1934, pp. 574, 576.

In the part relevant to C, states Lewis "will
occasionally throw a bouquet to some author--a few
are thrown to Mr. Auden--but to say that Mr. Auden
is 'brilliant and interesting,' and to misquote a
line is not criticism. It would be easiest to assume

that Mr. Lewis has no good opinion of any other
living writer, but unfortunately there is one high
light in this book which does little credit to his
taste: 'Mr. Roy Campbell in his *Georgiad* has produced
a masterpiece of the satiric art, which may be placed
beside the eighteenth-century pieces without its
suffering by that proximity.' This in a book in which
The Waste Land is referred to with contempt, as are
also the novels of Mr. E.M. Forster, and in which
Mrs. Woolf is attacked with a great deal of malice
and without any show of evidence that Mr. Lewis has
read either of her best works, *The Waves* or *To the
Lighthouse.*"

JII.19 Lewis, Wyndham. Letter to the editor under heading,
        "The Criticism of Mr. Wyndham Lewis." *The Spec-
        tator*, November 2, 1934, p. 675.

        As part of rejoinder to Spender's review [see
        above], Lewis replies in countering Spender's remarks
        about his championing of C as a satirist, "Anyone has
        a right to their opinion of the books of Mrs. Woolf--
        as also of those of Mr. Roy Campbell: though both
        these rights are denied me by Mr. Spender. To admire
        Mr. Campbell's books 'does little credit to one's
        taste,' I am told: whereas *not* to admire overmuch
        those of Mrs. Woolf is simply 'malicious.'"

JII.20 Gray, Cecil. *Peter Warlock: A Memoir of Philip
        Heseltine.* London: Cape, 1934. (P. 212.)

        At Heseltine's urging, Gray published a number of
        C's poems in his journal *The Sackbut*. [See E8a, b, c.]
        Of this set of poems "in the manner of Rimbaud" Gray
        states, "Long before any of the regular literary critics,
        Heseltine had divined in these immature poems the remark-
        able talent which is today acclaimed as one of the fore-
        most in modern English poetry."

JII.21 Hamilton, George Rostrevor. *John Lord, Satirist.
        A Satire.* London: Heinemann, 1934.

        After devoting several lines to the satires of
        each of "Humbert" and "Osbert," in Part II this verse
        satire in iambic pentameter couplets has four lines
        on C evidently aimed primarily at *The Georgiad*:

        Next, river-like *Roy Campbell*, when he rages,
        Swollen with gossip, through a score of pages

> Whose genuine wit, though aided by bad taste,
> In floods of roaring rhetoric runs to waste.

JII.22   Meyerstein, E.H.W. "Letter to W.R. Childe" (dated
         1935). *Verse Letters to Five Friends*. London:
         Heinemann, 1954.

         Contains the following lines on C:

> And Campbell, who (forgive me, but I wound
> Myself as well) the most inspired I found
> Of all since Brooke and Flecker, de la Mare
> Exempt, is he yet killing bulls (Beware,
> O Philistine!), or fishing at Martigues,
> And will he ever make unholy league
> With pitiful post-Squirearchs?

JII.23   Palmer, Herbert Edward. *The Mistletoe Child. An
         Autobiography of Childhood*. London: Dent, 1935.
         (Pp. 300-01.)

         Though they never met, Palmer and C corresponded
         and it was Palmer who did much to introduce C's work
         to the British public. They quarrelled in newspaper
         writings about Blake and who of the two of them was
         the better poet, but it was not until C established
         himself in southern France and took up bullfighting
         that Palmer "got less interested in him."

JII.24   Guibert, Armand. "Préface" to his translation of
         Adamastor [see A3d].

         Recounts C's youthful experiences in Africa, in
         England and as a seaman, his sojourn in France and
         removal to Spain. Comments on *The Flaming Terrapin*
         and *The Georgiad* before discussing more fully the
         Adamastor and *Flowering Reeds* collections. Regards
         the influences of modern French poets on C's work as
         sometimes detrimental. Sees "St. Peter of the Three
         Canals" as reminiscent of Claudel's "La Rapsode
         Foraine." Believes C's poetry does not owe its
         strength and being directly to his South Africanism
         and finds the satiric pieces on S. African themes
         not part of his "essence," wishing to maintain that
         C's true development is in the direction of becoming
         a "true son of the Mediterranean": "... il ne s'est
         pas refusé le luxe d'une langue opulente, colorée,
         volontiers romantique; mais le miracle méditerranéen
         s'est opéré au-dedans de lui, puis dans son rythme,
         et dans son vocabulaire, à mesure qu'il se laissait

pénétrer des plus secrètes influences de son climat
d'élection."

JII.25 "The Rise of Roy Campbell." *The Poetry Journal*, 1
(April 1937), 9-10.

A brief appreciation. References made to *The
Flaming Terrapin*, *The Wayzgoose*, *Adamastor*, *Poems
1930*, *The Gum Trees*, *Choosing a Mast* and *The Georgiad*.
"When in dead lands men like brutish herds ...,"
opening stanza, and "The Secret Muse" quoted. "His
work has a quality that can positively hurt; a savagery of words that becomes beautiful by reason of its
intensity; his pattern, his rhythm, is divorced from
the trite and the usual."

JII.26 Lewis, Wyndham. *Blasting and Bombardiering*. London:
Eyre and Spottiswoode, 1937.

Describes C's marriage in chapter headed "The
Wedding of Roy Campbell" and offers opinions on C's
politics and postwar sensibility: see pp. 222-25
passim.

JII.27 Weygandt, Cornelius. *The Time of Yeats*. New York,
1937. (Pp. 425-27.)

Considers mainly *The Flaming Terrapin*, but touches
also on "The Albatross," "Tristan da Cunha," "To a
Pet Cobra," "To a Young Man with Pink Eyes," "Poets
in Africa," "Solo and Chorus," and more slightly,
"Mass at Dawn" and "The Sisters." "Campbell is as
Scottish as Davidson. He has Davidson's belief in
the superman, Davidson's insistence on the truth
though the heavens fall, Davidson's soreness at the
way things are in the world.... The man can write,
there is no doubt of that. He is master of the verse
forms he attempts. The danger is that when his anger
passes, as pass it must with the years, the glow will
go out of his writing.... It will be a pity if there
will not come to him before he is old that tranquil-
lity in which emotion must be remembered before it
can be transmuted in a perfect art of words."

JII.28 Garnett, David, ed. *The Letters of T.E. Lawrence*.
London: Cape, 1938.

In a letter to Jonathan Cape and one to Edward
Garnett, L expresses his excitement over *The Flaming
Terrapin*. These letters show how he, together with

Augustus John, was instrumental in getting C's first
book published. Contains also a letter to C.J.
Greenwood, of Boriswood Limited, on the subject of
Broken Record.

JII.29 MacNeice, Louis. *Modern Poetry: A Personal Essay.*
        London: Oxford University Press, 1938. (Pp. 151-
        52).

        As part of general observations on the state of
        poetic diction in English, states, "And though admit-
        ting it to be a *tour de force*, I deplore the high-
        falutin of Roy Campbell (though this vice lies not
        only in the diction of his verse but in its movement).
        ... Our diction should be masculine but not exhibi-
        tionist."

JII.30 Palmer, Herbert. *Post-Victorian Poetry.* London,
        1938. (Pp. 249-54.)

        Makes comparisons with Redwood Anderson, Siegfried
        Sassoon and Rimbaud; notes influences of Dryden,
        Pope, Byron and the French Symbolists, and discusses
        The Flaming Terrapin, The Wayzgoose, The Georgiad and
        Mithraic Emblems briefly and *Adamastor*, "so far his
        best book," more extensively. In referring to
        "African Moonrise," states, "... swagger and mockery
        have always been two of the half-dozen driving forces
        of Roy Campbell's art, and are as constituent of his
        virtues as his vices. Other vices are only too plain
        ... even in 'Tristan da Cunha' and 'The Albatross.'
        ... But it is remarkable how good a medium he has
        made of such outworn things as anapaests in his poem,
        'The Palm.' Perhaps as a satirist he has overstepped
        himself...."

JII.31 Butler, P.R. (Lt.-Col.). Letter. *The Times Literary
        Supplement*, February 18, 1939, p. 105.

        Attacks the review, February 11, of *Flowering
        Rifle.* [See JIII.XI.1.]

JII.32 Commentary under "Education and Criticism," relating
        to rev. of *Flowering Rifle*, Feb. 11, and rejoinders
        in letters by C, Feb. 25 [see F4], and others.
        The Times Literary Supplement, March 4, 1939, p.
        135.

        "To read Mr. Campbell's poem and 'Poems from Spain'
        is to realize that the belief in instinct exemplified

by the one and the belief in reason exemplified by the other--beliefs of which each opponent can see nothing but the perversity--can only be reconciled in an imagination capable of seeing what is positive in both and by that vision lifting the conflict on to the creative level. The poet who could do that would really be serving the cause of civilization."

JII. 33 Reply of reviewer of *Flowering Rifle* to critical letter from C [see F5]. *Blackfriars*, 20.231 (June 1939), 460-61.

Agrees that criticism of the poem should be on literary grounds and says that this is what his was. The book is "lyrical invective at best," not an epic but a brassy, mechanical exercise, and "the language of the less prosy parts is worn out 'poetical' currency, full of bathos." Capitals are used "to galvanize the cliché into some shadow of life." States he omitted mention of "the anti-semitism, half-assimilated theology (especially of the Cross), special pleading, venomous flogging of dead horses" because he was confining himself to a literary criticism.

JII. 34 Walker, Oliver. "Footnote to Voorslag 1 and 2." *Trek*, 7.13 (December 18, 1942), 14; 7.14 (January 1, 1943), 8.

A treatment of the collapse of the *Voorslag* venture and the genesis of *The Wayzgoose* that would have it that C wrote the poem "to vindicate his *amour-propre*," with no thought of publishing it, but that "fullest satisfaction could not be secured by hiding the satire away and there were too many jackals yowling at his heels during those months of idleness ... not to let them have the full broadside."

JII. 35 MacDiarmid, Hugh (Christopher Murray Grieve). *Lucky Poet: A Self-Study in Literature and Political Ideas*. London: Methuen, 1943. (Pp. 7-8.)

"Roy Campbell, the South African poet, libelled me in his book of reminiscences, *Broken Record* (1934), the publication of which I had held up until the offending page was removed, and *inter alia* he fell foul of me for using the name of 'Hugh MacDiarmid' 'to conceal the fact that he has a mean, lachrymose little patronymic of his own.' MacDiarmid is, of

course, the Campbell clan name, and perhaps Roy
Campbell's resentment had some justification on
that score."

JII.36   Plomer, William. *Double Lives: An Autobiography.*
         London: Cape, 1943. (Pp. 166-67.)

Succinct coverage of the joint editorship of
Voorslag and the *Turbott Wolfe* controversy. Refers
to C's composition of "The Serf," "The Zulu Girl"
and "Tristan da Cunha"; discusses T.S. Eliot's letter
on the latter [see JII.1] and writes, "Now it so
happened that I had read to Campbell ... some extracts
from a letter to me from Oxford in February, 1922, by
my old Rugbeian schoolfellow, D.R. Gillie, including
a translation of a few lines from Kuhlemann's poem,
and a mere phrase or two in these had kindled Campbell's imagination." [See also JI.25.]

JII.37   "Roy Campbell in Durban. Hospital Patient at Spring-
         field." *Natal Mercury*, April 4, 1944.

An interview with C following his being invalided
out of the army in N. Africa. A leg injury dating
back to the Spanish Civil War and several bouts of
fever "had brought his medical category down." C
quoted concerning an article on him in the *Egyptian
Gazette* and his satirical answer in *Jambo*, as well as
on his intention to join either the B.B.C. or the
Spanish Institute in Madrid.

JII.38   Goldring, Douglas. *The Nineteen Twenties.* London:
         Nicholson & Watson, 1945. (P. 110.)

With reference to the controversy over the *New
Statesman*'s rejection of C's review of *The Apes of
God* by Wyndham Lewis, reports that the public exchange
of letters between Campbell and Ellis Roberts, who as
acting editor had rejected the review, "kept literary London diverted for some weeks" and that Ellis
Roberts himself subsequently wrote a largely eulogis-
tic review of *The Apes of God* for the *New Statesman.*

JII.39   Guibert, Armand. "Deux Sud-Africains Citoyens du
         Monde." *Renaissance* (Johannesburg), 4.8 (February
         1946), 6-8.

About the variegated lives led by C and the Afrikaans
poet Uys Krige. C's youthful freedom and wanderings
prepared him for his later, often exotic travels.

However, though seemingly footloose and thought lazy
at school, he actually immersed himself in English
literature and learned enough French to penetrate
the modern French poets and enough Latin to smooth
the way for his later study of Spanish and Portuguese poetry. Touches on C's whaling experience
and his life in Toledo and Rome. Notes his friendship with the pianist Maurice Ohana in Nairobi.

JII.40   Monteith, Malcolm. "Plain Facts about Roy Campbell."
         Spotlight, August 30, 1946, pp. 22-23.

A compressed biographical summary giving along with
what is familiar some interestingly fresh and specific details, such as those of C's life when first in
Provence and in Toledo, and his war service; the
assertion is made that during the Spanish Civil War
C took part in the battles of Brunete and Teruel and
was wounded at Talavera, and yet another version is
given of the Campbells' escape from Toledo.

JII.41   Sylvester, A.D.B. Letter. *The Listener*, December 5,
         1946, p. 799.

Attacks A.L. Rowse for championing C in a previous
letter as "the spirit of that mythical archetype, the
Temperamental Celt" and condemns his admiration for
C's "immoderate, extreme self-dramatising." Such
hysteria ("I am the Enemy") "is wrecking Campbell's
work as it wrecked that of Wyndham Lewis. But it is
easy to see why Mr. Rowse admires Campbell: the bun-
gling rhetorician doffs his hat to the inspired one."

JII.42   S., M. [Mary Armstrong Sullivan]. "Roy Campbell,"
         *Catholic Authors: Contemporary Biographical Sketches
         1930-1947*, edited by Matthew Hoehn, O.S.B., B.L.S.
         2 vols. Newark: St. Mary's Abbey, 1947. I, 103-05.

Contains quotations from *Broken Record* and gives
some details of C's Spanish experience. "General
Quiepo [sic] de Llano mentioned him with honour in
his despatches of April 1937." Some inaccuracies.
Mostly a recital of well-known biographical
ingredients.

JII.43   Slater, Francis Carey. *Selected Poems*. London:
         Oxford University Press, 1947.

"'Soar again, young eagle' / (to Roy Campbell),"
p. 140.

JII.44 Tyndall, William York. *Forces in Modern British
        Literature 1885-1946.* New York: Knopf, 1947.
        (Pp. 109-10.)

"Roy Campbell, the South African poet, was another
lesser Lewis, and his disciple. Having produced gor-
geous dithyrambs and pseudo-classical satires upon
Bloomsbury bohemians, especially Lesbians, he wrote
Broken Record (1934), an autobiography to explain his
position. Like Lewis an enemy of Jews, communists,
and softies, he sees Fascism, Italian and German, as
the only hope for the Western tradition. He salutes
Maurras and Léon Daudet as masters, attacks Hugh
MacDiarmid, and expresses devotion to bull-throwing,
shark-catching, and pugilism. This furious convert
to Catholicism made Franco's cause his own. In
Mithraic Emblems (1936), singing the Spanish civil
war, he sees fascists as 'Christs in uniform.' As
full of ornament as a Victorian parlor, but more
violent, his verses unite modern fury with nineteenth-
century technique."

JII.45 Hiener, Wilhelm. "Roy Campbell" [poem]. *Trek*, 13.1
        (January 23, 1949), 23.

JII.46 De Richter, Charles. [Article on C.] *Nouvelles
        Littéraires*, January 27, 1949. [Not seen.]

JII.47 West, Rebecca. Letter, under heading, "The Meaning
        of Treason." *The Times Literary Supplement*,
        December 23, 1949, p. 841.

"In my book *The Meaning of Treason* I refer to 'Roy
Campbell, a poet of undoubted genius,' as having
been a member of the British Union of Fascists.
Mr. Campbell informs me that he was not a member of
this organization and that he has never been a Fascist.
I regret that my misinterpretation of his position
should have led me to make this incorrect statement,
and I will expunge it from all future editions of my
book. My regret is all the deeper because I am very
conscious of the honour due to Mr. Campbell as a poet
and as a soldier who volunteered at the first possible
moment to serve in the Second World War, and who was
gravely wounded in the course of his service."

JII.48 Bullough, Geoffrey. *The Trend of Modern Poetry.*
        3rd edition. Edinburgh: Oliver & Boyd, 1949.
        (Pp. 118-20.)

C is "best when most under control, in the descriptive strophes of *The Flaming Terrapin*, Part V, in
the humorous pieces of *Talking Bronco*, and above all
in the lyrical descriptions, "The Zulu Girl," "The
Zebras," "The Serf," where his love of life is not
embittered by hatred." Discusses *The Georgiad*, *The
Flaming Terrapin* and *Adamastor*. Says the latter two
were "allegories of creative vigour marked by a colourful description and loose handling which recalls
Kipling's Good Workmen in Heaven: 'They shall splash
at a ten-league canvas with brushes of comets' hair.'"

JII.49   "*Nine* Salutes Some Passing Figures." *Nine*, 2.1
         (January 1950), 65.

Comments allude to C's physical encounters with
Stephen Spender, Geoffrey Grigson and Louis MacNeice:
"After Mr. Stephen Spender had been rescued by Popular
Front Action from being gored in a church hall,
Mr. Gee Gee was accosted while on his lawful occasions, in the vicinity of Portland Place. He was
cornered, it appears, and tossed playfully.... The
status quo was fittingly restored when Mr. MacNeice
flung his cloak at the Toro in a Tavern, made a swift
pass, and, they say, drew a little blood."

JII.50   Sadler, M.J.   "Roy Campbell." *Common Sense*, 11
         (April 1950), 163-65.

A general estimate depicting C as a "snob colonial"
unaware that changes in social class structure have
been the key to the modern condition and only regaining community with humanity in the Second World War.

JII.51   Mulvey, Charles D.   [Letter, replying to JII.49.]
         Nine, 2.2 (May 1950), 166.

Sets about to correct several statements, chiefly
the last: "Later when Mr. Roy Campbell and Mr. Mac
Neice were in conversation, differences of opinion
arose. There were two blows struck by Mr. Campbell
to the great discomfiture of Mr. MacNeice. At this
point, I came between them and the conversation between the two poets was resumed amicably and cordially."

JII.52   "Une Grande Figure de Camarguais." *Le Provençal*,
         July 10, 1950.   [Not seen.]

JII.53   Gardner, W.H.   "Poetry and Actuality."   *Theoria*
         (Pietermaritzburg), 3 (1950), 19-31.

         In part provides a commentary on "The Zulu Girl"
         and "The Serf," seeing the latter as pendant to the
         former. The tension of opposite suggestions culminates
         in the ambiguity of "harvest" in "The Zulu Girl" and
         in the ironic quality of "fallow" in "The Serf."

JII.54   Tschiffely, A.F.   *Bohemia Junction*.   London: Hodder &
         Stoughton, 1950.

         Boxers, circus folk, horse showmen and dog snatchers
         of the sort C knew described, p. 32. C's associations
         with John Gawsworth, Augustus John and Nina Hamnett
         referred to, p. 250, and his later friendship with
         Gene Tunney, p. 315.

JII.55   Davis, E.   "The Spoilt Boy in Roy Campbell."   *Trek*,
         15.3 (March 1951), 12-14.

         Cannot understand why C, who through his early
         poems transformed S. African poetry, should have
         turned on his fellow S. Africans in *The Wayzgoose* and
         gone on to posturing in Spain and in *Mithraic Emblems*.
         Sees much of C's later work as consisting in bluff,
         "false rhetoricism." Adversely analyzes "Choosing
         a Mast" so as to demonstrate its "pseudo-poetic
         conceit," its "pernicious Irishism," and its being "a
         play on prepositions and not on ideas." Maintains
         success has been C's downfall and that to save his
         quality he must return to Africa.

JII.56   Krige, Uys.   "Roy Campbell."   *Trek*, 15 (October 1951),
         3-5.

         Opens much as does "My First Meeting ..." [see
         JI.29]. Stresses C's gentleness, sensitivity. Says
         he was not a great *causeur*, being given to jerkiness,
         pauses; but he was capable of wonderful images,
         flights.

JII.57   Lewis, Wyndham.   *Rotting Hill*.   London: Methuen,
         1951.   (P. 307.)

         In closing this depressing portrayal of postwar
         London, Lewis presents a vignette of C: "As I was
         nearing 'The Catherine Wheel,' Roy Campbell at the
         head of his group, responding to the mirth of his
         followers with a series of spasmish nods of the torso

of jovial assent, emerged from the famous public
house. From the expressions of those about him I
could see that he had been telling them how the bull
tossed the matador the full length of the arena, how
Campbell caught him and gently laid him down, executed
a tourniquet before the bull could reach them, but
when he did, head down, and kicking up the dust,
Campbell killed him with the fallen matador's espada.
He was now obviously walking out of the bull-ring,
stepping gingerly to the deafening applause of the
officionados [sic]."

JII.58   Scott-James, R.A. *Fifty Years of English Literature,*
         1900-1950. London: Longmans, 1951. (Pp. 233-34.)

Following making a general contrast between C and
Auden, Spender and Day Lewis, states, "There is
immense energy and zest for life in his verse which
rings with hammerstrokes; and he delights in violent
satire at the expense of all that seems to him affected
and nonsensical. He is a heady poet, to be read in
small doses. A page or two is like a tonic; but pur-
sued too far his verse has the monotony of a bag-
pipe."

JII.59   Spender, Stephen. *World Within World.* London:
         Hamish Hamilton, 1951. (P. 152.)

Alludes to C as supporter of Franco and suggests
comparison between C and the poet Nick Greene in
Virginia Woolf's *Orlando.*

JII.60   Gray, Alan. "The Genius of Roy Campbell: A Lyricist
         and Swashbuckler from Natal." *African World,*
         March 1952, p. 14.

An impressionistic, mainly biographical sketch,
clearly in response to the appearance of *Light on a
Dark Horse.* Closes with an overview of the poetry,
including saying, "His best poems owe their distinction to the internal tension set up between the
passion and the discipline of their construction."

JII.61   John, Augustus. *Chiaroscuro: Fragments of an Auto-
         biography: First Series.* London: Cape, 1952.
         (P. 114 and *passim.*)

Describes visiting C at Martigues, and knowing him
in London. "He had lent me the manuscript of his
first long poem, *The Flaming Terrapin.* I thought it

a most remarkable work, in spite of its unflagging
and, to me, rather exhausting grandiloquence. I
showed it to T.E. Lawrence, who, much excited, bore
it to Jonathan Cape, with the result of its publication in due course."

JII.62   De Villiers, D.L.S.   "Calling on Roy Campbell."
          The Cape Argus, June 13, 1953.

          Reports on a visit to C in Portugal, his reasons
          for living there and association with Rob Lyle. Says
          it was Lyle who suggested the title "Light on a Dark
          Horse" and that C was then working on "the second
          part of his autobiography."

JII.62a   Sutherland, John.   "The Great Equestrians."   *Northern
          Review* (Montreal), 6.4 (October–November 1953),
          21–28. Repr. in *John Sutherland: Essays, Controver-
          sies and Poems*, ed. by Miriam Waddington. Toronto:
          McClelland and Stewart, 1972.

          The essay discusses G.K. Chesterton, D.H. Lawrence,
          Roy Campbell and C.S. Lewis. Consideration of the
          "Talking Bronco" leads to: "Not all literature is
          heroic in intent but all literature that is worthy of
          the name is heroic in effect. It stimulates action
          and it stimulates to action. It breaks down the
          barriers between the imagination and reality....
          It not only talks like a bronco: it throws its heels
          about like one. It is the swift kick that sends us
          sailing into the freedom of action."

JII.63   Opperman, D.J.   *Digters van Dertig*. Derke Druk
          [3rd ed.]. Kaapstad: Nasionale Opvoedkundige
          Uitgewery Bpk., 1953.

          In this authoritative study of the Afrikaans liter-
          ary renaissance of the 1930's, the author illustrates
          and alludes to C's influence upon the chief Afrikaans
          poets of the period, among them especially I.D.
          du Plessis, N.P. van Wyk Louw and Uys Krige. He
          points out how C was, variously, an inspiration,
          someone to emulate and someone to improve upon. The
          study is most valuable in describing the far-reaching
          consequences of C's praise for Afrikaans as a language
          and literary medium in his article on Krige in *The
          Critic*, 3.2 (January 1935), 61–67, and in tracing
          the effects on Krige of his friendship with C.

JII.64 MacCarthy, Desmond. *Memories.* London: MacGibbon
and Kee, 1953. (Pp. 172-73.)

Defends "Bloomsbury" against attacks made by
writers and painters, including C, and sees the
latter's "Home Thoughts on Bloomsbury" as an exaggeration of a common misconception about the group.

JII.65 "'n Digter Doodgeswyg" ["A Poet Suppressed"]. *Die
Transvaler*, March 23, 1954.

In its coverage of C's speech following his receiv-
ing an honorary D.Litt. degree from the University of
Natal [for details of the publication of this speech,
see H54], states that C, now that he is back in S.
Africa, has given "the English press," particularly
the out of country papers, something to chew on. He
has attacked and mocked the misrepresentations of
S. Africa by the press and answered its frequent hostility with a belligerence of his own. That an
English-speaking S. African has so spoken the truth
makes him truly an object of gratitude for Afrikaners.
"Hy het naamlik op 'n manier, soos hy dit alleen kan
doen, die kritici van die Unie oor die behandeling
van die nie-blankes met striemende slae geneuker. Hy
het nog verder gegaan. Hy het diegene wat op so 'n
naartige wyse na 'n splint in die oog van die Unie
sook, herinner aan die balk wat in hul eie oog is."
Like Ethel Campbell for her poems in praise of the
Afrikaner nation and its prowess, her brother "wat
nou 'n geleentheid afgewag het om in die hartjie van
Natal woorde to spreek wat lankal gesê moes wees het,
sal die Afrikaner nou ook dank betuig."

JII.66 Walker, Oliver. "Roy Campbell's Apology." *The Forum*
(South Africa), 3 (July 1954), 56-57.

Attacks C for apologizing in a radio broadcast from
Natal for *The Wayzgoose* ("ashamed of my previous ill-
nature"). Surveys C's accomplishments with mingled
praise and blame and notes that in CP49 he included
The Wayzgoose but left out *Flowering Rifle*, "that
long, bilious Fascistic poem."

JII.67 Mathews, Marthiel, and Jackson Mathews. Preface.
Charles Baudelaire. *The Flowers of Evil* (Selected
and edited by Marthiel and Jackson Mathews). New
York: New Directions, 1955. (P. vii.)

"Roy Campbell is the first poet of reputation to attempt the whole of the *Flowers of Evil* in English. We believe he succeeds in a large number of poems, but he is most successful in the hard-driving didactic ones."

JII.68   Hamnett, Nina. *Is She a Lady? A Problem in Auto-biography.* London: Wingate, 1955.

Gives an account of C at a boxing match in Camden Town, p. 54; of the early editorship of *Coterie* (to which C contributed), p. 72; and of W.B. Seabrook, a friend of C's, pp. 87-88.

JII.69   Regnery, Henry. Letter. *The Nation* (New York), February 11, 1956, p. 128.

Concerning John Ciardi's characterization of C's qualities of mind in his review of *Selected Poems* [see JIII.XIX.4], states, "I consider Mr. Ciardi's remark not only stupid and libellous but extremely cowardly."

JII.70   Crompton, Yorke. "The Poetry of Roy Campbell" [poem]. *Nine*, 4.2 (April 1956), 27.

JII.71   Kirk, Russell. "The Last of the Scalds." *Sewanee Review*, 64 (1956), 164-70.

Headily appreciative and anecdotal, this supposed review of four of C's books only glances at these but vividly manages to convey the C persona. The statements about C's poetry reading in Chicago are a sample: "There laughed and roared the Scald, the bard of violence and beauty, faith and hope. Libellous and reckless as the old scalds, as honest and as unabashed, Roy Campbell read his poems, and beamed on everyone, and presently made his way to a Clark street bar, where no one knew him and he sang sea-shanties for pure good humor, and they passed the hat in his honour...." Says C translated St. John of the Cross when in hospital in Spain; quotes from *Lorca*, *The Georgiad* and *Broken Record*.
See also his *Eliot and His Age: T.S. Eliot's Moral Imagination in the Twentieth Century.* New York: Random House, 1971. Pp. 39, 374.

JII.72   Aldington, Richard. *Introduction to Mistral.* London: Heinemann, 1956. (Pp. 90-92, 191-92.) [Dedicated to F.S. Flint and Roy Campbell.]

Quotes "Horses on the Camargue" and regards C as the English-speaking poet most able to interpret Mistral because of immersion in his world. "Roy Campbell is the only English-speaking poet who has lived in Rhodanie as one of the people, earning his living as a fisherman of Martigues or as one of the most successful and popular *raseteurs* in the bull-fights and *gardian* at the *ferrades* [round-ups].... His poem on the horses of the Camargue is an original in the sense that it is built from his own experience and emotion, and the inspiration of Mistral's lines started his poem as it might have been started by a passage of Virgil or Homer.... it also interprets the lines far more accurately and eloquently than any other English version."

JII.73 Rose, Brian. "Roy Campbell: a tribute." *South African P.E.N. Yearbook 1956-57*, p. 28.

Comments on the relationship of C and F.C. Slater.

JII.74 Plomer, William. "South African Writing." *London Magazine*, 4.2 (February 1957), 52-56.

Gives reasons, including discovery of Mediterranean affinities, for indebtedness to C's example of the S. African poets Uys Krige, Guy Butler, F.T. Prince, David Wright, Roy MacNab and Anthony Delius.

JII.75 Obituary. *The Times* (London), April 25, 1957, p. 13.

"No poet of the last thirty years has done more original work or compromised less with the current fashions of the literary world.... to call him a poet of the right is merely to use a convenient label. It does not explain the beauty of his lyrics nor the marvellous sweep of his narrative descriptive power. The restlessness that sent him roaming from place to place and sampling all manner of odd jobs, afloat and on land, was symptomatic not of inner uncertainty but of a magnificently virile consistency. He knew what he wanted from life and from art; there was no room for half measures or pale shades in his philosophy."

JII.76 Rousseau, I.J. "Roy Campbell." *Natal Mercury*, April 25, 1957.

Recalls meeting C at Oxford and states he has had a greater influence on Afrikaans than on English-speaking

S. Arican poets. He reports that a documentary film
was planned on *The Flaming Terrapin*, with English,
Afrikaans and Zulu sound tracks, set against a background of African wildlife!

JII.77   Du Plessis, Enslin. "I Knew the Real Roy Campbell."
         The Cape Argus, April 27, 1957.

         "The real Roy Campbell was far removed from the
         Roy Campbell of legend. He was tender-hearted, kind
         and friendly, modest and mild--full of Christian
         humility.... He was a man of very rich and boisterous
         humour.... He was often laughing up his sleeve when
         people (including the victims of his impish sense of
         humour) took him seriously.... He was always ready
         to lapse into laughter with, as well as at, the vic-
         tims of his scorn.... His gift for hyperbole was
         almost as great as that of Rabelais."

JII.78   Lancaster, R.D. "Roy Campbell" [poem]. *The Times
         Literary Supplement*, May 3, 1957, p. 277.

JII.79   Bolitho, Hector. "Roy Campbell."   *The Queen*,
         May 14, 1957, p. 43.

         Recalls he had offended C in 1928 by telling him he
         should not hold back from publishing much of the poe-
         try he had written. Irked, C wrote him subsequently:
         "I have nursed my revenge for a long time ... I am an
         extremely vindictive person, and if there is one
         thing I resent more than anything else it is the as-
         persion of laziness. Though I was born in South
         Africa, I do not possess the colonial temperament
         with its loafing, invertebrate characteristics...."
         C quoted as saying he publishes only when he needs
         money. Later he told Bolitho he had liked a book of
         his and invited him to tea.

JII.80   Payn, Bill. "Roy Campbell." *Durban High School
         Magazine*, June 1957, pp. 27-31.

         Reminisces about the youthful C in Durban, mainly
         his and Mary C's stay at the C family home. "He was
         then suffering from some heart trouble and had grown
         a magnificent Assyrian beard."

JII.81   Arber, Muriel Agnes. "Roy Campbell and the Comet,
         April 1957" [poem]. *The Poetry Review*, 48.3
         (June-July 1957), 138.

JII.82　Curle, J.J. "For a South African Poet" [poem]. *The Poetry Review*, 48.3 (June-July 1957), 149.

JII.83　Van den Bergh, Tony. "Roy Campbell: Flaming Toreador." *The Poetry Review*, 48.4 (July-September 1957), 135-38.

Anecdotal; by a friend of latter days, one of the group of Rob Lyle, Charles Mulvey and A.F. Tschiffely. Says that after coming to London from Oxford, C, representing S. Africa, competed in the rodeo at the White City, London. Other incidents and comments made by C reported on. For instance: "He would stride into the 'Catherine Wheel,' Kensington, wearing bull-fighter's hat, astrakhan coat and chaperejos and dangerously brandishing a knobkerrie."

JII.84　"Vaquero in Vacuo." *The Times Literary Supplement*, November 8, 1957, p. 672.

Sees Tennyson as the basic influence on C. Refers approvingly to "St. Peter of the Three Canals," "The Road to Arles," "The Albatross" ["Stretching white wings in strenuous repose"] and "The Sisters." Maintains C was never really a European and thus found Spain, between Africa and Europe, congenial. In outlook he took the view by turns of the peasant and the aristocrat.

JII.85　Ley, Charles David. Letter. *The Times Literary Supplement*, November 22, 1957, p. 705.

Provides some useful information on C and the Spanish Civil War and on his movements and activities thereafter.

JII.86　*Homenaje a Roy Campbell de los Papeles de Son Armadons*. Madrid-Palma de Mallorca, 1957. [Pamphlet, 14 pp.]

Tributes and reminiscences by Robert James Kenyon, Camilo José Cela, Antonio Tovar, Charles David Ley and José Manuel Caballero Bonald. C's poem "Soci dou Félibrige" ["Of all the immortality concocters"] quoted at the first; the rest in Spanish.

JII.87　Krige, Uys. "Roy Campbell as a Lyrical Poet." *The Bulletin of the English Association (S. African Branch)*, 2 (1957).

An abbreviated version of JI.26 (q.v.).

JII.88 De Mauny, Erik. "The Progress of Translation," *The*
        Craft of Letters in England: a Symposium, edited by
        John Lehmann. Boston: Houghton Mifflin, 1957.
        Pp. 218-33.

        Contains references to C's translating, with com-
        ments. "French poetry since Baudelaire has bristled
        with difficulties for the translator, yet there have
        been several notable ventures. Among the more suc-
        cessful I would include Norman Cameron's version of
        A Season in Hell ... Roy Campbell has produced a
        number of strikingly good translations from Baude-
        laire."

JII.89 Miller, G.M., and Howard Sergeant. *A Critical Survey*
        of South African Poetry in English. Cape Town:
        Balkema, 1957.

        "To Campbell, wild creatures such as those of the
        veld, with their grace of movement and untamable
        spirit, have always served as symbols of the life of
        freedom and independence which he would have for
        human beings, and his physical contests with them have
        been a source of spiritual exultation. This proud
        vision of beauty 'volted with delight' is probably
        South Africa's greatest gift to him. It is revealed
        in his scornful attitude towards the smugness and
        unadventurous mediocrity of modern city life, its
        meaningless pursuits and employments, its mechanical
        patterns and drab order of society, in both his
        prose ... and in his poetry."

JII.90 Wagner, Geoffrey. *Wyndham Lewis: A Portrait of the*
        Artist as Enemy. New Haven, Conn.: Yale University
        Press, 1957.

        Attempts to indicate the extent of C's indebtedness
        to Lewis for social and political views by parallel-
        ing treatment of subjects in passages from their
        works: social criticism of the working class in *The*
        Vulgar Streak, *Rotting Hill* and *Broken Record*, pp.
        37-38; the socialists' 'responsibility' for racial
        discrimination in *Paleface*, *America and Cosmic Man*
        and *Broken Record*, p. 48; attacks on liberalism in
        The Art of Being Ruled and *Light on a Dark Horse*,
        p. 68; communism as a product of the middle class in
        The Revenge for Love and *Broken Record*, p. 65;
        socialist exploitation of the working man in *Rude*
        Assignment and *Light on a Dark Horse*, p. 74; and

anti-feminist views in *Time and Western Man* and *Broken Record*, p. 203.
See also his "Roy Campbell: Triumphant Torero." *Catholic World*, 179 (1954), 180-85.

JII.91 Graves, Robert. "A Life Bang-full of Kicks and Shocks." *New York Times Book Review*, January 5, 1958, p. 6.

Compares and contrasts Hemingway and C. Both had a romantic love affair with Spain during the Spanish Civil War, but "Hemingway rooted for the Loyalists ... Campbell eulogized the heroic Nationalists who were singlehandedly sweeping away the Reds and Jews (Campbell was a sad Jew-baiter)...." Calls José Antonio de Rivera the hero of *Flowering Rifle*; quotes C's dismissive note on García Lorca. Desires to make the point that C did not fight in Spain. "Although Campbell writes as though he had carried his 'flowering rifle' in the forefront of General Franco's crusade, the truth is that he was evacuated from Spain early in August, 1936--we met on the refugee boat--and returned there as a well protected war correspondent...." Writes of C's style: "As a poet Campbell slowly polished his provincial, and therefore Tennysonian, style--until he developed a grandiose gasconading manner which has its charm in short quotation, but soon fatigues."

JII.92 Sitwell, Edith. "Roy Campbell." *Poetry*, 92 (April 1958), 42-48.

The eulogy opens, "On Easter Monday, the 22nd of April, 1957, the English-speaking people lost one of the only great poets of this time, a poet whose every line conveyed vigor and fire...." Speaking of C himself, says, "... his whole character reflected the great stretches of grandeur, the exuberant color of his native South Africa." Refers to poems in such phrases as, "such a great and terrible poem as *To a Pet Cobra*"; "superb strength and savagery" of the latter part of *Mazeppa*; "exquisite, cool, vital, dancing sound" of lines from *The Palm*; and "water-lapping beauty, ineffable sound" of the opening of St. John's *Upon a Gloomy Night*. Believes *Vision of Our Lady over Toledo* "is amongst his greatest work."

JII.93 Gardner, W.H. "The Poet and the Albatross." *English Studies in Africa*, 1.2 (September 1958), 102-25.

The use of the albatross as symbol by poets since
Coleridge, including Baudelaire, Hopkins and Roy
Campbell. "... Coleridge and these three poets all
had something in common: all were sensitive, passionate, and attracted in one way or another towards
Christianity and the problem of evil; all were, moreover, to some degree 'maimed'--psychically, morally
or physically--paradoxically, in such a way that their
poetry derived additional force from their disability.
... both Baudelaire and Campbell treated the de-skied
Albatross as a symbol of their own inspired but mis-
understood poetic selves. Yet neither poet could con-
fidently retain the fiction that the Poet-Albatross
was more important than the Christ-Albatross."

JII.94   John, Augustus. "The Flaming Terrapin: Roy Campbell--
         Poet from South Africa." *The Sunday Times* (London),
         October 12, 1958. Reprinted in *Finishing Touches*.
         London: Cape, 1964. Pp. 123-27. [See JII.105.]

         Recounts meeting C with T.W. Earp, painting his por-
         trait, C's visit to him with his fiancée and subse-
         quent meetings. Scorns C's bullfighting pretensions
         and participation in the Spanish Civil War, but
         defends his continued liking for C: "I am not taken in
         by these purely literary exercises in bombast.   I
         suspect this affectation of gigantic strength and
         ruthless courage. Vain as an exhibitionist child, he
         looks round for applause...." Praises his translations
         of St. Juan de la Cruz and Eça de Quieroz, and much
         of *Portugal*. Is glad C changed his attitude towards
         gypsies, but deplores the "abject servility of his
         references to Salazar."

JII.95   Duque, Aquilino. "Prólogo," *Roy Campbell: Poemas*
         (Selección, versión y prólogo de Aquilino Duque).
         Madrid: Ediciones Rialp, 1958. Pp. 9-12.

         C's poetry a poetry of action, the witness to his
         many-sided life as wanderer and "troubadour," some of
         it no doubt imaginary. C was a curious fusion of
         aggressiveness, muscularity, generosity in victory,
         Mediterranean Christianity, pride in strength and
         love of liberty. His work reflects strongly Herbert
         Spencer and Nietzsche, and self-mythologizing tenden-
         cies. Describes C's verse of direct and sensuous
         language as rhetorical and musical (before him
         Rimbaud and Baudelaire had the grand utterance) and
         emphasizes its mystical and ecstatic imagery. Sees

his crowning by the Félibre at Arles in 1953 as the high point for him and believes that, had he lived, his poetry would have increasingly been imbued with his Spanish experience. Underlines the popular quality of C's poetry and its need of a popular audience: "Esta poesía, fulgurante y clamorosa, necesitaba un público que la coreara estremecido; sin el referéndum popular a esta poesía le hubieran faltado sentido y proyección. Era, en cierto modo, poesía juglaresca, y así vivió su creador vagabundo: llamando la atención de sus posible auditorios con volatines y acrobacias; imprecionando a sus oyentes con proezas de forzudo e historias tartarinescas."

JII.96 Meyerstein, E.H.W. *Some Letters*. Edited by Rowland Watson. London: Neville Spearman, 1959.

Letters 49, 85 and 298 indicate an acquaintance with C when he was in Kent and mention V. Sackville-West, her poem *The Land*, and a book on Rossetti reviewed by C.

JII.97 Cartwright, A.P. "'Poet Tossed Words as Juggler's Indian Clubs.' (S.A. Hall of Fame No. 7)." *Natal Daily News*, April 11, 1960.

Details of C's youth and time at Merton College, Oxford.

JII.98 Gardner, W.H. "Library Service and Library Co-operation." *South African Libraries*, 28 (October 1960), 31-35.

Gives details of his research on C, including a confirmation of a report in a Barcelona newspaper of C's bullfighting prowess, quoted from by C in *Broken Record*.

JII.99 Sitwell, Dame Edith. "Campbell, the Brave Giant." *The Observer*, November 20, 1960, p. 24.

Recalls first meeting C at Oxford with William Walton. Did not see each other again for many years. Says he possessed "flashing eyes of the kingfisher's blue" and that he would have been more at home in the Tudor age; goes on to retell several anecdotes illustrative of C's exotic adventures and prowess. "Faith, hope and courage never failed this great poet, whose virtues were those of bravery, love of this wonderful world, whose faults were brought about

by a complete miscomprehension of certain people....
He has been accused of being a fascist. He *never*
was a fascist. But he was a Christian, and he was
loyal to his Sovereign."

JII.100   Entwhistle, William J., and Eric Gillett. *The Litera-*
          ture of England A.D. 500-1960. London: Longmans,
          1960; 1st ed. 1943, with title ending "1942."
          (Pp. 175-76.)

"... *Flowering Rifle* (1939) showed his exultant,
fiercely held nationalism at its fiercest. It also
exhibited the virtues and defects of his satirical
approach, with its indiscriminate and sometimes ill-
considered condemnation. *Talking Bronco* (1946)
showed that Campbell's methods and outlook did not
change. Under the indiscriminate condemnations which
he scattered so lavishly there is a vision and, sometimes, a tender humanity which are seen at their
best in *Skull in the Desert*.... *Light on a Dark
Horse* (1951) should not be missed, and his one book
for children, *The Mamba's Precipice* (1954), should
be in the essential library of every young person."

JII.101   Strong, L.A.G. *Green Memory*. London: Methuen, 1961.
          (P. 226.)

In recalling personalities met at Oxford in 1919,
writes: "Another writer who did not belong to the
University was Roy Campbell. I had first met him a
year or two earlier, a pale and scared looking
slender boy of nineteen, emerging from a cupboard
at Tommy Earp's, in which he had been hiding from
some tradesman to whom he owed money. No introduction could have been less in character, when one
thinks of the swashbuckling figure he grew into."

JII.101a Rexroth, Kenneth. "Roy Campbell," in his *Assays*.
          Norfolk, Conn.: New Directions, 1961. Pp. 125-28.

An unrestrained attack occasioned by the publication of CP57.

JII.102   Howarth, Patrick. *Squire: Most Generous of Men*.
          London: Hutchinson, 1963. (P. 247.)

Considers a pamphlet attacking Squire's criticism
of D.H. Lawrence "legitimate protest" in contrast to
C's onslaught in *The Georgiad*, "a personal attack
... devoid of wit, taste or literary merit, and of a

viciousness which is astonishing even in that
repellent work."

JII.103 Rose, W.K., ed. *The Letters of Wyndham Lewis*.
London: Methuen, 1963.

Contains five letters to C (d. April 6, 1932;
July 3, 1934; October 25, 1936; June 28, 1950;
July 14, 1951) and two letters to Mrs. C (d. August,
1936; January 5, 1944). References to C occur in
the letter to Augustus John [September-October,
1930]; in that to C.H. Prentice, February 2, 1931;
and in that to Geoffrey Grigson, pp. 401-02. Editorial references to C are found on pp. 190, 205.

JII.104 Grobler, P. du P. "Dirk Opperman: 50 Jaar."
Lantern, 14 (December 1964), 10-21.

In the course of the essay on Opperman makes brief
comparisons with C, pp. 10, 17. Opperman the
greatest poet the province of Natal has produced.
Despite similarities between him and C, his ability
to produce a better imagery that is more original
and precise, and his superior power of abstraction
make him the better poet: "... waar Campbell meermale
in die concreta bly steek, slaag Opperman feitlik
altyd daarin om die konkrete met 'n geestelike
inhoud te vul." But C outdoes O in satiric verse--
finds O's *Kuns-mis* too "literary."

JII.105 John, Augustus. *Finishing Touches*. London:
Jonathan Cape, 1964. (Pp. 123-27.) [See JII.94.]

JII.106 Povey, John F. "The Myrrh of Parting: A Study of
the Theme of Exile in South African Poetry."
University of Toronto Quarterly, 35 (1965), 158-75.

Devotes pp. 160-62 to a discussion of C.

JII.107 Krige, Uys. "Roy Campbell." *Pretoria News*,
November 6, 1965. [Not seen.]

JII.108 Lewis, C.S. *Letters*. Edited by W.H. Lewis.
London: Bles, 1966. (Pp. 13-14.)

Gives particulars on the gatherings of the Inklings
and notes C's membership and participation. At one
meeting he read his translations of "a couple of
Spanish poems."

JII.109   Jennings, Hubert.   "Don Roy Quixote Campbell," *The
          D.H.S. Story 1866-1966.*   Durban: The Durban High
          School and Old Boys' Memorial Trust, 1966.   Chap.
          17, pp. 123-30.

          Briefly contrasts C unfavorably with Fernando
          Pessoa, who also attended the D.H.S., and then after
          quoting the segments in *Light on a Dark Horse* devoted
          to C's feud with A.S. Langley, the headmaster, sets
          out to correct this record and to suggest the subse-
          quent effect on C of his experience of Langley.

JII.110   Holt, Basil.   "Roy Campbell's Early Years."
          Africana Notes and News, 17 (June 1967), 268-77.

          C's forebears, birthplace (incl. photo) and home
          of youth, parents and brothers and sister, upbringing,
          early artistic and literary endeavours treated.
          An interesting inclusion is quotation of account
          of the visit to the Campbell home by Sir John Evelyn
          Wrench and his sister, taken from the latter's *The
          Overseas Club Tour in South Africa.*   Discusses in-
          fluences, mostly Rupert Brooke's, apparent in un-
          published juvenilia, which are quoted extensively.
          (See also discussion arising from this article:
          Rowland Hill, "Roy's Sister Ethel," *Africana Notes
          and News*, 17 (December 1967), 387-90; identifies one
          of the targets in *The Wayzgoose.*)

JII.111   Benson, Frederick R.   *Writers in Arms: The Literary
          Impact of the Spanish Civil War.*   New York: New
          York University Press, 1967.   (Pp. 27, 29, 37.)

          Refers to denunciations of pro-Loyalist writers by
          Wyndham Lewis, Evelyn Waugh and C, and states that
          C was in the vanguard of European Catholics who called
          for a "great crusade to expel the heretics whose
          'dogmatized utopias' threatened to destroy the re-
          ligious and social traditions of Catholic Spain."
          Quotes from *Flowering Rifle* and observes, "Few men
          committed to either cause [the Nationalist or the
          Loyalist during the Spanish Civil War] were willing
          to testify to the humanity of the other."

JII.112   Salter, Elizabeth.   *The Last Years of a Rebel: A
          Memoir of Edith Sitwell.*   London: The Bodley Head,
          1967.   (Pp. 18-19.)

          A reference to Albert de Lacerda's having been a
          good friend of C's leads to reporting ES's views on

C's Baudelaire translations--"his translations
emerged as poems in themselves"--and is followed by
an anecdote about C's physically attacking a critic
who had insulted ES. "Roy Campbell represented a
great deal to her. Not only was he a poet whom she
greatly admired, but he was that rare thing in her
life, a champion.... She had an Elizabethan appreciation of a man who could use his hands as well as
his head and she responded to Roy Campbell's cham-
pionship with an entirely feminine gratitude."

JII.113 Cargo, Robert T. *Baudelaire Criticism 1950-1967: A
         Bibliography with Critical Commentary*. University:
         University of Alabama Press, 1968.

         Supplies bibliographical details of the editions
         of C's translation of the *Poems of Baudelaire* and
         lists selected reviews.

JII.114 Fielding, Daphne. *Emerald and Nancy: Lady Cunard
         and Her Daughter*. London: Eyre and Spottiswoode,
         1968.

         Appendix C, a catalogue of the production of the
         Hours Press, gives bibliographic details of C's
         Poems, 1930.

JII.115 Harvey, C.J.D. "Wine and English Literature,"
         Spirit of the Vine, edited by D.J. Opperman. Cape
         Town: Human and Rousseau, 1968. Pp. 298-300.

         Illustrates from C's poems in CP49 that "There are
         many direct references to wine in his work and (a
         sure sign of a special affinity) it occurs again and
         again in his imagery...." Discussion includes some
         of the poems in *Mithraic Emblems* and the text is
         accompanied by a reproduction of the holograph ms.
         of poems IV and VIII in the sequence of the "Mithraic
         Frieze" poems.

JII.116 Pama, C., ed. *The South African Library: Its His-
         tory, Collections and Librarians 1818-1968*. Cape
         Town: A.A. Balkema, 1968. [In English and
         Afrikaans.]

         In article on MSS collections held, W.H.P.A.
         Tyrrell-Glynn states: "Onder die letterkundige manu-
         skripte is daar van Roy Campbell, digter uit Natal,
         stiervegter en avontuurlustige swerwer, o.a. *The
         flaming terrapin*; *Mithraic emblems* en *The wayzgoose*,

asook briefwisseling ná 1926 wat deur prof. W.H.
Gardner gebruik word by die skryf van 'n volledige
biografie van Campbell."

JII.117   Ready, William. *The Tolkien Relation: A Personal
          Inquiry.* Chicago: Regnery, 1968.

          Describes the meeting between C and J.R.R. Tolkien
          and C.S. Lewis. Asserts Tolkien's profound admira-
          tion for C. "It was like calling to like, Tolkien
          and Campbell."

JII.118   Wright, David. "For Roy Campbell" [poem; no. VI of
          Seven South African Poems], *The Penguin Book of
          South African Verse*, comp. by Jack Cope and Uys
          Krige. Harmondsworth: Penguin Books, 1968.
          P. 728.

JII.119   Lee, Laurie. *As I Walked Out One Midsummer Morning.*
          London: Andre Deutsch, 1969. (Pp. 145-55.)

          An account of his meeting and stay with the Camp-
          bells in Toledo in 1935 (?); dwells on C's gargantuan
          drinking and its effects.

JII.120   Press, John. *A Map of Modern English Verse.* London:
          Oxford University Press, 1969.

          Contains "Autumn" as a sample poem of the 1930's,
          p. 214, and extracts from "Contemporary Poetry" in
          Scrutinies ..., ed. by Edgell Rickword (London,
          1928), given on pp. 119-20. Comments, "Roy Campbell
          was, in many ways, the mirror-image of his detested
          MacSpaunday. His tough South African upbringing,
          his polemical brand of Roman Catholicism, his itch
          to pummel his opponents and his hatred of cliques in
          power all drove him to fight in Spain on Franco's
          side, and to waste his talent on vulgarly monotonous
          diatribes against Communist degenerates. What sur-
          vives of his copious verse is a handful of lyrics
          and translations unblemished by the musty quarrels
          of the decade."

JII.121   Wall, Bernard. *Headlong Into Change: An Autobiog-
          raphy and a Memoir of Ideas since the Thirties.*
          London: Harvill Press, 1969. (Pp. 178-82.)

          Refers to initial publication of translations of
          poems of St. John of the Cross in *The Changing World.*
          Traces the steps by which his friendship with C

turned to coldness; summarizes account of the in-
famous attack on Spender. Praises C as translator
of St. John, but states, "Yet Roy was an uneven
translator. His version of Baudelaire was pure
Campbell. How could a man from the Veldt and the
Camargue understand the hothouse atmosphere in which
the great Baudelaire worked out his tortured and
neurotic consciousness...?" Refers to the friendship between C and Dylan Thomas.

JII.122   Horner, Dudley Barrie, comp. *Francis Carey Slater
          (1876-1958): A Bibliography.* Johannesburg:
          University of the Witwatersrand, 1970.

          Lists a number of writings on Slater by C; also
          gives published source of letters to Slater and a
          poem by Slater on C.

JII.123   Kershaw, Alister, ed. *Richard Aldington: Selected
          Critical Writings, 1928-1960.* Carbondale: Southern
          Illinois University Press, 1970.

          Contains version in English of Aldington's tribute
          to C first published in French in *Hommage à Roy
          Campbell* [see JI.27] and in English in *The European*
          [see JI.28].

JII.124   Sitwell, Edith. *Selected Letters.* Edited by John
          Lehmann and Derek Parker. London: Macmillan, 1970.
          (Pp. 201-02; 206-17.)

          Prints a letter to C d. July 14, 1955 that comments
          on his illness, his friendship with William Empson
          and her hope of shortly being received into the
          Roman Catholic Church as C's and Mary C's god-
          daughter. Another letter, d. September 23, 1957,
          most movingly speaks of C's death and tells of a
          reading she gave of his poems.

JII.125   Sisson, C.H. *English Poetry 1900-1950: An Assess-
          ment.* London: Rupert Hart Davis, 1971. (Pp. 232-
          34 *passim.*)

          Furnishes a number of opinions and anecdotes, in-
          cluding: "He was once taken to Max Gate to meet
          Hardy but was too awed to enter the house, and
          stayed in the car, drinking whiskey from a hip
          flask, while his friends went in."

JII.126   Beeton, D.R.   "Roy Campbell." *Unisa English Studies*,
          10.3 (September 1972), 43-50.

          Transcript of a program in a series on South
          African poetry broadcast by the S.A.B.C. in 1966.
          Comments freshly upon and quotes some of the better
          known poems; as well, looks attentively at some of
          the poems of "Mithraic Frieze." Places some emphasis
          on South Africa's effect on C and on C's attitude
          towards his country of birth, at the same time sug-
          gesting the view of C the South African reading
          public has come to adopt. "Campbell ... was engaged
          in a lifelong love-hate struggle with South Africa.
          The Zulu Girl produced the best in this love-hate
          conflict, in which the warnings, the forebodings,
          seem to be born of a deep concern. South Africa
          did not always arouse Campbell's best, or his most
          complex response, however, and a poem such as *The
          Wayzgoose*, written ostensibly as a clever satire,
          never allows itself to be engaged with any real
          feeling, and often becomes little more than name-
          calling."

JII.127   Middleton, D.M.A.F., and Freiherr von der Valken-
          stein.   "Roy Campbell: the effect of his political
          ideas on his poetry." *Zambezia: a journal of
          social studies in Southern and Central Africa*
          (University of Rhodesia), 2.2 (December 1972),
          55-66.

          "A forceful and sometimes lyric poet, he was in-
          capable of the sustained thought, especially in
          politics, which could sustain poets like Dante or
          Milton. His thought is often incoherent, prejudiced,
          and, in its finer aspects, unrealised. He was pre-
          pared to accept a few slogans and took no responsi-
          bility for any further consideration. These failings
          go to the very roots of his verse--faulty metrics,
          frequently unclear or inappropriate imagery ...
          obscurity which arises from ... failure of technique."

JII.128   Daniels, Mary F., comp.   *Wyndham Lewis: A Descriptive
          Catalogue of the Manuscript Material in the Depart-
          ment of Rare Books, Cornell University Library.*
          Ithaca, N.Y.: Cornell University Library, 1972.

          Lists 6 letters from Lewis to C and 1 to Mary C,
          all but one of them (to C, d. May 15, 1950) in Rose
          [see JII.103]. The "Calendar of Manuscript Materials

and Correspondence of Other Writers" lists: "Roy
Campbell, 1901-1957--50 letters to Wyndham Lewis
[n.d.]-1954."

JII.129 Hope, Christopher. "Old Big Mouth." *Bolt*, 8
(June 1973), 30-36.

Rev. of *Lyric and Polemic: The Literary Personality
of Roy Campbell*, by Rowland Smith [see JI.58].
"Dr. Smith sees polemic finally prevailing over
lyric. But by his own account of Campbell's poetic
development it is difficult to see how there could
have been any other conclusion. Dr. Smith has
written a good, useful book. Up until now there has
been nothing like it. No one who is interested in
poetry in South Africa can ignore it."

JII.130 Parsons, D.S.J. Review of Rowland Smith, *Lyric
and Polemic: The Literary Personality of Roy
Campbell* [see JI.58]. *University of Toronto
Quarterly*, 42 (Summer 1973), 420-21.

Finds analyses of individual poems judicious and
penetrating, among them notably poems in *Mithraic
Emblems* and *Talking Bronco*, and calls those of successful adaptations of French originals "most illu-
minating and felicitous"; but objects that the too
exclusively psychological approach leads to some
neglect of "formative intellectual influences and
cultural conceptions," to a too great stress merely
on lightheartedness in *The Georgiad* and *The Wayzgoose* and to an insufficient recognition of the
traumatic effect upon C of the Spanish Civil War.
Regrets C's translations not dealt with.

JII.131 Rosenbaum, S.P. "Bertrand Russell: The Logic of a
Literary Symbol." *University of Toronto Quarterly*,
42.4 (Summer 1973), 301-27.

In the course of presenting and evaluating the
literary symbolic uses of Russell by various writers,
the essay devotes a couple of pages to C's treatment
of him in *The Georgiad*. "Campbell is exploiting
here the mathematical logician turned popularizing
moralist. *The Georgiad* was written in the wake of
Marriage and Morals and *The Pursuit of Happiness*....
As a reactionary ... Campbell was contemptuous of
Russell's political as well as moral ideas ...
Russell is presented along with George Bernard Shaw

as a propounder of boring, joyless utopias ... where
fear of strife dominates love of life."

JII.132   Nicolson, Nigel. *Portrait of a Marriage*. New York:
          Atheneum, 1973.

          Includes depiction of the life led by his parents
          at their summer home in Kent when the Campbells were
          guests there for several months in 1928, and provides
          the revelation, "Vita [Sackville-West] fell in love
          with Mary, to the fury of Roy, who wrote *The Geor-
          giad*, a highly uncomplimentary portrait of Long Barn
          and the Nicolsons in revenge."

JII.133   Pujals, Esteban. *La Poesía Inglesa del Siglo XX*.
          Barcelona, 1973. (Pp. 107-10, 124-25.)

          Compares and contrasts C's poetry with that of
          Auden, Day Lewis and Spender, with Auden's especially,
          and stresses the importance of Spain in C's poetry,
          quoting--and providing verse translations in Spanish
          for--parts of "Hot Rifles" and *Flowering Rifle*.
          Also briefly discusses C as a World War II poet,
          with commentary on "Luis de Camoens" and "Snapshot
          of Nairobi," and compares and contrasts his African
          war poems with those of Roy Fuller.

JII.134   Ullyatt, A.G. "Horses on the Camargue: Roy Campbell."
          Crux, 8.2 (May 1974), 5-8.

          An appreciative three-part analysis of the poem
          stressing its mythic and "Gothic" characteristics.
          Written for high-school students.

JII.135   Opperman, D.J. "By die Dood van Roy Campbell"
          [poem], *Groot Verse-Boek*. Kaapstad: Tafelberg,
          1951; 5th ed., 1974. Pp. 266-67. Reprinted from
          Dolosse. Kaapstad, 1963.

JII.136   Sperber, M.A. *And I Remember Spain*. London, 1974.

          Flowering Rifle treated on pp. 154-59. [Not seen.]

JII.137   Paton, Alan. Rev. of Rowland Smith, *Lyric and Polemic:
          The Literary Personality of Roy Campbell* [see
          JI.58]. *Research in African Literatures*, 6.1
          (1975), 120-25.

          "Smith makes it clear that he is dealing with
          Campbell's poetry and the personality it reveals,

and that he is not writing a biography. But the
biographical background is good and indispensable."
Sketches four stages he himself perceives in C's
career.

JII.138　Rosenthal, Marilyn. "Spanish Civil War Poets in the
English Language," *Poetry of the Spanish Civil War.*
New York: New York University Press, 1975. Pp.
102-204.

Discusses Rukeyser, Auden, Spender, MacDiarmid
and C. Though dependent on Ford's study [see JI.44]
for analysis of *Flowering Rifle*, is more systematic
in exposing its errors of fact and its distortions.
Interestingly compares and contrasts the poem with
MacDiarmid's *The Battle Continues* [see JI.21].

JII.139　Simon, Myron. *The Georgian Poetic.* Berkeley:
University of California Press, 1975. (P. 91.)

Draws some parallels between Osbert Sitwell's
"The Jolly Old Squire" and *The Georgiad.* Sees C's
poem as concentrating its satire on J.C. Squire, but
recognizes its attack on the Neo-Georgians as part
of Modernist polemics includes "the epicene world
of Bloomsbury."

JII.140　Gordimer, Nadine. "English-Language Literature and
Politics in South Africa." *Journal of Southern
African Studies*, 2.2 (April 1976), 131-50. (P.
136.) [Reprinted in C. Heywood, ed. *Aspects of
South African Literature.* London: Heinemann, 1976.]

C as a self-imposed exile "provides a fascinating
example of the strange and complex mutations brought
about by the effect of politics upon writers and
literature in South Africa." He believed the self-
justifying myth that he had left S. Africa because
he had found the color bar abhorrent. He had written
"biting and elegant attacks on white complacency"
and "sensuously incomparable poems about blacks."
But he dismissed political and social aspiration as
crowd emotion and was elitist rather than humanitar-
ian. Says C left S. Africa out of vanity--he felt
he was not appreciated by the whites and romanticized
himself as "African" abroad. Finally he was cut off
from all but the whites he had rejected.

JII.141　Three letters. *Contrast* (Cape Town), 39 (April
1976, Volume 10, No. 3), pp. 72-74.

    a. Barend J. Toerien gives his account of C's
       attack on Spender.
    b. Robert Greig wonders why "Dr. Paton has passed
       on the Campbell biography to someone who is
       not a South African."
    c. Alan Paton reassures Mr. Greig on the points
       in his letter concerning his successor.

JII.142 Fraser, G.S. Rev. of Rowland Smith, *Lyric and
      Polemic: The Literary Personality of Roy Campbell*
      [see JI.58]. *Journal of Southern African Studies*,
      3.1 (October 1976), 122-24.

      Smith brings out the sources of C's lyricism clearly
    and uses biographical material to demonstrate the
    loveable and the violent in him; in his study he
    shows he knows true poetry outlasts quarrels. But,
    Fraser asserts, the book "... does not put its finger
    on what seems to me the central thing about Campbell,
    and a number of other 'colonial' writers of genius
    ... who come to metropolitan England to escape from
    a crude, unjust, and over-simple society and find
    the complications and sophistications, the poses,
    falsities, treacheries of the London world, hard to
    digest imaginatively. They feel they are being
    patronized and they are right." Argues for more of
    a view of C as a less intellectual but often more
    colorful adherent of the elitist cultural conserva-
    tism represented by Eliot, Pound, Yeats, the later
    Auden and at times D.H. Lawrence. Believes it should
    also be stressed that of European contemporaries
    Lorca was closest to C in major respects despite
    political and other differences.

JII.143 Gray, Stephen. "The Myth of Adamastor in South
      African Literature." *Theoria* (Pietermaritzburg),
      48 (May 1977), 1-23.

      In discussing C's contribution to the interpreta-
    tion of Camões' mythic giant, attempts through an
    analysis of "Rounding the Cape" to account for C's
    abandonment of South Africa and deliberate self-
    exile. "... Adamastor is the figure that represents
    all that Campbell has 'hated or adored'; he is taking
    leave of all the paradoxical emotions of the anti-
    romantic young poet's relationship with South Africa,
    land of violence and sadism.... the down-trodden
    Adamastor, off the sweat of whose back we have lived,
    is ready to hold sway again. Campbell's valediction

is a resigned and uneasy statement of the failure of
white civilization." During the essay the writer
enters the controversy occasioned by Alan Paton's
most recent bio-critical writings on C. For Paton's
rejoinder, see his letter in the next issue.

JII.144 Watson, George. *Politics and Literature in Modern
Britain*. London: Macmillan, 1977. (P. 92 and
passim.)

Quotes from C in *Light on a Dark Horse*, chapter 22,
on the "real issues" of the war in Spain in 1936--
that there could be no compromise between East and
West, between Credulity and Faith, between "irrespon-
sible innovation" and tradition--and comments: "Past
versus present, tradition versus innovation: these
were the stark alternatives supposed to underlie the
inescapable choice between Right and Left."

JII.145 Parsons, D.S.J. "The Roy Campbell Collection."
Notable Works & Collections (University of Saskatchewan Library), 6 (June 1978), 1-5.

In describing the University of Saskatchewan's
collection, compares it with collections elsewhere
and notes degree to which it complements these.
Stresses the collection's evidence for the dating of
individual poems and the body of unpublished material
held, including translations of plays by Lorca and
correspondence and notes relating to C's war experience and the last decade of his life.

JII.146 Walcott, Derek. *The Joker of Seville & O Babylon!
Two Plays*. New York: Farrar, Straus and Giroux,
1978.

Note preceding *The Joker of Seville* contains the
statement: "I began laboriously by trying to translate into alternating rhymes of eight-foot lines
directly from the old Spanish, but soon gave up.
What I surrendered, having read once through Roy
Campbell's mainly blank-verse translation, was the
exactness of vocabulary, but what I hope I have kept
is the rhyme scheme and tempo."

JII.147 Alexander, Peter. Review of *Roy Campbell* by John
Povey [see JI.63]. *Research in African Literatures*
(U. of Texas), 9.1 (Spring 1978). [Not seen.]

III. SELECTED REVIEWS

JIII.I *The Flaming Terrapin*

1. *The Spectator*, May 3, 1924, p. 714.

    "Mr. Roy Campbell's verse is rowdy and alarming:
    The Flaming Terrapin ... stands like a giant among
    the bagatelles and delicacies of most modern poets.
    And, like a giant, it is primitive and unsophisticated.
    He is definitely coarse in technique and his clatter
    and hiss of rhythm will stun.... Such is the general
    level of Mr. Campbell's voice, invigorating, hefty,
    prodigious."

2. *The Times Literary Supplement*, May 29, 1924, p. 337.
    [Coll. in Edgell Rickword, *Essays and Opinions
    1921-1931*, ed. by Alan Young. Cheadle, Cheshire:
    Carcanet, 1974, pp. 44-46.]

    Primitive simplicity and directness of vision
    praised. "Vision is the essential of poetic style,
    for without it imagery degenerates into rhetoric.
    Rhetoric which enables the poet to sustain his in-
    spiration is not to be despised in itself, and without
    rhetorical power Mr. Campbell would not have been
    able to carry through his design on a scale remark-
    able for so young a poet." Praises quality of com-
    parisons and bold associations in imagery, also vary-
    ing of couplets with insertion of quatrains. Notes
    ability to vary moods and introduce exotic landscape
    "in very much the same way as the central stanzas of
    'Bateau Ivre,' and it is probably the first instance
    of the direct influence of Rimbaud in English verse."
    Complains of some unrealized or over-familiar imagery,
    tendency to overstatement and confused construction--
    two or three climaxes before the poem is half done.

3. *The Birmingham Post*, June 6, 1924.

    Points out the weaknesses of the poem and concludes
    that it is easier to praise isolated passages than
    the whole.

4. Rev. by Edward Garnett. *The Nation & the Athenaeum*,
    June 7, 1924, pp. 323-24.

    "It is absurd, of course, to try to measure the
    poetic treasure-house by the yardstick of prose. The

poet's achievement lies in the leaping fountain of
imagination, in its profusion of invention, in its
lavish exuberance, and wealth of emotion. Its pictures are so concentrated and its transitions so
abrupt that it is not easy to grasp the effect of the
whole, even at a second reading. One must add that
though there are many reverberations from the seven-
teenth-century classics, such as Dryden and Milton,
and also of Shelley, and even of moderns, the original
feeling of the whole transmutes these borrowings, and
the poet's youthful, magnificent audacity sweeps all
before it."

5. *The Manchester Guardian*, June 19, 1924.

   C's "very first book is not just a promise but an
   achievement." Likens the imagery of ocean to that in
   Masefield's *Dauber*.

6. *The Liverpool Daily Post and Mercury*, June 25, 1924.

   "The conception of the poem is magnificent, touching
   what we have for want of another term to call subli-
   mity, and the language in which it is realised is
   full of virility, fire, colour suggestion, its only
   fault being, perhaps, that it attracts too much
   attention to itself to leave the intellectual intention it has to convey, quite clear and significant."

7. *The Outlook*, June 28, 1924.

   Perceives strong traces of Shelley in the poem but
   claims C often rivals rather than imitates him.
   States the poem is also analogous to Rimbaud's *Le
   Bateau Ivre* and Alfred Mombert's *Die Schöpfung*.

8. *The Adelphi*, 2.1 (June 1924), 86.

   "... we should have known it was the work of a
   young man, though few young men begin with such an
   astonishing verbal and imaginative gift as Mr. Campbell. Naturally he is drunk with it; and knows no
   more than we what the poem is about. Everything and
   nothing."

9. Rev. by Richard Hughes. *The Spectator*, July 19, 1924,
   pp. 98-100.

   "The style is almost pure Marlowe-Vachel Lindsay,
   with occasional touches of Dryden.... But

unfortunately the poem, as a whole, is not quite so impressive as it is in parts. In the first place, its central notion is not sufficiently sublime or original really to tax the poet's powers of expression, as the powers of a great poet are always taxed.... And in the second place, Mr. Campbell is always noisy, always expresses his meaning by exaggeration...."

10. *South Africa*, August 8, 1924.

Acknowledges the poem's zest, energy and originality, but warns of the danger of excess while calling it "one of the finest South African poems since Pringle's 'Afar in the Desert.'" Adds, "He is coming to England to publish a book of poems, and we shall be curious to see if they are as good...."

11. Rev. by A.E. Coppard. *The Saturday Review*, 138 (August 16, 1924), 171-72.

"... a vast invigorating energy, full of the pounding thunder of cataclysmic storm and the shock of oceanic dawns ... repays a debt to Marlowe and Webster, to Milton as well as to 'Moby Dick.'" Commends the "descriptive magnificence" and "occasional epigrammatic irony"; says "quieter passages have many exquisite images ... the meditative quality is deeply moving." Closes with, "Beyond a little economy in adjectives Mr. Campbell has nothing more to learn of poetic technique--he has only to develop."

12. Rev. by Humbert Wolfe. *The Westminster Gazette*, August 23, 1924.

The Flaming Terrapin would have to figure in any discussion of whether the epic is dead. After a fashion C has written "the *Paradise Lost de nos jours*." But if C is not exactly Milton, he is at least not Masefield at second hand. Though clearly suffering from "the malady of youth," C is alive and "does not hesitate gently in an anaemic countryside; he does not conceal himself behind jollities of sport; he has learned nothing from 'E.M.'--but unfortunately, unlike so many of E.M.'s pupils, he has forgotten nothing of the duty owed to poetry, which is, quite simply and fearlessly to say what you have in you...."

13. Rev. by F.L. Lucas. *The New Statesman*, 23 (August 23, 1924), 572-73. [Coll. in *Authors Dead and Living*. London: Chatto & Windus, 1926, pp. 217-23.]

Calls *The Flaming Terrapin* a gallimaufry--a mixture of the atmospheres of The Apocalypse, Lucan, *The Ancient Mariner*, *Moby Dick*, Dryden and the Sitwells. Feels sure time will calm the vehemence, experience teach the poet form; but hopes the spontaneity remains.

14. Rev. by Francis Bickley. *The Bookman*, 66 (August 1924), 277-78.

"The poem then is ... a myth of burgeoning life, and if, in parts, it seems a mere chaos of whirling words, it often moves with the true *élan vital* of which it is meant to be the expression. If, too, one prefers to reserve judgment as to its success as a whole, there is no question of its incidental triumphs--the brilliancy of many descriptive passages and the rightness and originality of its innumerable metaphors ... no question, either, of the vigour of Mr. Campbell's mind."

15. Rev. by Babette Deutsch. *The Literary Review*, September 6, 1924, p. 4.

"One may neglect the obvious flaws: the facile allegorical passages, the unnecessarily confused mythology, the crowding metaphors, too heavy for their frame, the abuse of the meter. One dare not neglect the gift of a man who sees the waves mounting into the night."

16. *The New York Times Book Review*, September 14, 1924, p. 14.

"Terrific image after terrific image astounds the mind, and the impact gradually disintegrates it."

17. *The Boston Evening Transcript*, September 27, 1924.

Makes comparisons with Francis Thompson and Coleridge and comments: "His rushing torrents of language leave one dazed and breathless, as if a swollen and thunderous stream had swept by. Metaphors, similes and strange words and phrases cascade one after another so rapidly that the reader finds it hard not to let the sound completely dominate the sense."

18. *The Left Wing*, October 22, 1924.

   Enthusiastic but not blind to faults. Sees the
   opening of Part V in particular as Shelleyan.

19. Rev. by Hamish Miles. *The Dial*, 77 (November 1924),
   423-25.

   "Mr. Campbell has contrived to declaim a poem
   which, so far as its prodigious eloquence is concerned, leaves all his contemporaries gasping--or
   politely smiling at an outburst of energy so ridicu-
   lously primeval. It might be easy enough to carry
   out a white-fingered dissection of its structural
   flaws: the symbolism wavers sometimes into disjointed
   and bewildered images, the shorter, galloping lines
   of the fifth part ... are disappointingly ineffec-
   tive, and the towering effects of the horrific (and
   it would be hard to match, since Thomas Beddoes,
   Mr. Campbell's sense of this element) are distorted
   sometimes by sheer, merciless accentuation into per-
   spectives of a Doré-esque falsity. But so doing
   one would leave untouched the core of its vitality,
   the overweening energy of its writer's impulse....
   even if he seems now and then to be lashing himself
   forward with his thongs of epithets, one is left
   justifiably amazed. It is something, after all, to
   have the power to amaze."

JIII.II *The Wayzgoose*

1. *The Natal Advertiser*, February 17, 1928.

   "We are amused as we reflect what sort of a passion
   he will fall into when the greater world outside
   Durban asks what manner of man it is who, with repu-
   table antecedents in his native town and bearing a
   family name that has won honour in a dozen different
   ways, flies into tantrums of this sort and wastes so
   much good paper and valuable time in besmirching,
   befouling, traducing and lampooning people who always
   did their best, according to their lights, to treat
   him with cordiality, regard and such poor hospitality
   as they had at their command."

2. *The New Statesman*, 30 (March 3, 1928), 662.

   "Mr. Campbell hits more often than he kills. Small
   consolation for him, hitting and blowing to pieces

one poor Colonial cock-bird, be its pretensions
never so ridiculous. He must annihilate in bulk; he
must massacre by coveys; he is really very angry ...
The Wayzgoose shows that feverish ingenuity which
sometimes distinguishes an abusive letter.... has
much to say and will sacrifice no jot of it: contin-
uity and construction go to the wall ... the citadel
of Dullness fell flat before Dryden's trumpet blast.
Mr. Campbell's bombardment is delightfully vigorous;
still, he has only loosened some desultory scabs of
plaster from the wall."

3. The Times Literary Supplement, March 8, 1928, p. 166.

   "The styles and manners of both Pope and Dryden
   are assimilated in Mr. Campbell's satire, and there
   are many echoes of these poets wittily introduced....
   The satire is violent and yet polished, as satire
   should be.... If we are to look for energy from the
   Dominions we can find it best not in those whom
   Mr. Campbell satirizes but in his satire. The heroic
   couplet, the continued antithesis, and all the
   elaborate tricks of eighteenth century satire are
   not inimical to energy.... It is not a question of
   laying the victims dead with a neat stroke, for this
   is merely vindictive satire, but of animating them
   into activity, of creating what nearly amounts to
   fictional characters. And this Mr. Campbell does
   very well, both dexterously and energetically, having
   had created for him by the seventeenth and eighteenth
   century satirists precisely the right medium for the
   purpose."

JIII.III Adamastor

1. The New Statesman, 35 (April 19, 1930), 53.

   After praising The Flaming Terrapin but calling
   The Wayzgoose "a spendthrift attack on provincialism,"
   considers Adamastor on the whole good--"There are
   acerbities and flawed angers in Mr. Campbell's new
   book but, happily, the epic-romantic imagination pre-
   dominates. The grave and simple stanzas which
   Mr. Campbell prefers to employ may lack novelty of
   cadence, but they bring forward the powerful images
   with full effect." Has praise for "The Albatross,"
   "Tristan da Cunha" (with some caveats about rising
   into "the void of rhetoric") and, above all, for

"The Zulu Girl"--one of the very few "epic lyrics"
in the language. Has little to say about the satiric
poems and suggests C at best when objective, not dis-
turbed by emotion "or embarrassed by his own Equa-
torial wealth of imagery."

2. Rev. by Richard Church. *The Spectator*, May 3, 1930,
    p. 745.

    "Today we are privileged to hear, clearly and in-
    dubitably that eternal miracle, a great word master,
    a Merlin, a Lavengro. Mr. Roy Campbell has found
    our English language weary with intellectual age and
    drawing over the close fire of education. He has
    stung it to life, to rebellion and has made it proud,
    eloquent and young again."

3. *The Times Literary Supplement*, May 15, 1930, p. 410.

    "When an impulse rouses [C] he becomes a magician
    of symbols, serious, comic, serio-comic ... Mr. Camp-
    bell will play a trick, as it were, with ... metaphors
    by adding metaphors for them too [as in "The Festi-
    vals of Flight"].... The intricacy of Mr. Campbell's
    wit has nothing laboured in it, as a rule...."
    Criticizes "The Sleeper" but admires "the great sim-
    plicity" of "Autumn." Concludes: "He is rich to the
    point of embarrassment in learning, not perhaps the
    academic kind, but the learning of a curious ardour
    ranging the geographical and mythological worlds;
    his vocabulary is magnificent in its swift provision
    of words of every grade and opportunity; his versi-
    fication is athletic, finely strung, quick-turning."
    Thinks "Mass at Dawn" one of the "most remarkable
    pieces."

4. *The Nation & the Athenaeum*, May 17, 1930, pp. 224,
    226.

    "Mr. Campbell *is* best when he is briefest. Some
    of the verses of 'The Albatross,' which is longish,
    are magnificent, but as a whole it is repetitious
    and shapeless. The one exception to the rule is the
    very fine 'Tristan da Cunha,' and even that might
    be briefer with advantage. For the rest, of the
    pick of these pieces--'The Zulu Girl,' 'African
    Moonrise,' 'The Sisters,' 'Horses on the Camargue,'
    and 'An Open Window'--none is over fifty lines....
    Yet if with the familiar virtues, fine language,

imaginative range, new and vigorous metaphor, go the
familiar vices, an overintensity, an occasional quite
comic inappropriateness.... The fact is that Mr.
Campbell does protest too much. He urges the superiority of the poet over the blind mob, but not content to live in that superiority he must keep
talking about it...."

5. Rev. by E.H.W. Meyerstein. *The Saturday Review*,
   May 24, 1930, p. 662.

   Holds that with the exception of "Tristan da
   Cunha" and to a lesser extent "The Palm," the
   Adamastor collection does not satisfy the expecta-
   tions raised by *The Flaming Terrapin*. In these other
   poems C derives too much from Charles Churchill,
   Baudelaire and Rimbaud and in general "must temper
   his spleen with ideas," as well as avoid being "an
   odd recrudescence of Byronism."

6. Rev. by C. Henry Warren. *The Bookman* (London), 79
   (October 1930), 50.

   Condemns the "couple of pages of unworthy satirical
   fragments at the end" but is full of praise for such
   poems as "Tristan da Cunha," "The Zulu Girl,"
   "Autumn" and "Mass at Dawn." Believes that C,
   "Purged of some unnecessary rancour ... may one day
   give us some really peerless poetry; for he has an
   intensity of vision that often reaches white heat."

7. Rev. appeared originally in the *Sunday Referee*.
   [Reprinted in Edgell Rickword, *Essays and Opinions
   1921-1931*, edited by Alan Young. Cheadle, Cheshire:
   Carcanet, 1974, pp. 257-58.]

   "["The Albatross"], the sombre 'Tristan da Cunha,'
   and the beautiful poem 'The Palm,' deliciously
   handled in a metre that might easily have been disas-
   trous, are to me the highest peaks of achievement in
   a volume which well bears out the promise of the
   earlier *Flaming Terrapin*.... in one or two pieces
   which are less successful one may notice a lack of
   intellectual suppleness ... later tendencies seem to
   be away from this danger-area--for which the subtle
   intellectualism of Paul Valéry's poetry is perhaps
   to be thanked...." Campbell has a peculiar gift of
   sarcasm which is extraordinarily successful when involved with a lyrical theme, as it is in "Festivals
   of Flight" and "Poets in Africa."

8. *The New York Times Book Review*, January 25, 1931,
    p. 2.

    "In *Adamastor* Campbell proves that he is a poetic
    force for the rejuvenation of poetry, abundantly
    alive, starkly individual and cyclonic of utterance."

9. Rev. by Bernice Kenyon. *Outlook*, April 15, 1931,
    p. 536.

    "Roy Campbell is a genius--one of the very few to
    whom that misused term can safely be applied."

10. Rev. by Harriet Monroe. *Poetry*, 38.2 (May 1931),
    98-100.

    Finds the collection disappointing after *The Flam-
    ing Terrapin* and after having expectations raised
    excessively by critics like Edith Sitwell and Arnold
    Bennett. "Instead of being swept along by a poetic
    tornado, I listened coldly to much over-rhetorical
    oratory expressive of an egoistic bitterness not un-
    common among modern youth...." Faults "A Song for
    the People" and "To a Pet Cobra," but singles out
    "The Festivals of Flight" as "perhaps the most
    interesting poem in the book." Comments on the beau-
    tiful and trenchant metaphors in it and "The Alba-
    tross." Perceives some likenesses between the
    latter and George Sterling's work and concludes:
    "One would like to urge upon this talented South
    African-English poet George Meredith's plea for
    'more mind'; also a stronger bit upon his Pegasus."

11. Rev. by Dudley Fitts. *The Hound and Horn*, 4.4
    (July-September 1931), 631.

    Comments that in these short lyrics there is little
    opportunity for combining the heroic and the bombas-
    tic as in *The Flaming Terrapin* but that there is the
    same expressive force and lack of polish. "His is
    not the artistic unaffectedness of Robert Graves; it
    is a fundamental ingenuousness, which is extremely
    attractive, but which does much to dissipate the im-
    pact of his work."

JIII.IV *The Georgiad*

1. Rev. by Geoffrey Grigson. *The Saturday Review*,
    November 7, 1931, pp. 593-94.

    "... if it is impossible to resuscitate Coleridge
    or a savager Oldham, Dryden or Pope, we have at least

the benefit of Mr. Roy Campbell's irruption....
The reviewers now to a degree unparalleled can
mutually make literati out of dunces and for a time
can conceal the mean nature of any animal. Asses,
therefore, who have had their ears cut off by friendly
reviewing, should open the 'Georgiad' with trepida-
tion." Says C "cannot be called petty, for if some
of his victims are negligible, they stand for much,
and his satire attacks beyond them other things and
cults...." He "would not see Mr. Campbell's peculiar
violence diminished" and "would not belittle the
'Georgiad,'" but owing to its seldom touching the
"consummate brevity" of *The Dunciad*, its occasional
weaknesses and incoherence and "passages of dullness
and ineptitude," it could have been a greater poem.

2. *The New Statesman*, 2 (November 14, 1931), 620.

    The Georgiad panned briefly--"dismal dish, cold
scrambled eggs"--under "Brevities on Books."

3. *The Times Literary Supplement*, December 3, 1931,
    p. 980.

    "The subject is not a novelty; quite a long time
has elapsed since Mr. Osbert Sitwell's 'Way Down in
Georgia.' Nor is it a new departure in Mr. Campbell
... we should not care to say whether Pope in the
'Dunciad,' Churchill *passim* or Byron in 'English
Bards and Scotch Reviewers' is predominantly his
great example.... In profusion of ironical and
boisterous imagination he is as strongly individual
as in the lyrical rhapsodies which have made him,
still young, a force in modern poetry. The victims
of his present skirmish will be among the first to
be grateful for the entertainment which he offers.
But who are these victims? A number of our contemporaries are certainly named or as good as named ...
but Mr. Campbell brings on a central figure ...
Androgyno" who "vanishes from our attention behind
great columns of digression.... Mr. Campbell's re-
sources of illustrative form and term are such that,
with all respect for his energetic baiting of modern
verse, one hopes he has settled that account and is
ready to engage higher themes once more."

4. Rev. by John Linnell. *The Fortnightly Review*, New
    Series, 131 (Old Series, 137), (January 1932), 127.

The book is racy, vigorous, pungent, brilliant--
"But Mr. Campbell defeats himself by the very excess
of his purgative methods ... Herakles ... never published abroad a detailed list of the varieties of
filth ... he discovered [in cleaning out the Augean
stables].... Still less did he so demean himself as
publicly to increase with his own excrement the mass
of corruption already existing."

5. Rev. by D.H.V. *The Spectator*, February 6, 1932,
    pp. 186-87.

    The Georgiad regarded unfavorably as compared to
    the other poems reviewed (*Red Roses for Bronze* by
    H.D. and *The Sale of St. Thomas* by Lascelles Aber-
    crombie). There is "a great gulf fixed between
    Mr. Campbell and H.D. ... in whose work form and
    sense are completely and clearly fused." Owing to
    C's failure to generalize his attitude, his poem is
    far less effective than Abercrombie's. C criticized
    for technical unproficiencies and an unwisely chosen
    subject. "It is unlikely that this labour of hate
    will add to Mr. Campbell's existing poetical reputa-
    tion. Neither literary back-scratching, which he
    opposes, nor literary back-biting, which presumably
    he favours, can be of much assistance to the cause
    of poetry...."

JIII.V *The Gum Trees*

1. *Revue Anglo-Américaine*, December 1931, p. 166. [Not
    seen.]

JIII.VI *Taurine Provence*

1. Rev. by John Marks. *The Spectator*, November 25,
    1932, pp. 761-62.

    "Mr. Hemingway does not take corridas in France
    seriously. Mr. Campbell takes them very seriously;
    he uses the passion for the bull-adversary as an
    incantation against Bernard Shaw, the War, the
    Peace, bank-clerks, psycho-analysis, the whole of
    devitalized Humanity in general. He is an enthusiast
    of Provençal joustings and bull-games, Provençal
    culture, Mithraism and the Spanish corrida. The
    seventy pages of his lively superficial little essay
    do not tell us much about tauromachy, but they

contain a great deal of fire-spitting and some
genuinely delightful appreciations of good things
and sound values; these are Mr. Campbell's, the
poet. The topography, food and wisdom of Provence
he admires and understands. The Spanish corrida he
likes but does not understand. (This is even more
apparent in his text than in his drawings.) The
'abrivade,' 'bourgine,' trident-game and 'razet' are
simple, exciting pastimes; the bullfight proper is
una cosa muy seria, which attracts Mr. Campbell;
but his taste is for the romantic, for seeing 'the
Amazon Mme. Calais in her splendid harness perform-
ing feats.' Here, with a vengeance, is 'a vision of
the salvation of civilization from tradesmen and
pedestrians by equestrians and cattlemen.'"

JIII.VII *Flowering Reeds*

1. *The Times Literary Supplement*, April 27, 1933;
   p. 299.

   Says in these poems C "has withdrawn, or emerged,
   into a narrower, more objective field of experience."
   Discusses their descriptiveness, dependence on ex-
   tended simile and symbolism. Cites "The Olive Tree I"
   as one of the best poems: "In this poem, thought,
   feeling and image are finely knit together"; others,
   however, such as "On the Top of the Caderau," are
   defeated by their excessive energy. Judges that
   "Within the limits which Mr. Campbell sets himself
   (or by which perhaps he is bound) he is generally
   successful. He is at his best in 'Choosing a Mast,'
   'The Olive Tree,' 'The Gum Trees' ... and 'Overtime,'
   a poem with wider implications than most of the
   others.... One should also mention several adroit
   translations from Rimbaud and Baudelaire."

2. Rev. by J.V. Healy. *Poetry*, 42.3 (June 1933), 166–67.

   "Mr. Campbell is no insignificant poet. *The Wayzgoose* and *The Georgiad* are among the best satires of
   this generation ... *Adamastor* shows lyrical promise,
   but this later book indicates a retrogression in the
   poet's growth." Complains of C's tendency towards
   turgidity and imprecise or merely mannered phrasing.
   "He is more interested in his tumid tenuity of style
   than in what he has to say." Pays tribute to C's
   originality of usage but deplores the profusion of
   "pre-raphaelite imagery" in this collection.

JIII.VIII *Choosing a Mast*

    1. *Revue Anglo-Américaine*, February 1933, p. 256. [Not
       seen.]

JIII.IX *Broken Record*

    1. Rev. by V.S. Pritchett. *The Fortnightly Review*,
       New Series, 136 (July 1934), 122.

       "Mr. Campbell hits hard when his colonial scorn is
       roused; that is to say, his blows would be good if
       they landed, but they spend themselves in the air
       most of the time and the interest wanes. When he
       has real matter to hand, such as the coming of the
       sardines to his native coast, or the memory of some
       Rhodesian hunt, he can write those pages of clear
       and sonorous prose which we expect from the most word-
       intoxicated poet of our generation. But from his
       random opinions, heaven protect us--and him."

JIII.X *Mithraic Emblems*

    1. Rev. by Geoffrey Stone. *American Review*, 8 (December
       1936), 164-76.

       Essentially a review of *Mithraic Emblems*, though
       Stone ranges more widely. Discusses C's Mithraism
       and cowboy and bullfighting imagery. "Occasionally
       ... the symbolism degenerates into an unpleasant
       sentimentality, as, when the Crucifixion is called
       'the final toss' on 'the black horns of the Cross.'
       And the expression of religious concepts in cowboy
       language often strikes the falsely hearty note of
       manufactured *genre* poetry. Yet in the title-poem
       ... this symbolism is combined into a strangely
       effective work...." Quotes from and discusses
       "The Seven Swords," "Let Spender over wowser-
       problems fret," "The Voice of the Rails" and
       "Toledo, 1936." Is critical: "Mr. Campbell has a
       lot to account for on the debit side. His verse
       is plainly written in haste, and speed is a worthier
       attribute in the arena than in the Muses' garden.
       For all his facility in language, he is apt to
       repeat too often a good phrase.... His scorn of
       the unworthy at times degenerates to mere bravado
       ... noisy rhetoric ... his verse is distressingly

uneven, and will descend from a pure and perceptive
lyric note to he-man swashbuckling.... Yet in
balancing the ledger, the ultimate figures must be on
the credit side...."

JIII.XI *Flowering Rifle*

1. *The Times Literary Supplement*, February 11, 1939,
   p. 93.

   Calls *Flowering Rifle* "less a poem than a bombardment" and finds it suggestive that one who has
   claimed to champion the organic should vent such
   "monotonous and mechanic" violent invective. Complains
   of the lack of truly destructive wit, the "deadening
   repetition of the same abuse clothed in the same trite
   similes" ("'Right' and 'Wrong' for him are 'Right' and
   'Left'") and the exulting in the name of religion
   over the braining of opponents by "the thundering
   hammer of the Cross." Sums up: "For all its arrogance
   and denial of reason as a factor in the growth of
   humanity the poem does fling down a crude challenge
   to 'liberal' democracy to prove not only its intelligence but its spiritual value. That Mr. Campbell
   has had personal experience of both régimes in Spain
   and is fighting with the Nationalists gives a realis-
   tic basis to his poem. But the rhetorician in him is
   always in command."

2. *Spain* (pub. by Spanish Press Services Ltd.), 6.7
   (February 16, 1939), 139-40.

   Written from "thorough first-hand experience," the
   poem "deserves praise as something more than a satiric
   epic and a fighting argument ... more than haunting
   passages of religious love and human comradeship under
   arms...." C "has asserted to the poets of his generation that their departure from the tradition of
   Christendom has led them to sterility and death in
   their philosophies...." C has exposed the continual
   lies of press and radio, but his poem is no Hymn of
   Hate; rather, it "is based upon the idea of redemption
   and of renaissance rather than of extermination."
   The poem is an attempt to restore to European literature "the glory of Christian arms, such as was heard
   in the *Song of Roland* ... Roy Campbell ... fights
   under Christ and his Spanish Leader for the ultimate
   triumph of the Christian cause."

3. *New English Weekly*, March 2, 1939.

    Uses quotations from Charles Churchill to condemn
    the "inhumane insanity" of C's "bad poem." Wonders
    who is supposed to read it--the Right reads only
    Punch, the Left is made up of such unpleasant, des-
    pised people. Quotes the section dealing with the
    fate of the disabled Republican tank to epitomize
    condemnation.

4. Rev. by Stephen Spender. *The New Statesman and
    Nation*, 17 (March 11, 1939), 370.

    The whole work fails to exist independently of the
    reality that inspired it and "has no unity of design,
    no sustained argument, no plot, no single vision.
    It is a kind of three-decker sandwich consisting of
    one layer of invective against the intellectuals of
    the Left, the International Brigade, the Spanish
    Republican Army, etc; a second layer of autobiography
    concerning the exploits of Mr. Campbell and his
    flowering rifle; and a top layer of rhapsody about
    Franco and his colleagues, who are treated as nothing
    less than angels." Beneath "ignoble sweepings of
    every kind of anti-Semitic and atrocity propaganda"
    there are buried "stones of a certain lustre." How-
    ever, Spender adds, "There are several passages in
    this book which make me feel physically sick."

5. Rev. by J. Arteaga De Leon. *Spain* (pub. by Spanish
    Press Services Ltd.), 7.7 (May 18, 1939), 140.

    Flowering Rifle is "a strange combination of poetry
    and invective, facts and poetic feeling, political
    satire and lyricism. The grim monotony of the rhyming
    couplets and the sharp and brutal language of camp
    and stable give the poem the force of a battering ram
    against the ideas and people of a world that was an
    enemy to Spain.... It serves also to condemn the Red
    shadow of Communism and its allies, who are legion."
    The poem contains sincerity, vision, devotion, inten-
    sity, as well as bite and bludgeon, a fanatical
    militancy.

JIII.XII *Collected Poems, 1949*

1. Rev. by G.S. Fraser. *The New Statesman and Nation*,
    38 (December 17, 1949), 738.

"Mr. Campbell is, I think, sometimes betrayed by
his skill and fluency in writing rhymed invective
into mere vulgar abuse. And I think that his personal feuds sometimes rob him of a craftsman's sense
of proportion. Yet, when the dust has settled on
these quarrels--and on wider political quarrels, on
which I have not touched--Mr. Campbell's place, I
would think, among the dozen or so more important
poets of our time is assured. Future readers will
not go to him for insights into a troubled civilization to which ... he has never really belonged ...
but is there another lyrical poet of our time who
combines, just as he does, vigour, directness, tech-
nical control, and the most vivid sense of natural
beauty?"

2. Rev. by C.E. *Forum* (South Africa), 12.49 (March 11,
    1950), 26-27.

    Appraises the earlier poetry typically; then goes
    on to lament over C's lack of compassion in later
    work and failure to realize his superiority as a poet
    over the many poetasters he spent so much time and
    energy lambasting--"Attired as a *matador* he repeatedly
    enters the arena to torment, with magnificent passes
    of the cape, and to slaughter, not a worthy opponent,
    a full-grown fighting bull, but a peaceful, weak-
    kneed calf."

3. *The Times Literary Supplement*, March 24, 1950, p. 184.

    "... taste has been altering to his advantage. He
    is romantic, he is sensuous, and he is violent; and
    to that extent he is more 'contemporary' than he used
    to be. When in the further revolution of taste,
    clarity itself returns to favour, as return it inevi-
    tably will, Mr. Campbell will reap the benefit."
    Surveys C's career and comments on most of the major
    poems. Complains, "Quite in a minority are the 'quiet'
    poems ... and even in these the reader may look far
    for any evidence of loving-kindness.... We may be
    offered the *circumstances* of poetic emotion: something
    may be beautifully observed, and likened revealingly
    to something else ... but the observation and the
    simile are all.... And what repels us is not that he
    finds the common man inferior, not that he scorns his
    grovelling condition, but that he relishes it."
    Ends: "Mr. Campbell's best performance has been to
    extol, in memorable and shining words, all sorts of
    bravery...."

4. Rev. by L.F.D. *The Manchester Guardian*, April 28,
    1950.

    The poems prove C to be "one of the best modern
    poets.... His verse is rich, virile, and technically
    excellent. It can flow lyrically, it can be tinged
    with mysticism (in a ritual, sensuous way); in satiric
    pieces become devastatingly sharp; or take on a mono-
    lithic grandeur. It is by turns religious and pagan,
    noble or bawdy, without losing tone or poise. And
    Mr. Campbell is one of the best translators alive.
    He can also be funny.... Of course, the list of
    virtues ends with a 'but.' Mr. Campbell's temperament
    has a broader sweep than his intellect. He is im-
    posing rather than subtle."

5. Rev. by David Wright. *Poetry London*, 18 (May 1950),
    27-30.

    Explains C's poetry, especially his satire, as an
    outcome of his S. African origin. Singles out *The
    Georgiad*--a lineal descendant of *Mac Flecknoe*--for
    praise, while acknowledging it contains C's worst
    faults: excess and length. Champions C's lyrics,
    quoting from *Choosing a Mast*, "Horses on the Camargue"
    and "Luis de Camões," and states, "Mr. Campbell
    manages to take a seat at table with Dryden and Lord
    Byron, with contemporaries as distinguished and dif-
    ferent as Mr. T.S. Eliot and Mr. Dylan Thomas."
    After discussing the translations from St. John of
    the Cross and quoting from *En Una Noche Oscura*, ob-
    serves: "This is the kind of thing at which Mr. Camp-
    bell is at his best.... it is as a great and sustained
    lyric poet he will be remembered."

6. Rev. by P.D. Cummins. *The Poetry Review*, 41.3 (May-
    June 1950), 148-50.

    "Campbell is one of the few living poets capable of
    confounding the *zeitgeist* of negation with passionate
    affirmations...."

7. Rev. by Richard Church. *John O'London's Weekly*,
    June 6, 1950, p. 19.

8. Rev. by Eric Gillett. *The National and English Review*,
    135 (July 1950), 136-40.

    Reviews CP49 along with Auden's *Collected Shorter
    Poems, 1930-1944* and in the comparison appreciatively
    favors C for affirmation, religion, lyricism.

9. Rev. by Vincent Cronin. *The Month*, New Series, 4.1 (July 1950), 71-72.

"... the quality of participation in what he describes gives new urgency to age-old themes. There is no ideological lip-service to the masses here, but an active sympathy for people whom Mr. Campbell has lived with and understands and loves." Says the short, descriptive poems are the best and that, while superior to them, C owed much in technique to his "Georgian contemporaries."

JIII.XIII *The Catacomb* (journal edited by Rob Lyle and Roy Campbell)

1. Rev. by D.S. Carne-Ross. *Nine*, 2.3 (August 1950), 261.

Says C's ebullient personality and fiercely satirical, combative spirit everywhere present in this journal of right-wing, Catholic political, social and cultural persuasion. Such a reaction against "the Spender-Grigson *ethos*" was inevitable, but "It is a pity Mr. Campbell and his band of *bravi* sometimes spoil their case by unbalanced and ill-mannered overstatement."

JIII.XIV Translation of *The Poems of St. John of the Cross*

1. Rev. by Kathleen Raine. *The New Statesman and Nation*, 41 (June 16, 1951), 685-86.

Except for Allison Peers' literal translation, C's is virtually the first adequate one. "He has produced the Spanish rhymes and metres as closely as possible, and yet his English versions have the freshness of original poems--with occasional exceptions, like 'loving ardours flushed' where a phrase or a word introduced in order to get a rhyme might have been happier." Says the translation "bears the mark of a labour of love, and a deep immersion in the atmosphere of St. John's poetry and thought...."

2. Rev. by John Frederick Nims. *Poetry*, 80 (June 1952), 153-58.

We should be grateful to C "for bringing to a wider audience poetry so important and so neglected--even though his translation is a very poor one. It gives some idea, more or less accurate, of the content of

the poetry, but it gives no idea whatsoever of the
properly poetic: those qualities of imagery, diction,
and rhythm that make the author one of the finest
poets of any literature." After providing a series
of examples of lapses, concludes: "Most of the examples ... are from the first quarter of the Cántico:
they are typical. Open the *Poems* anywhere and you
find, across from St. John's simplicity, directness,
and freshness, an English that is affected and bookish; idioms out of tune, connotations dissonant,
syntax involved and straining. Any translation of
poetry is a disappointment, a series of compromises
and defeats for the translator. Campbell writes so
glibly he has the air of being triumphant--whereas he
is continually misrepresenting the poetry of St. John."

JIII.XV *Light on a Dark Horse*

1. Rev. by Dylan Thomas. *The Observer* (London),
    December 16, 1951, p. 7.

    "In the first half of this often beautiful and
    always bee-loud autobiography, Roy Campbell writes of
    his young blazing days in young Durban and the African
    wilds; and out of the clamour and colour and violence
    and enormous loyalties of those days, out of that fan-
    tastic world of hippos and lily-trotters, flamingos
    and lions, mambas and koodoo bulls and cloud-born
    aloes, comes much of his fiery, flowered, percussive,
    venomous, boasting and devoted poetry.... I acclaim
    the first twelve chapters, written by a poet of
    genius. But, for much of the rest, I think it throws
    rather a bad light on an old war-horse."

2. Rev. by V.S. Pritchett. *The New Statesman and Nation*,
    43 (January 5, 1952), 17.

    "Half of this autobiography is a superb account of
    a childhood and youth in Natal and Rhodesia and a
    short, amusing picture of Bohemian London in the
    Twenties; the other half, which describes quarrelling
    with men, bulls and horses in France and Spain, is
    nothing like as good."

3. *The Listener*, January 31, 1952, pp. 191, 193.

    "Were it not for the intrusion of ... shabby notions,
    Light on a Dark Horse could be unhesitatingly

recommended for its fascinating pictures of South
Africa and Southern Europe, for its relish of
strength and danger and sensual delights. Unfortunately the shabby notions are there, particularly
in the chapters on literary life in London in the
'twenties and of Spain in the thirties. For those
who can take such matters in their stride *Light on a
Dark Horse* should prove the most interesting and
unusual poet's autobiography published in this
century."

4. *Newsweek*, 40 (September 15, 1952), 104.

    The book "begins with a terrific picture of his
    South African boyhood ... ends like something lyrical
    but obscure by ... Ezra Pound." Says, from the
    account, C's marriage "seems to have caused only a
    little less public excitement than that of the Duke
    of Windsor." Amidst the confusions of the latter
    part of the book one catches sight of someone "a little
    like the youthful Teddy Roosevelt and once in a great
    while a glimpse of the author emerges."

5. Rev. by Peter Russell. *Nine*, 3.2 (Summer-Autumn
    1952), 363-68.

    Contrasts C's and Stephen Spender's autobiographies.
    In particular praises C's style and powers of descrip-
    tion. "Campbell's all round nature, his genial
    interest in every human activity which is not ignoble
    or debased, makes his autobiography one of the most
    absorbing and stimulating books of the century. It
    has none of the pompousness of Burton or Doughty yet
    has all their courage and poetic imagination."

6. Rev. by Robert Phelps. *The Nation* (New York),
    October 18, 1952, p. 360.

    "Properly, a poet can be a hero only for another
    poet.... When he undertakes to be his own, he must
    either be very innocent--that is, hardly a poet at
    all--or, like Yeats, able in some canny corner of him-
    self to work with masks ... Campbell is innocent. It
    is not only the number of dashing things he does but
    the confident candor with which he beholds himself
    doing them that makes his book so ingratiating....
    Heaven only knows what ever made him bother to write
    poetry."

7. Rev. by Hugh Kenner. *Poetry*, 82 (June 1953), 169–75.

> "Awareness of himself in action, detailed knowledge
> of the animal and vegetable kingdoms, and an assort-
> ment of impressive athletic skills may be said to con-
> stitute Mr. Campbell's poetic equipment.... His
> prose is a better *substitute* for poetry than his
> verse is."

See also JIII.XXIV.2

JIII.XVI *Lorca*

1. Rev. by Geoffrey Brereton. *The New Statesman and
    Nation*, 44 (October 18, 1952), 456.

> "Lorca's vitality, Mr. Campbell argues ... owes
> nothing to political considerations.... what we have
> is a poet rooted in the Andalusian soil yet, paradox-
> ically, universal." C's thesis is that Lorca combined
> popular tradition with his own rendering of "the most
> cultivated artifice of baroque poetry." But the re-
> sult is confusing because C "explodes his Lorca at us,
> showering fragments not only of Gongora, but of half
> a dozen other poets of the *Siglo de Oro* ... first we
> should know whether we are concerned with a Master
> Alchemist or a *pierrot lunaire*, and this question is
> not squarely faced. Yet this too full-hearted study
> does communicate something of its own excitement.
> Its particular interest is that it contains several
> hundred lines of Campbell's own translations of Lorca,
> most of them new. In their skill and self-effacement
> they are the best tribute to the original."

2. Rev. by Stephen Spender. *The New Republic*, 128
    (February 2, 1953), 18–19.

> C's volume is an "admirable discussion not only of
> Lorca, but also of the French symbolists, of Spanish
> poetry, and of poetry in general." Notes C "insists
> on the paradox that Lorca is both regional and acces-
> sible" and that "when he tries to be 'cosmopolitan'
> in the poems about Whitman and New York he becomes
> 'parochial and provincial.'" The second half of the
> review, however, dilates upon the criticism that "This
> lively book is marred seriously by what is an error
> in presentation, and less slightly by the kind of
> polemics which lead Campbell into inaccuracies about

his political opponents." Says, "The mistake is that
all the quotations from Lorca appear in Campbell's
own translations ..." and, "It is necessary to stop
the creation of a myth that until the appearance of
this essay Lorca's name has been used only to make
political capital for the extreme Left in England."
Refers to the work of Gerald Brenan and the introduction to the translation of Lorca by Spender and Gili,
"the best-known selection of Lorca's work in an
English translation."

JIII.XVII Translation of *Poems of Baudelaire*

1. Rev. by C.J.D. Harvey. *Ons Eie Boek*, 20.3 (1952),
    117-18.

    Finds a remarkable similarity in the technical aims
    of Baudelaire and C and attributes the success of the
    translation to this: "Like Baudelaire, Mr. Campbell
    has since his early days increasingly aimed at natural,
    forceful colloquial language, confined, however, in a
    strict metrical form and using a regular scheme of
    true rhymes.... As it is just here, in the matter of
    finding rhymes, that so many otherwise creditable
    attempts at translating rhymed verse come to grief,
    this probably accounts for the great superiority as
    poetry of his translations." Points out the deep in-
    fluence on C of Baudelaire from the beginning as
    observable in poems like "The Albatross" poems,
    "Buffel's Kop," "The Zulu Girl" and "The Skeleton
    Navvy."

2. Rev. by J.G. Weightman. *The New Statesman and Nation*,
    45 (January 24, 1953), 97.

    "Mr. Campbell is modest about his Baudelaire. Un-
    like his St. John of the Cross, it was written, he
    says, without supernatural aid.... Certainly a great
    deal of work has gone into this volume and our first
    remark must be that the gist of the meaning is, on
    the whole, there.... But we are soon aware of the
    usual serious deficiencies of verse translation....
    Mr. Campbell cannot give us the solemn echo of
    Baudelaire's verse, just as he cannot give us his
    general sensuousness.... However, to say that
    Mr. Campbell's translation is, on the whole, a
    shambles, is not to be fiercely critical. Hardly
    anyone could do better, and most of us would do far
    worse."

3.   Rev. by J.G. Weightman. *The Twentieth Century*, 153
     (February 1953), 135–41.

     Thinks the best translation is that of *Sépulture*, a
     minor example of the "black" poems he considers C
     does best, he being less successful with Baudelaire's
     highest flights. Analyzes the rendering of *La Mort
     des Amants* to show what he believes are deficiencies
     both in the translation and in poetic quality to be
     found throughout much of the collection. Qualifies
     the analysis, however, by saying, "To see how compara-
     tively good this defective rendering is, one has only
     to compare it with that of Arthur Symons."

4.   Rev. by J.H.F. McEwen. *The Month*, New Series, 9.3
     (March 1953), 180–83.

     Translation of the whole of *Les Fleurs du Mal* called
     "a remarkable achievement." Praises that of *L'Examen
     de Minuit* as a sample of the "rumbustious, hard-hitting
     Baudelaire who particularly appeals to Mr. Campbell,
     and with whom he is at his most felicitous." But says
     his touch is sometimes less certain in purely lyrical
     passages--criticizes failures in simplicity and pre-
     ciseness in renderings of *La Mort des Pauvres* and *Le
     Crépuscule du Matin*. All things considered, however,
     "Seldom indeed has so noble a tribute of affection
     been paid by one poet to another."

5.   *The Listener*, 49 (April 2, 1953), 573–74.

     "Mr. Roy Campbell has produced a thoroughly workman-
     like translation which is, on many occasions, better
     than the model." Feels it a pity, though, that the
     translations, like the originals, are so often uneven.
     In seeking reasons for these inequalities, states, "He
     has a religious type of mind, admittedly, but it does
     not quite fit in with Baudelaire's to make a complete
     collaboration.... Possibly the chief trouble lies in
     the fact that he started off on the wrong foot in his
     desire to find a compromise between the modern and
     the archaic. It is all too seldom that he catches
     what W.H. Auden calls 'the poetry of departure.'"

6.   Rev. by T.W. *The Poetry Review*, 44.2 (April–June
     1953), 348.

     Dissents from C's desire to be "as colloquial as
     possible"; to be so "is not necessarily a virtue
     when you are translating a fastidious artist." Says

it is natural to compare C's version with the best
already done. "Those by Lord Alfred Douglas, Margaret
Jourdain, and Eugene Mason may be cited, and these
remain untoppled from their pedestals. Liberties
taken by Mr. Campbell with his rhymes do not justify
themselves in many of the sonnets, but he triumphs in
'The Giantess,' and in several others finds words as
daring and as dazzling as those of the great original."

7. Rev. by Wallace Fowlie. *Poetry*, 82.2 (May 1953),
   86-95.

   Selects *L'Imprévu* (translated as "The Unforeseen")
   as a good example of C's "principal virtues as a
   translator"--exceptional mastery of rhyme, vigorous
   and natural rhythm, fidelity to the original with few
   liberties taken in the translation of key words. "I
   like the firmness and colloquial boldness of these
   translations.... Those who love Baudelaire in French
   will always quibble over some points in any translation, but there are fewer points here than usual.
   Whereas the general rendering of these poems cannot
   be questioned, the translation of a few specific
   words is surprising...."

8. Rev. by Jackson Mathews. *The Sewanee Review*, 62.4
   (Autumn 1954), 663-71.

   Notes C first poet of reputation to translate all
   of the *Fleurs du Mal* and briefly surveys other translations. For several reasons, though he is uneven,
   C has been able to furnish "a good number of the finest translations of certain poems that have yet been
   done in English." Believes C at his best in the
   hard-driving didactic poems (sees his "To the Reader"
   as the finest version). Less sure with the lyrics,
   C has nevertheless written some "beautiful English
   poems" (e.g., "Elevation," "The Splendid Ship,"
   "Sorrows of the Moon") and excels in the "tough"
   poems like "De Profundis Clamavi" and "The Unforeseen":
   in these C "has made an important part of Baudelaire
   for the first time fully known in English...."
   Argues, however, that C's viewing of Baudelaire
   through the eyes of a Catholic convert, as in "The
   Unforeseen," makes him miss Baudelaire's complex
   irony. Complains C tends "to neglect and sacrifice
   figurative structure in favor of *verbal color* and
   sound effects," and to indulge at times in padding,
   as in the overuse of "seems." Objects to C's

slanginess, forced rhyming and too frequent resort
to feminine and rich rhyme. C's lack of sympathy
with some of Baudelaire's poems caused him to be
slapdash in their treatment.

JIII.XVIII Anon. *On the Four Quartets of T.S. Eliot*. Foreword by Roy Campbell

1.   *The Times Literary Supplement*, September 11, 1953,
        p. 576.

        "In his foreword Mr. Campbell after some rather
        vague and random flings at 'official criticism,'
        recommends this essay as an example of 'the independent
        personal approach.'"

JIII.XIX *Selected Poems*

1.   Rev. by Randall Jarrell. *New York Times Book Review*,
        April 17, 1955, p. 4.

        "... when I looked for the life in Campbell's poems
        all I could find was literature." Quotes from *The
        Flaming Terrapin* and "The Palm" and says: "he is the
        Byron not of our days but of Byron's.... It is hard
        to believe that it is we who are reading this, and
        not our great-great-grandfathers. When we come across
        echoes of Rimbaud's drunken boats and Baudelaire's
        digging skeletons, it surprises us as much as if we
        had seen them in Shelley or Byron. It is a very bad-
        tempered Byron who writes these poems; his heart no
        longer bleeds, but only barks and bites ..., when
        he is at all contemporary I like him best; but usually
        he is what Edith Sitwell calls him, 'a literary
        tornado.'"

2.   Rev. by Edith Sitwell. *The Saturday Review*, 38
        (June 18, 1955), 19.

        Quotes Nietzsche's praise of Petronius and says,
        "Speed, fire, and power: these are the three spirits
        informing Dr. Campbell's poetry." Praises speed in
        "The Albatross," power in "Horses on the Camargue"
        and the "tragic splendour of that great yet terrible
        poem 'To a Pet Cobra.'" Goes on to give high praise
        to "The Palm" and "En Una Noche Oscura." Quotes
        Whitman on "the rhyme and uniformity of perfect

poems" and states, "... the perfume palpable to form
arises from Dr. Campbell's poems. Their fulfilled
purpose is delight."

3. Rev. by Roberta Teal Swartz. *Kenyon Review*, 17.4
    (Autumn 1955), 650-56.

    Cites as among C's best poems "The Sisters," "The
    Zebras," "Raven II," "The Sling," "The Palm," "To a
    Pet Cobra," "The Snake" and the opening "Dedication."
    Comments on *The Flaming Terrapin* and *The Georgiad*
    and when discussing imagery states, "The scintilla-
    tions of scales or feathers, the proportions and
    movements of trees and beasts unknown to us, the
    admiration of persons, gentle and close, descriptions
    like those of Spenser illuminate the lyrics, or cas-
    cade from him in the satires like the toads and
    vipers that fell from the lips of the bad sister in
    the fairy tale. His humor is rollicking, his wit
    erudite. The disappointments and mistakes are those
    of action--repetition of words, phrases and symbols,
    bad taste, a touch of the morbid here and there, and
    a *scattered* sensibility. He avoids sentimentality
    almost completely, however, and his technique is
    almost impeccable...."

4. Rev. by John Ciardi. *The Nation* (New York),
    December 10, 1955, p. 515.

    "No poet writing in English has equalled Campbell's
    violence.... None has presented a mind--to me at
    least--more despicable, a mind compounded of storm
    trooper arrogance, Sieg Heil piety, and a kind of
    Nietzschean rant, sometimes mixed with a ponderously
    uncomical sense of satire. The center of that mind
    --and its poetic style--is all sledgehammers. It
    would be comforting to one's sense of liberalism to
    report that the result is merely thud-thud. What
    must be reported instead is that the sledgehammers
    are sometimes magnificent...." [See JII.69.]

JIII.XX *Collected Poems, 1957*

1. Rev. by Geoffrey Grigson. *The Observer*, September 29,
    1957.

    "... there is no more tenderness behind his poetic
    face than behind the face of a beetle." Asks, "Does

a livingness, a living activity of style and language,
then forgive him? Is enough left when his views are
cut out?" Says he is not sure and that C "used
couplets without enough internal drama of variety,
bullying them to convey too often a nearly imbecile
monotony of denunciation." Concludes: "Some of this
volume, then, is rabid, some of it is folly slashed
by a greater fool; who in one poem takes the hoopoe
for his heraldic crest, forgetting that hoopoes nest
in dirt and repeat a tedious two-note song." Suggests
that C was like Camões in first finding the wonders
of Africa and the Indian Ocean and then the contrasting
staleness of the West, but that C never admitted "that
the oceanic beaches are now for the most part crowded
with the iridescence of empty tins."

2.   Rev. by Edwin Muir. *The New Statesman and Nation*,
     January 11, 1958, p. 49.

     "Comparing *Flowering Rifle* and *Talking Bronco* with
     Campbell's early poetry, one has the feeling of look-
     ing on while the partisan and the man of action kill
     the poet. Campbell's name will live by such poems as
     'The Golden Shower' in this volume and by a number of
     poems in the first. But it is sad to think of his
     journey from his pagan paradise to this rowdy corner
     of the inferno."

See also JIII.XXI.3.

JIII.XXI *Portugal*

1.   Rev. by V.S. Pritchett. *The New Statesman and Nation*,
     54 (November 30, 1957), 736-37.

     "... when we have allowed for the vulgar Celtic
     inflation and the plain nastiness, ... a vivid and
     intimate account of Portuguese life...." C has written
     as well as anyone about the mysterious origin of the
     Lisbon fado. "... the Portuguese and ourselves are
     in his debt for his translations of the lyrical poets
     and above all for his renderings of Camoens."

2.   *The Times Literary Supplement*, December 6, 1957,
     p. 736.

     "Neither travel-book nor guide-book, as he says,
     this projection of the author's personality upon

congenial themes yet contrives to impart a deal of
precious information, much of it esoteric."

3. Rev. by Rose Macaulay of *Portugal* and CP57. *London
   Magazine*, 5.4 (1958), 58-61.

Complains of the way in which C's hate and scorn
for loathed figures keep intruding upon his descriptions in *Portugal*. Observes: "He is much better
under the sea, among intimidating fish, though this
leads to a diatribe on excessive love of animals....
Yet Mr. Campbell was himself attached to horses and
bulls, and his chapter on the Campinos is (though ill-
written) of a good deal of interest." In discussing
his treatment of Lisbon, states, "... he tells us
that it has now been restored to its original greatness
by the combined efforts of Our Lady of Fatima and her
faithful servant Salazar." Proceeds to: "Much better
is the section on Portuguese literature, which takes
us completely and reverently through the centuries;
the chapter on poetry is written with considerable
knowledge and some lively translations, and is the
best thing in the book." In coming to the relationship between C's prose and his poetry, says: "His
prose [in *Portugal*] is oddly shoddy and illiterate,
in a poet with his gift for phrase; perhaps he should
have written only verse. This new volume of his
collected poems contains some vivid and memorable
passages, which at times transcend and redeem the
boasting and hate they carry." Speculates on what
effect C's eventually abandoning his passionate fixa-
tion on the Spanish Civil War might have had on his
poetry.

JIII.XXII *Collected Poems, 1960*

1. Rev. by John Wain. *The Spectator*, March 4, 1960,
   pp. 326-28.

Is critical of the translations from the French,
but says C was "very well placed to translate Spanish
and Portuguese poetry ... whatever these poets are
actually like in their original texts, Campbell was
drawn to them all by one quality: a hard magnificence,
a burning, jewelled intensity which suggests baroque
and Moorish architecture." Singles out the translation of Alonso Gamo's "You a Wing among the Wings of
Birds" and Lorca's "Song of the Horseman" for special
praise.

2. Rev. by Grace Banyard. *Contemporary Review*, 197
    (March 1960), 184.

    "Roy Campbell's translations from the French,
    Spanish and Portuguese, from Horace and St. John of
    the Cross, are such that, in the phrase of Edith
    Sitwell's Foreword, 'the whole book is full of
    wonders.' The essential Lorca, the lilting sadness,
    for example, seems to have been caught in 'Song of
    the Horseman'...."

3. Rev. by Leonard Clark. *Time and Tide*, April 2, 1960,
    p. 383.

    C was a superb translator "with a special feeling
    for the Iberian peninsula." Says his most important
    translations those of St. John of the Cross and Lorca.
    "Although some may quarrel with the accuracy of the
    translations, none will deny the trenchant mind and
    passionate heart which informs them."

4. Rev. by Eric Gillett. *National and English Review*,
    154 (April 1960), 141-43.

    "... as Mrs. Campbell points out in her preface, he
    began to translate from Rimbaud and Baudelaire when
    he was eighteen, and went on translating all his
    life.... St. John of the Cross, Lorca, the Spanish
    and Portuguese provided Campbell with his most con-
    genial originals. The exact logical processes of
    French thought were too strait for his generous and
    often fierce mind. He enjoyed the bawdiness of Horace
    because he thought it honest and witty, and his trans-
    lation of the 'Ars Poetica' is lively enough but it
    has not the inevitability of a classical or a defini-
    tive version."

JIII.XXIII *Poems of Roy Campbell*, chosen and introduced by Uys
    Krige

1. Rev. by Geoffrey Durrant. *Standpunte*, 14.1 (October
    1960), 65-70.

    "Dr. Krige suggests by a few reservations and hints
    that he is fully aware of Campbell's limitations; but
    he rightly--in an edition which is so well suited to
    school use--gives his chief attention to Campbell's
    striking virtues. This is as wise as it is generous,
    for a good teacher will no doubt help his pupils to

see the faults for themselves, and so provide the
necessary protection against the moral falsity of a
good deal of the later work."

JIII.XXIV *Selected Poetry*, edited by Joseph M. Lalley

1. Rev. by Jeffrey Hart. *National Review*, December 31,
   1968, pp. 1330-31.

   In being raised on the borders of the British Empire
   and always more or less at odds with its center,
   London, C was rather like Kipling; he was also like
   Hemingway in being a sportsman and "something of a
   brawler." He "designed his verse to be everything
   modern poetry--as he thought--was not: vigorous,
   passionate, manly, disciplined." But he was a better
   man than poet. "... the poetry written by such contemporaries ... as Eliot, Pound, Stevens, and Marianne
   Moore represented a highly exacting art, far more
   disciplined than his." Says his translations more
   satisfactory than his original work. Lists the faults
   in C's work but commends a short lyric like "The Dead
   Torero" and the effectiveness of his satire--"though
   if it is twentieth century satire you want, Eliot's
   early poems are the place to go." Adds: "It is to
   Campbell's everlasting credit, however, that he had
   the right instincts about the war in Spain....
   Flowering Rifle is bombastic and unreadable, but he
   saw the essence of modern history laid bare."

2. Rev. by Patrick Anderson of *Light on a Dark Horse* and
   Selected Poetry. *The Spectator*, August 23, 1969,
   pp. 241-43.

   The autobiography makes one see how much C "admired
   the stoicism and ferocity of the animal world, but
   how seldom he himself was violent." The first half
   of the book, moreover, is mostly about the natural
   world in such a way that "a poet's sensitivity to
   form and colour is combined with practical information
   patiently and courteously delivered; there are also
   good, sometimes tall stories and the whole thing is
   laced with a breezy humour tending to the grotesque."
   Inquires why, then, the book is not "a masterpiece"
   and confesses to bafflement while suggesting it might
   be because of a combination of boastfulness, digres-
   siveness, "inability to establish the incidents in
   terms of the inner life" and make them "more than the

defiant gestures of a muddled, immature personality";
above all, it might be "a failure of the shaping
imagination ... of intelligence." Perhaps C, as a
poet, rather despised prose. However, does not,
judging by *Selected Poetry*, find him a good poet.
"He simply bobs by you, fiery-faced but curiously
relaxed, on the groundswell of English prosody and
amongst the flotsam of fire, lyre, strife, life,
corn, morn. But there are one or two splendid epigrams and I would except Rimbaud-dominated lyrics
such as 'The Zulu Girl' and 'The Sisters.' Generally
a good translator...."

Section K
Research Collections

Abbreviations Used in Section K

A	autograph
AL / draft	draft of autograph letter
AL / draft inc	incomplete draft of autograph letter
ALS	autograph letter signed
ALS's	autograph letters signed
A MS	autograph manuscript
A MS / frag	incomplete manuscript passage
A MSS	autograph manuscripts
APCS	autograph post card signed
APCS's	autograph post cards signed
file	a related sequence kept as a unit
TC	table of contents
TccL	typed carbon copy of letter
TccL's	typed carbon copies of letters
TccMS	typed carbon copy included with manuscripts
TccMSS	typed carbon copies included with manuscripts
TLS	typed letter signed
TLS's	typed letters signed
T MS	typescript included with manuscripts
TS	typescript

KI. KILLIE CAMPBELL AFRICANA LIBRARY,
UNIVERSITY OF NATAL
DURBAN, NATAL, SOUTH AFRICA

I. *Manuscripts*
   1. A MS of *Poems*, 1930.
   2. A MSS of juvenilia (five poems).
   3. A MS of "Upon a Gloomy Night" (some differences from published version).
   4. A MS of several short humorous verses on other poets, written in Scots dialect and headed, "The Godly Fore."
   5. About 20 A MS / frags of poems.
   6. TccMS of unpub. poem entitled, "To the Royal Family Visiting South Africa" [1947].

II. *Correspondence*
   Includes
   1. ALS's from C: to his cousin Dora, when he was ten years old (with drawings); several--mostly written in youth--to various family members; 2 to Mary C written c. 1924; some 20 to his wife or daughter Tess written when on active service (several profusely illustrated with pen and ink sketches); to Peter Russell.
   2. TS copies of ten letters from C to his mother, written between 1939 and 1942.
   3. ALS's from Mary C to Killie Campbell (C's cousin), including one refuting that he was ever a fascist.
   4. ALS from Philip Heseltine to C, d. February 28, 1923, congratulating him on having written *The Flaming Terrapin*.
   5. ALS from Edmund Blunden to C, d. June 30, 1939, on *Flowering Rifle*.
   6. TLS's
      a. From Killie Campbell: to Archbishop Denis Hurley about Dr. W.H. Gardner's research in Spain on C; several others mentioning C.
      b. From Lincoln MacVeagh of the Dial Press / d. September 13, 1927: to C's mother, stating desire to publish C's next book after *The Flaming Terrapin*.

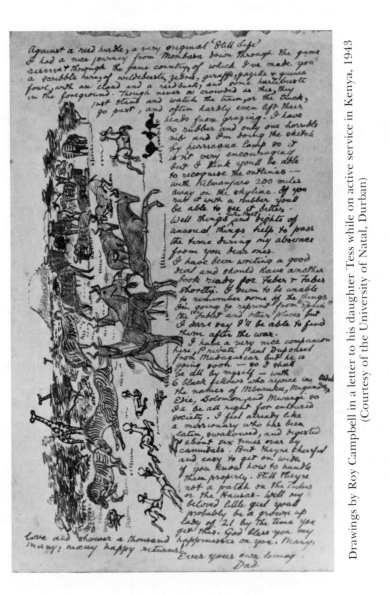

Against a reed hurdle, a very original "Still Life"
I had a nice journey from Mombasa down through the game
reserve & through the game country of which I've made you
a scribble here, of wildebeeste, zebra, giraffe, gazelle & guinea
fowl, with an eland and a reedbuck; and some hartebeeste
in the foreground. Though never as crowded as this, they
just stand and watch the train, or the truck,
go past, and often hardly even lift their
heads from grazing. I have
no rubber and only one horrible
nib and I'm doing the sketch
by hurricane lamp so it
isn't very encouraging
but I think you'll be able
to recognise the outlines —
with Kilimanjaro 200 miles
away on the skyline. If you
rub it with a rubber you'll
be able to see it better.
Well things and sights of
unusual things help to pass
the time during my absence
from you dear ones.
I have been writing a good
deal and should have another
book ready for Faber & Faber
shortly. I seem to be unable
to remember some of the things
I'm going to reprint from "Flowering
the "Flaming" and other places but
I dare say I'll be able to find
them after the war.
I have a very nice companion
here, Private Paul Duponsel
from Madagascar but he is
going soon — so I shall
be all by myself — with
6 black fellows who rejoice in
the names of Mbwuku, Mugandi,
Erie, Solomon, and Mwangi so
I'll be all right for cultured
society. I feel already like
a missionary who has been
eaten, swallowed, and digested
about six times over by
cannibals. But they're cheerful
and easy to get on with
if you know how to handle
them properly. Still they're
not a patch on the Zulus
or the Hausas. Well my
beloved little girl you'll
probably be a grown up
lady of 21 by the time you
get this. God bless you my
love and shower a thousand happinesses on you. Many,
many, many happy returns.
Ever your own loving
Dad.

c. From Tess C to Killie C; also ALS.

III. Bibliography of C's writings; comp. by V.M. Barrat and
     KCAL. [1954.] 7 pp. [Unpub.]

IV. *Printed Materials*
    1. Copies—a number of them signed—of most of the
       English first editions of C's works and translations,
       including the deluxe editions of CP49 and *Broken
       Record*; also a copy of *Homenaje a Roy Campbell* ...
       [see JII.86].
    2. *The Life of Sam Campbell Told in Verse*, by Ethel C
       [see JI.5]; also copies of her other books of poetry.
    3. Newspaper clippings of C's "Modern Poetry and Con-
       temporary History" [see H8] and many Durban newspaper
       clippings referring to C.
    4. Copies of some 40 studies of C, from South African
       journals mostly.
    5. Typed copies of reviews or excerpts from reviews of
       The Flaming Terrapin in English and U.S. papers and
       journals.
    6. Scrapbook of biographical materials and reviews from
       magazines and newspapers.

V. *Typescripts of Radio Broadcasts*
   1. Broadcasts by C [for these, see Section G and Note]:
      a. "Calling South Africa." [Dated March 1942 by
         KCAL.]
      b. "A South African Poet in Portugal."
      c. "Some South African Writers."
   2. Broadcasts about C;
      a. "A Tribute to the Late Roy Campbell." B.B.C.
         broadcast, April 28, 1957.
      b. Smith, Sydney Goodsir. "Roy Campbell, a Personal
         Tribute." Scottish Home Service Broadcast,
         June 18, 1957.
      c. Tribute transcribed from S.A.B.C. tape recording
         [1957].
      d. Tribute by Rob Lyle *et al*. B.B.C. broadcast,
         September 11, 1958.

VI. *Notes by Killie Campbell*
    On C's publications and appearances in journals, espec-
    ially ones in South Africa; on the whereabouts in
    South Africa of MSS.

VII. *Portraits, Photographs*

Pictorial material held includes portrait of C by Mary C
(oil on canvas, 60 x 51 cm) and three photographs of
the bronze bust of C executed by Hugh Oloff De Wet.

KII. THE SOUTH AFRICAN LIBRARY,
CAPE TOWN

I. *Manuscripts*
1. *The Flaming Terrapin.* A MS of Parts I and II, and
   part of Part III. 26 leaves.
2. *Mithraic Emblems.* A MS, including cover with title.
   7 leaves. [The "Mithraic Frieze" poems.]
3. *Tristan da Cunha.* A MS. 3 leaves.
4. *The Waysgoose* [sic]. TccMS / with A corrections and
   emendations. 26 leaves.

II. *Correspondence*
1. ALS's and APCS's:
   a. From C to C.J. Sibbett (friend and patron), c.
      1928-c.1934: supply details of life in Provence;
      reasons for move to Spain; writing of *Broken Record*
      in Barcelona; long ALS / d. April 1931 full of
      praise of Wyndham Lewis, a marvellous description
      of pines, and explaining dislike of writing
      letters--corrects them in draft as he does poems.
   b. AL / drafts from C to C.J. Sibbett, 1950-56: about
      life in London; Sibbett's having been the one who
      got him reading Camoëns; details of forthcoming
      move to Portugal and giving of lectures at the
      University of Salamanca; plans to live half the
      year in Portugal and half in Spain and to rent two
      houses in London so as to avoid taxes and in all
      make a thousand pounds a year; ALS from Galamares,
      Portugal, d. 1956, asking if Sibbett has a copy of
      the *South African Nation* in which a fragment of a
      long poem of his now lost appeared; on being very
      ill, having diabetes; numbers of APCS's.
   c. From Mary C to Sibbett, 1950-51.
   d. ALS from Augustus John to C / d. May 25, 1929,
      expressing hope of visiting him at Martigues in
      October and congratulating him on bullfighting
      exploits.
   e. ALS from F.C. Slater to Sibbett about C, d.
      '3.2.51'.

2. TccL from D.H. Varley (S.A.L. librarian) to C, d.
   May 4, 1949, asking for confirmation of account given
   in earlier letter to Sibbett, in which C had said of
   the writing of *The Wayzgoose* that the words and
   phrases formed themselves automatically and that only
   48 hours elapsed between the start and finish of com-
   posing the poem.

III. *Printed Materials*
   1. Unpub. M.A. thesis on C by R.V. Davis [see JI.22].
   2. Newspaper clippings with references to C from *The
      Cape Argus*.
   3. Copies of the *South African Nation* from 1917 on.
   4. Copies of *The Waste Paper Basket of the Owl Club*,
      1926, with line drawings by C illus. "Tristan da
      Cunha," and 1934 [see E18, E52].

KIII. BERG COLLECTION,
NEW YORK PUBLIC LIBRARY

I. *Manuscripts*
   1. From *Adamastor*. A MS / poems. 21 pp., including some
      prelims, TC. "Amphisbaena" [sic]: many diffs. from
      pub. version; "Mazeppa": diffs. in stanza two from
      pub. version.
   2. *The Death of the "Sanglier."* A MS / prose. 9 pp.
   3. Introduction to exhibition catalogue of paintings by
      Enslin du Plessis. A MS / prose. 3 pp. "He has
      never suffered that staleness which comes from having
      to vitiate one's creative work with the drudgery of
      breadwinning.... Du Plessis is profoundly erudite
      both in painting and literature, and his conversation
      on either subject is full of knowledge and experience.
      He is the opposite of the naif."
   4. [From *The Wayzgoose*.] A MS / poem inc. 10 pp.
      "Along whose track the wretch to safety squirms...."
      [Variants.]

II. *Correspondence (11 folders)*
   1. 16 AL / drafts and 1 APCS to Enslin du Plessis, 1930-
      1938. In four groups: those from Martigues, France;
      those from Altea, Alicante, Spain; those from
      Toledo, Spain; those from Binsted, Sussex, England;
      also, 1 from Rome.

a. From Tour de Vallier, Gour, Martigues: subjects
   raised include the success of *Adamastor* (and reviews of it) and of the Hours Press collection;
   visits at different times of Hart Crane, Liam
   O'Flaherty, William Plomer; references made to
   Elliott Seabrooke the painter, Laurens van der
   Post, friendship between Aldous Huxley and Drieu
   de la Rochelle, correspondence with F.C. Slater;
   some details given of a long letter to him from
   William Plomer objecting to *Satire and Fiction*.
b. From Quintana, Altea, Alicante: include socio-
   political comment on communism, Hitler's persecution of Jews, Christianity; announces his baptism
   and marriage in the Catholic Church and excitement
   over prospect of living in Toledo; vividly describes
   where he is living and reports on his progress in
   writing *Mithraic Emblems*; allusions made to seizure
   of his possessions before he left France and present
   ascetic life; refers to stays with him of Uys
   Krige and Helge Krog and the prospects for a London
   production of one of Krog's plays.
c. In APCS / d. June 21, 1935, from Toledo, rhapso-
   dizes over the city, reveals he had had to have a
   spinal operation in Madrid. Chief content of
   letters from Toledo: Uys Krige as man and poet;
   Krige's and Armand Guibert's approval of the
   "Horizon" poems; his being beaten up by Asaltos
   "for no reason at all"; his being in the bullring
   and a newspaper report of his success as a
   rejoneador; his being briefly in prison because of
   alleged debt; the increasing street-fighting and
   his and his family's special confirmation in the
   Cardinal Archbishop's private chapel "as a reward
   for protecting the Carmelites during the fighting
   at the risk of our throats."
d. From Glebe House, Binstead [sic], Arundel, Sussex:
   mostly concerned with difficulties in getting
   Mithraic Emblems reviewed and "A Yarn with Old
   Woodley" pub.--reports Oswald Mosley had offered
   to get it pub. but gives assurances he is not
   going to let Mosley "recruit" him; expresses anti-
   democratic sentiments, supports Mussolini's
   Abyssinian campaign; refers to having sat to
   Wyndham Lewis for "an equestrian portrait" and to
   impending departure for Portugal. Letter from
   Rome refers to dispatch of *Flowering Rifle* to
   Longmans, the Anschluss, the Nazi treatment of the
   Jews, Italian censorship, the League of Nations,

the mysterious "suppression" in England of two
books of his, Bloomsbury.

2. ALS (from "Roy Campbell, l'Anglais, Jouteur de la
Joyeuse Lance Martigale, Martigues, B du R") to
Robert Bowyer Malise Nichols [d. April 25? n.y.].
9 pp. Discusses several of Nichols' poems and compares "The Tower" with "Tristan da Cunha"; admits to
having appropriated a line from one of Nichols' poems
for latter; assures N neither he nor Edward Thomas,
Rupert Brooke or Lascelles Abercrombie is satirized
in *The Georgiad*, and refers to Lady Dorothy Wellesley
and Victoria Nicholson; thanks N for his help with
promotion of *Adamastor* but asks him to stop [Arnold]
Bennett from reviewing his work; expresses pleasure
at [Aldous] Huxley's approval of his poetry and recalls association with him, thinks his character
Gumbril must be based on him as he then was.

3. AL / draft to unnamed recipient who sent him a book,
which he liked, by E.H.W. Meyerstein.

4. ALS / draft to Edith Sitwell introducing Archbishop
Hurley and giving an account of his saving of the
Carmelite archives in Toledo, his being sentenced to
death "by the Tcheka" and escape during a bombardment of the Alcazar.

5. AL / rough draft of a rowdy, abusive letter to Randall
Jarrell, which includes a cocky quatrain, resulting
from Jarrell's review of *Selected Poems* [see
JIII.XIX.1].

6. 2 ALS's from Mary C to Edith Sitwell.

KIV. POETRY COLLECTION,
STATE UNIVERSITY OF NEW YORK AT BUFFALO

I. *Manuscripts*

1. A MS / draft inc. 14 odd lines of working of a poem:
"Through blood and fire the evening frowns ... harsh
fragrance as of thyme will wake us."

2. A MS / draft inc. Part of *Choosing a Mast*, here
headed "The Pines"--"Their boughs like running
water swirl and shine ... Eagles to that high place
will sometimes come." 12 lines, some dropped in
pub. version.

3. A MS / draft inc. Segment of "Solo and Chorus" from
"The Conquistador."

4. A MS / prose frag. Description of Marseille.

II. *Correspondence (all AL / drafts)*
   1. Several, and 1 APCS, to Maurice Wollman, about inclusion in an anthology.
   2. Several to Peter Russell, mostly about contributions to *Nine*.
   3. Several to John Gawsworth, about the London scene, reviewing, contributions to a journal.
   4. 1 to the Trustees of the Civil List Pension Fund on behalf of a John Metcalfe.
   5. Several letters and 1 APCS to Kenneth Marshall of Zwemmer's Bookshop concerning *The Georgiad* and Marshall's role as agent in negotiating for its publication.
   6. APCS to C.J. Greenwood of Boriswood Limited.

III. *Printed Materials*
   1. A good collection of first editions, many with dust jackets, including broadside by C *et al.*, *Watlingia* (1947), copies of the translations of Helge Krog's *The Copy* and *Happily Ever After?* and numbers of works to which C made contributions.
   2. Offprints of several studies of C and newspaper clippings.
   3. A complete run of *The Catacomb*.

KV. THE ACADEMIC CENTER LIBRARY,
UNIVERSITY OF TEXAS AT AUSTIN, TEXAS

I. *Manuscripts*
   1. A MS. Roy Campbell's translation of *The Poems of St. John of the Cross*.
   2. 4 A MS exercise books with A revisions (notably of "Orpheus," "To Aimé Tschiffely" and "Preface" to CP57).
   3. A MSS / drafts. Poetic workings I: of about 12 poems and translations, mostly unpub.
   4. A MSS / prose frags and A MSS / verse drafts. Misc. unidentified passages; several pages each on the Spanish Civil War (incl. C's own involvement), from *Taurine Provence*, for a review of P.D. Cummins' *One is One*, of a description of Lisbon harbor, of a lecture given at the University of Salamanca; poetic workings II: sundry fragments and satiric doggerel; A MS of "Autobiography in Fifty Kicks."

5. A MS of about half of the translations of *Les Fleurs du Mal*.
6. Armstrong, T.I.F., "Roy Campbell; Some Bio-bibliographical Notes by his Friend John Gawsworth, dedicated to Richard Aldington": A MS / second draft signed "John Gawsworth" with A emendations; d. July 1961. 34 pp.
7. Unidentified work: A MS / frag with A revisions. Passage about autobiog. incident in Spain--"This digression is to show you what the real Basques are like ..."; A MS / poem with A emendations: "I ask, 'Why has it dawned another day?'"
8. A MS / notebooks of translation of *The House of Bernarda Alba* by Federico García Lorca.
9. Dylan Thomas's notes for his review in *The Observer* of *Light on a Dark Horse*. A MS (about 11 sheets).
10. Typescripts: "The Poetry of Dylan Thomas" by C (appeared in *Shenandoah*, 1954); review of *The Poems of St. John of the Cross* by Herman Peschmann.

II. *31 A MS Notebooks*
1. Part of Portuguese literature section of *Portugal*, mostly on Pessoa.
2. A farrago of poems and bits of poems; at the end a difficult few pages on Pessoa containing an interesting descr. of the Campbells' house garden in Durban and conjecture about Pessoa's home, also in Durban.
3. Mostly various workings of "Caramba!"
4. Largely reworking of a segment of "Talking Bronco" and part of "The Carmelites of Toledo." Also, an unpub. poem on Toledo after its being taken by the Nationalists during the Spanish Civil War.
5. Further reworkings of "Orpheus."
6. Contains a listing of poetic output, mostly of poems in CP57, but some from CP49 and a number from CP60 ("Si Kulu Lez' Isiswe" included). A MSS of "An Epistle from the Talavera Front," "Driving Cattle to Casas Buenas" and of an unpub. related fragment, "In Memoriam: 'Mosquito,'" "The Born Too Late" and "Pillion to Talavera."
7. Longish poem on Rhodes and Kruger; sundry fragments; "Spooring an Angel" bits.
8. Poem ded. to Rob Lyle after death of Thomas, Tschiffely and Mulvey (rough of "Dedication"); part of "Nativity"; sundry prose bits, mostly attacks on T.E. Lawrence.
9. Passage on Olive Schreiner; poem, "Tragelaph and Hippotragus" ("Papyrus"); odd, half done poem on the changing self.
10. A bit of "Talking Bronco." Otherwise, melange.

11. Translator's preface to "Classic Plays of Spanish Theatre" and sundries, incl. AL / inc containing ref. to Robert Frost's daughter.
12. More passages for *Portugal* and what looks like a rejected section of "Talking Bronco." Verse squib contra Robert Payne.
13. Section of journal giving various drafts of a letter on Spanish poets and poetry and the "censoring" of some of them in England and C's efforts to combat this; references to an article in *Nine*.
14. More draft versions of "Orpheus" and "For Aimé Tschiffely."
15. Unsuccessful workings over of poem beginning, "Which only those can weather who have known." Unpub.
16. Has unpub. poem on Carlos Riba; also AL / draft inc to Douglas Jerrold, and of another to Alan Pryce-Jones.
17. Part of poem with autobiog. refs., but scarcely legible.
18. Drafts of poem descr. Lisbon and containing rather lachrymose references to follies and orgies, and pleas to God to teach the poet how to die. More on the Payne satire (see 12 above). Translation of Morales' "On a Foal that Died on a Moonlit Night."
19. Draft of squib against "shrill monkeys who screech when they see him"--refs. to Bayliss, West, Milne, Rolfe, Logue, David Paul. Frag.--"In darkness / the ramadan of Bashan / and only with their voices moulding ..."; part of a trans. from Spanish.
20. List of titles pub.; gloomy poem on state of poetry and poets (c. 1955).
21. Drafts of trans. of Portuguese poems; unidentified prose passage.
22. More workings of "To Aimé Tschiffely" and draftings of letter to the *TLS* on attempts to silence discussion in England of certain Spanish poets.
23. Draft of a discussion of Portuguese poetry.
24. Melange and repetitions.
25. Melange and repetitions.
26. Manuel Bandeira's "Renunciation" ("Counsel" in CP60), reworked five or six times.
27. Melange; mostly reps. of "Homage to Ezra"--"'I have been around, gramercy ...'"
28. More workings of "Orpheus."
29. More passages for *Portugal*; a part of trans. of Horace's *Ars Poetica*.
30. More workings of "Orpheus."
31. Draft fragments of a review of A.L. Lloyd's trans. of Lorca's poems [see H50]. AL to Peter [Russell?] about translations of Lorca.

III. *Correspondence*
  1. From C: 20 ALS's to Mary C, most when C was on active
     service; 5 or so to his mother; several to daughter
     Teresa; to Herman Charles Bosman (file); to Jocelyn
     Brooke; to Edmund Blunden (file); to Richard Church
     (file); about a dozen to Mrs. Tullah Hanley and 2
     APCS's to Thomas Edward Hanley (from whom most of the
     collection was acquired by the Academic Center
     Library); to Amy Hanley; to Ronald Duncan; to Edward
     Garnett (file); to John Lehmann; to Thomas Moult; to
     Herbert Edward Palmer (file); to Frederick Prokosch;
     to Rob Lyle (file); to Nesta Sawyer; to Stephen
     Spender.
  2. To C: from Edith Sitwell (file; also to Mary C); most
     of the letters from Wyndham Lewis reproduced in Rose
     [see JII.103].

IV. *Miscellaneous*
    File pertaining to books by C, reviews, appearances in
    anthologies.

KVI. WYNDHAM LEWIS COLLECTION,
CORNELL UNIVERSITY

Correspondence
    Mostly AL / drafts undated: 30 letters and 11 APCS's.
    1. AL / drafts:
       a. 5 from the Weald, or Long Barn, Sevenoaks, Kent,
          dealing mostly with C's writing and submission of
          "The Albatross" to L for *The Enemy*.
       b. 10 from Tour de Vallier, Gour (1 fr. Querolles),
          Martigues, Bouches du Rhone, variously about C's
          projected biography of L, his reading of L's works,
          reviewing of *Paleface* and *The Apes of God*, the re-
          jection of review of latter, *Satire and Fiction*,
          arrangements for L's visit to Martigues, comments
          on issues of *The Enemy*.
       c. 2 from Calle San Pedro 28.3.I, Barcelona, one
          praising *One-Way Song*.
       d. 1 from Altea, Alicante. This and remaining letters
          and cards mainly concern personal affairs or are
          rather cryptic.
       e. 2 from Airosas 13, Toledo.
       f. 1 from Glebe House, Binsted, Arundel, Sussex.
       g. 1 from Estombar, Algarve, Portugal.

h. 2 with London addresses.
i. 1 from Bormes Village, Var, France.
j. 1 from Quinta dos Bochechos, Galamares, Portugal,
   mentioning visit by Henry Regnery and wife and
   daughter.
k. Remaining 13, lacking inside addresses, seem mostly
   to have been written in England.
2. Places of origin of APCS's: ? from Martigues; 1 from
   France; 1 from Airosas 13, Toledo; 2 from Glebe House,
   Binsted, Sussex; 1 from [England]; 1 from Portugal;
   1 from 19 Via Donatello, Rome; 1 from 17 Campden
   Grove, W.8 [London]; 1 from Dr. Roy Campbell, c/o
   Marine Biological Commission, 167 Springfield Road,
   Durban [South Africa].

KVII. UNIVERSITY OF SASKATCHEWAN LIBRARY

I. *Manuscripts*
    1. Plays
       a. TccMS with A corrections of translation of *The
          Trickster of Seville* by Tirso de Molina. 84 pp.
          Also TccMS of opening page of radio version.
       b. A MS in 4 notebooks of translation of Calderón's
          Love After Death, with A corrections. 98 pp.
       c. T MS, heavily corrected, mostly in pencil, of
          translation of Lorca's *Yerma*. 56 pp.
       d. TccMS with some A corrections of translation of
          Lorca's *Blood Wedding.* String-bound in folder.
          63 pp.
       e. A MS in foolscap size notebook with boards of
          translation of *Fuente Ovejuna* by Lope de Vega.
          78 pp. Some pencilled corrections, queries by a
          reader. Also A MS/frag of translation of *Numancia.*
    2. Novel
       A MS in 2 notebooks, with some A corrections, of
          translation of *The City and the Mountains* by Eça
          de Queiroz. 241 pp.
    3. Published Poems
       a. MS as submitted to The Bodley Head of CP57. Pref-
          ace handwritten; typed TC. Poems in order with
          A annotations, editor's markings; some poems in
          A MS, others T MS, some in printed form on pages
          taken from sources where previously pub.--e.g.,
          poems from *Talking Bronco.* Some poems dated, with
          place given--scratched by editor. For *Flowering*

        Rifle, 1939 printed text as annotated and altered
by C used. Additional T MSS or TccMSS of many of
the later poems, some with A corrections, also
held.

  b. Group of A MSS: "Drunken Boat (from the French of
Arthur Rimbaud)"; "Si Kulu Lez' Isiswe (Fragment
of Zulu War Song. 1906 Rebellion)" and a second
Zulu song poem; "La Mancha in Wartime, 1936";
lines from "The Golden Shower"; "Spooring an Angel";
"On a White Foal Dying ..."; "To a Bull in Bronze";
"The Cat II"; "Conversation"; "To a Madonna
(Baudelaire)"; "Poor angel! that harsh note was
meant to sing"; "My being turns to smoke in the
mad strife - Bocage."

  c. A MSS of poetic workings: a notebook of workings of
"Orpheus"; several workings of "To Aimé Tschiffely."

4. Unpublished Poems

  a. A MSS: "Ode to Salvador Dali"; "I can say grace
for Housman, Hardy," Part I; about a dozen parodies
and squibs intended for a collection to be called
Banderillas. Assorted fragments. All a page or
so each.

  b. TccMSS: "Christ in mourning for his declivity";
"El Mio Cid"; several further squibs. All a page
or less each.

5. Prose

  a. A MS of part of "Translator's Introduction" on
subject of Spanish dramatists. 4 pp.

  b. A MS of section intended for *Portugal* on Iberian
horses, horsemanship and cavalry. 6 pp.

  c. A MS. "The Life and Work of A.F. Tschiffely."
Talk given at the Argentine Embassy, London,
c. 1955. 15 foolscap pp.

  d. A MS / frag on the bullfight (for *Portugal*?).

  e. A MS of unpub. autobiog. prose dealing with Durban
days and C's time as student at the University
College of Natal, Durban.

  f. Disparate A pages of *Light on a Dark Horse* MS.
32 pp.

  g. A MS / notebooks with 18 workings of parts of
Preface to CP57.

  h. A MS of journal: entries for March 2-16, 1957.
C, laid up with bad hip, reading Lope de Vega and
Prudentius.

  i. A MS / draft of part of preface to *Nostalgia*.

  j. A MS / draft of part of an essay on ways his kind
of poetry differs from that of others.

Spooring an Angel.

The tiger on the roses,
The python in the ferns, he freaked with fire —
The presence that discloses
What nobody supposes:
The ~~god~~ harper with the sunbeams for his lyre.
With him to be their shepherd,
The zebras strum the wind with golden bars.
It was his gun that peppered
The beauty of the leopard
Like midnight with the buckshot of the stars.

Opening lines of holograph MS. of "Spooring an Angel" (KVII.I.3b)
(By permission of the Roy Campbell Estate
and the University of Saskatchewan Library)

k. A MS / frag on Isaac Rosenberg's having absconded
   with the Spanish gold deposit (for a letter?).
l. A MS / draft (for a letter?) about the death of
   Lorca, and some contemporary Spanish poets.
m. A MS / rough draft of page from the trans. of *The
   City and the Mountains* on the character Jacinto.
n. A MS / frag on escape from Toledo and claim to
   have been in Guernica after it was bombed.
o. A MS / frag on "Shakespeare's rhetoric of love."
p. A MS / frag on Numantia as symbol.
q. A MS / frag on T.E. Lawrence, with allusions to
   The Mint.
r. T MS of talk on "The Poetry of Edith Sitwell."
   8 pp. [See G7.]

II. *Collected Poems*
    Proof copy of CP49 with A corrections, emendations.
    Autograph copies or TccMSS of many of the poems in
    CP49 and CP57, some of those in CP60.

III. *Correspondence* (all but those to family and some to Lyle
     in draft):
     Most letters held postdate 1950. The majority are to
     his friend and literary associate Rob Lyle; the rest
     divide up into those written to recipients in the U.S.,
     those to people in England and those to family.
     1. To U.S. recipients: to the Editor of the *New York
        Times* objecting to biased reviewing of *Selected Poems*;
        to a woman he accuses of campaigning against him on
        account of his alleged anti-Semitism, to which he
        offers a rebuttal and objection to attacks on him by
        "Eberhart, Payne and the N.Y.T. critics"; to Harvey
        Breit defending himself against the "smears" of "the
        Jarrells, Paynes and Eberharts"; to a Dr. Schwartz
        about the delivery of some MSS to Mr. and Mrs. T.E.
        Hanley.
     2. To people in England: to Lord David Cecil supplying
        biographical information, chiefly on war service; two
        letters to Edith Sitwell: one commenting on postwar
        Spain, the Burgess-Maclean affair and his own member-
        ship in "the Secret Service for a whole year," and the
        other on hopes of reading poems on TV; to Alan
        [Pryce-Jones] on an article about Spanish poets in
        the *TLS*; to Brian [Howard?] about his relationship
        with Wyndham Lewis; to Mr. Reinhardt, the publisher,
        about changes to be made in *Portugal*; to the Editor
        of the *TLS* on the state of poetry in Spain after the
        Civil War, Vicente Aleixandre and "anglo-saxon"

misrepresentation of events in Spain during the
Spanish Civil War; to a Father Jones thanking him for
urging him to do a verse translation of St. John of
the Cross's *Cántico espiritual*, but suggesting Edith
Sitwell be asked to do so as he has to finish a com-
missioned history of the Spanish Civil War; to an unnamed recipient concerning Spender and Gili's translation of "caracola."

3. To family (1 APCS from France to Mary C, d. circa
1931; 8 ALS's, several APCS's to wife, daughters
spanning 1943-c. 1955): one ALS to Mary C (d. '5/9/43')
details life in E. Africa during the war (has small
drawings in india ink of askari camp layout and in-
terior of living quarters, of animals); one letter to
Anita about her ballet career; one letter to Tess and
her mother when they were on holiday for Tess's health;
the rest, to Mary C, concern chiefly events of the
N. American tours and 1954 visit to S. Africa, and *inter
alia* provide information on C's struggles with alco-
holism and poor health; one letter to his mother
(d. October 17, Año de la Victoria, from Toledo)
comments on the world situation and his plans for
joining up in the British army, and mentions his
recent involvement in social work in Spain.

4. Some 30 letters and several APCS's to Rob Lyle: partly
concerned with literary business, including Lyle's
projected biography of him, or the management of prop-
erties in Portugal; otherwise, personal. Also six
line drawings of animals, two of them in letter to
daughter Anita.

IV *Addendum*
Research materials consisting of TccL's, notes and photocopies given for the collection by D.S.J. Parsons.

KVIII. NATIONAL ENGLISH DOCUMENTATION
CENTRE, RHODES UNIVERSITY,
GRAHAMSTOWN, SOUTH AFRICA

I. *Correspondence*
Either ALS's, TLS's or TccL's; often ALS's with typed
copies.

1. Letters to C (any considerable number indicated in
parentheses): from Richard Aldington (file, 1951-57),
José M. Alonso Gamo, Leonard Bacon, Munro Beattie,

Louis Bonnerot, Colm Brogan, George Campbell, Hamish
Campbell, Charles Causley, Henri Chabrol (file),
Ralph Currey, Ronald Duncan, Ludovic A. Forbes,
Christina Foyle, W.H. Gardner, William Gormley, C.M.,
C.J. Greenwood (file), Armand Guibert (file--to C
and Mary C), T.E. Hanley, Tullah Hanley, Philip Hesel-
tine, Brian Higgins (file), Archbishop Denis Hurley,
Augustus John, Peter Kemp, Rev. John F. Kenney, Uys
Krige (file), Wyndham Lewis, Robert MacGregor, E.G.
Malherbe, John Masefield, Hugh Massie and Co., Diana
Mosley, Rev. John P. Murphy, Alan Neame, Cilette
Ofaire, William Plomer (file--to C and Mary C),
F.T. Prince, Henry Regnery (file--to C and Mary C),
Jack de Richter, E.V. Rieu, Izak Rousseau, C.J.
Sibbett, Edith Sitwell (file--to C and Mary C),
Sacheverell Sitwell, Martin Skinner, F.C. Slater
(file), Walter Starkie, Tambimuttu, José Mª Tironella,
Vernon Watkins.
2. A considerable collection of letters to Mary C from
numerous correspondents.
3. Letters from C: most copies are of ones also to be
found at the South African Library, at the Killie
Campbell Africana Library or at the University of
Saskatchewan Library. The following originals are
uniquely held: to Richard Aldington (file, 1951-57),
brother George and sister-in-law Agnes (file), Fernando Street Coupers (file), Angel Flores, C.J.
Greenwood (file, made available by The Bodley Head),
William Payn, John Pick (file), William Plomer (file),
Edward Roworth, F.C. Slater (file), Stephen Spender
(d. June 11, 1946), John and Audrey Sutherland, Gene
Tunney.

II. *Research Collections*
1. The bulk of the collection consists of research
materials amassed by the late Dr. W.H. Gardner for
the official biography of C: extensive correspondence,
numerous files of newspaper clippings, extracts from
or copies of some poems appearing in journals, many
reviews of C's works and a wide selection of articles
on him and passages from books. Also, Dr. Gardner's
notes and preliminary draft of his biography.
Perhaps of special interest are:
a. an account by Lloyd Duchemin of impressions of C
during his visit to Mount Allison University,
Sackville, New Brunswick, Canada in 1953.
b. photocopies of obituaries on C in European newspapers, and a file of newspaper obits.

    c. copy of a lecture on C by Dr. Walter Starkie, given
in Madrid, October 1959.

    d. Dr. W.H. Gardner's notebook of anecdotes about C.

    e. copies of articles for reference works and of a
lecture on C by Dr. Gardner.

    f. letters expressing adverse criticism of C's trans-
lations of the classic Spanish plays passed on to
Dr. Gardner by Eric Bentley.

    g. copies of C's own radio broadcast scripts [see G
Note] and of those he was responsible for as talks
producer for the B.B.C.

    h. transcription of Charles de Richter's article on C
in *Nouvelles Littéraires*, January 27, 1949.

    i. translation of an article in *Pueblo*, May 1951.

    j. translation of J.H. Bidarra de Almeida, "Don Roy
Quixote Campbell," *Noticias da Africa do Sul*,
May 1967.

    k. translation of article, "Uma Rua com o nome de
Roy Campbell," *Noticias da Africa do Sul*, August
1973.

    l. a collection of photographs, including one of
Mary C's portrait of C and one of the bronze bust
of C [by Oloff de Wet?].

2. Numbers of letters from Alan Paton to various correspondents and a file of his preliminary materials for
a biography of C.

Note: This collection, not seen by the compiler, was established at the National English Documentation Centre in
1978. [See Introduction.]

Appendix

ROY CAMPBELL ITEMS SOLD AT SOTHEBY'S,
18 JULY 1972*

1. Autograph drafts for sections of *Lorca: An Appreciation
   of His Poetry*. Mostly latter part of chapter III and
   most of chapter IV. 25 pp., five of them typewritten.
   Bought by Foyles for £220.00.

2. Autograph Ms. of 8 stanzas of "The Clock in Spain."
   Bought by F. Edwards for £60.00.

3. Autograph Ms. of "Portuguese or Brazilian Lullaby" in
   Portuguese and English versions; 12 lines each.
   Unpublished.
   Bought by F. Edwards for £120.00.

4. Autograph drawing of matador and bull.
   Bought by W. & G. Foyle for £55.00.

5. Autograph drawing of picador.
   Bought by S.T.L. Gleeson for £40.00.

6. A.L. to Edith Sitwell (1st page only); n.d.
   Bought by Landway for £16.00.

7. A.L.S. to wife during W.W.2; 1 p. & rough draft; n.d.
   Bought by W. & G. Foyle for £40.00.

8. 2 A.L.S. to mother, plus address panel; 2 1/2 pp.;
   11 November 1943; n.d. (1ᴊ51).
   Bought by W. & G. Foyle for £65.00.

9. A.L.S. to wife; 1 p.; n.d.
   Bought by W. & G. Foyle for £45.00.

*Taken from: Sotheby & Co.'s *Catalogue of Nineteenth Century
and Modern First Editions, Presentation Copies, Autograph
Letters and Literary Manuscripts*, Mon./Tues. 17/18 July 1972;
prices and buyers list supplied separately on request.

10.   A.L.S. to wife and daughter Teresa; 2 pp.; 19 March 1953.
      Bought by W. & G. Foyle for £85.00.

11.   Autograph Ms. of poem "Cid Campeador." Unpublished;
      40 lines.
      Bought by W. & G. Foyle for £90.00.

12.   Autograph Ms. of translation of Valéry's "The Bee";
      14 lines.
      Bought by F. Edwards for £28.00.

13.   P.C., signed, to wife; n.d. (?1939).
      Bought by W. & G. Foyle for £18.00.

14.   Wartime A.L.S. to wife; 1 p.; 8 July 1944.
      Bought by W. & G. Foyle for £35.00.

15.   A.L.S. to mother; 1 p.; 4 December 1944.
      Bought by F. Edwards for £55.00.

16.   P.C., signed, to Robert Lyle; 8 April 1954.
      Bought by Maggs for £42.00.

Index

Abbreviations Used in the Index

B.B.C.	British Broadcasting Corporation	news	newspaper
coll	collected by	N.Y.P.L.	New York Public Library
comp	compiled by	ptr	printer
des	designer, designed by	pub	publisher
dist	distributor	S.A.B.C.	South African Broadcasting Corporation
ed	editor, edited by	sel	selected by
iltr	illustrator	supp	supplemented by
jr	journal	trans	translated by

A name in parentheses is that of the author of the title preceding it, at times of an author whose work is listed because C translated it. Main titles are given in brackets after similar part titles so as to distinguish one from another; on occasion, as well, brackets enclose otherwise desirable identifications.

Whenever the title of a work varies slightly, it is indexed under the title of commonest occurrence. Likewise, names such as "Camões" are indexed under the form most frequently found.

Names with prefixes, including *Saint*, are also indexed under the part of the name following the prefix. Cross-references are given whenever an author is known by more than one name.

As a rule, the French and Spanish translations of C's poems are indexed under their titles in English.

Faber & Faber Ltd. (pub): A3a, 3e, 5, 7, 13, 14a, 16
The Faber Book of Comic Verse (comp Roberts): I26
The Faber Library - No. 10: A3a
"Fable" (Lorca): I50
"A Fable for my Children": A15
Facetti, Germano: C2f
"Fado: The Music of Lisbon/And the Gypsies": B6
"Familiar Daemon": E48, I41, 48, 80
"The Family Lumber-Chest": E104
"The Family Vault": A15
"Fantastic Engraving" (Baudelaire): I51
Farewell, Aggie Weston (Charles Causley): H43
Farrar, Straus and Giroux (pub): JII.146
"Fear" (Paço d'Arcos): C7; I79
"Febrile City Between the Mountains and the Sea" (Paço
    d'Arcos): C7; I79
"Federico García Lorca" [CP60]: C6; H31
"Félibre": I55, 56
The Félibre: JII.95
Feraud: B1
"The Festivals of Flight": A8; E20; JI.3; JIII.III.3, 7, 10
"Fetish Worship in South Africa": H7
Fielding, Daphne: JII.114
Fifty Spanish Poems (Juan Ramon Jimenez): H46
Fifty Years of English Literature, 1900-1950 (Scott-James):
    JII.58
"The Fight": E55; JI.8
Finishing Touches (John): JII.94, 105
The First Edition and Book Collector, London: E9; JII.11
"First Glimpse of African Shores" (Paço d'Arcos): C7
First Line and Title Index to the Poetry of Roy Campbell
    (Miller): JI.37
"First Meeting with Roy Campbell" (Krige): JI.29, 48
First Time in America (coll Arlott): I41
First Words: A Miscellany of Verse and Prose: D5
"Fishing Boats in Martigues": I82
Fitts, Dudley: JIII.III.11
Five Catholic Poets (Robinson): JI.46
"Five Poems of Lorca": E95, 96, 97, 98, 99
"Five Romanceros of Lorca": E89, 90, 91, 92, 93
"The Flame": A3d, 10; JI.27
"The Flame of Living Love" (St. John of the Cross): E83
The Flaming Terrapin: A1, 3c, 19, 20; I3, 4, 8, 15, 22, 28,
    33, 61, 69, 71, 84; JI.1, 11, 16, 20, 23, 42, 54; JII.2,
    3, 4, 10, 15, 16, 24, 25, 27, 28, 30, 48, 61, 76, 116;
    JIII.I.1-19; JIII.III.1, 5, 7, 10, 11; JIII.XIX.1, 3
"The Flaming Terrapin: Roy Campbell--Poet from South Africa"
    (John): JII.94